W9-BWU-255

Downstairs, Upstairs

Ohio History and Culture

Series on Ohio History and Culture

John H. White and Robert J. White, Sr., *The Island Queen: Cincinnati's Excursion Steamer*

H. Roger Grant, *Ohio's Railway Age in Postcards*

Frances McGovern, *Written on the Hills: The Making of the Akron Landscape*

Keith McClellan, *The Sunday Game: At the Dawn of Professional Football*

Steve Love and David Giffels, *Wheels of Fortune: The Story of Rubber in Akron*

Alfred Winslow Jones, *Life, Liberty, and Property: A Story of Conflict and a Measurement of Conflicting Rights*

David Brendan Hopes, *A Childhood in the Milky Way: Becoming a Poet in Ohio*

John Keim, *Legends by the Lake: The Cleveland Browns at Municipal Stadium*

Richard B. Schwartz, *The Biggest City in America: A Fifties Boyhood in Ohio*

Tom Rumer, *Unearthing the Land: The Story of Ohio's Scioto Marsh*

Ian Adams, Barney Taxel, and Steve Love, *Stan Hywet Hall and Gardens*

William F. Romain, *Mysteries of the Hopewell: Astronomers, Geometers, and Magicians of the Eastern Woodlands*

Dale Topping, edited by Eric Brothers, *When Giants Roamed the Sky: Karl Arnstein and the Rise of Airships from Zeppelin to Goodyear*

Millard F. Rogers Jr., *Rich in Good Works: Mary M. Emery of Cincinnati*

Frances McGovern, *Fun, Cheap, and Easy: My Life in Ohio Politics, 1949–1964*

Larry L. Nelson, editor, *A History of Jonathan Alder: His Captivity and Life with the Indians*

Ian Adams and Steve Love, *Holden Arboretum*

Bruce Meyer, *The Once and Future Union: The Rise and Fall of the United Rubber Workers, 1935–1995*

Joyce Dyer, *Gum-Dipped: A Daughter Remembers Rubber Town*

Melanie Payne, *Champions, Cheaters, and Childhood Dreams: Memories of the Soap Box Derby*

John A. Flower, *Downstairs, Upstairs: The Changed Spirit and Face of College Life in America*

A. Martin Byers, *The Hopewell Episode*

DOWNSTAIRS, UPSTAIRS

THE CHANGED SPIRIT AND FACE OF COLLEGE LIFE IN AMERICA

JOHN A. FLOWER

The University of Akron Press
Akron Ohio

All inquiries and permissions requests should be addressed to the
publisher, The University of Akron Press, Akron, OH 44325–1703

Manufactured in the United States of America
First edition 2003
07 06 05 04 03 5 4 3 2 1

Library of Congress Cataloging-in-Publication Data

Flower, John A., 1921-
   Downstairs, upstairs : the changed spirit and face of college life
in America / John A. Flower.
      p. cm.
   ISBN 1-884836-96-8 (cloth : alk. paper)
   1. Education, Higher--United States. 2. Education, Higher--Social
   aspects--United States. 3. Universities and colleges--United States--
   Administration. I. Title.
   LA227.4 .F58 2003
   378.73--dc22

                                                2003018073

The paper used in this publication meets the minimum requirements of
American National Standard for Information Sciences—Permanence of
Paper for Printed Library Materials, ANSI Z39.48—1984. ∞

TO MAXEEN,

whose love and belief in me motivate her to nip
my heels when I don't perform.

Contents

Acknowledgments   ix

Preface   xi

Introduction   1

1. Rain and Shine   24

2. The Pacific Theater   35

3. Back in the States   44

4. Michigan to Ohio   59

5. Vulgarities and Disrespect on Campuses:
    Lessened Academic Standards   82

6. Academic Freedom, Tenure, and Corruption
    in Intercollegiate Athletics   104

7. Exponential Increases in Knowledge and
    the Technology Developed to Teach and
    Communicate It   120

8. Diversity in Race, Culture, Class, and
    Affirmative Action   136

9. Students as Customers   164

10. Up Interstate 271 to Cleveland and
    Cleveland State University   178

11. Professional Politics and Bureaucracy   201

12. What Became Known as the Winbush Affair   209

13. Problems in Shared Governance: How They Relate to Detached Professors and Their Disconnects in Teaching Students   246

14. Rising College Costs, Less Support, Outdated Administrative Management, the Dilemma of Increased Part-time Faculty along with Graduate Student Unionizing   269

15. Morality and Ethics on Campus: The Replacement of Accepted Verities by Relative Values   293

Epilogue: The Impact of Today's Forces for Change: What Will Happen?   316

Notes   345

Index   367

Acknowledgments

MANY INTERACTIONS AND discussions with a wide circle of people were helpful as this book was being written. Some had meaning going beyond the normal give and take of academic and professional communicating. Michael Carley, Director of the University of Akron Press, supported my initiative from the time I first approached him with the project. In addition to running a university press he is an accomplished and recognized scholar in the affairs of nineteenth- and twentieth-century Russia. As the manuscript went through its various permutations the consistency of his involvement, always buttressed by concrete suggestions, provided direction as to the way I organized material. Professor Emeritus Lou Milic believes in the importance of the issues I set forth and discuss. He never countenanced on my part any divergence from the goal of straightforward communication. My two "inherited sons," Robert Stone and Jon Stone, successful in business but not authors, pointed out useful ways the book could have appeal beyond a traditional academic audience. Roy Lennox, senior managing director at Caxton Corporation, a major New York City hedge fund (who in a former life was an historian) helped in my efforts to express technical subjects in nontechnical language. Sanford Rosenbluth helped in bringing focus to issues that are inevitably fuzzy. Finally, Les Roberts, the well-known author of detective novels set in Cleveland, who read one of the early drafts, provided pungent and encouraging comments about the project—what is readable and what is not. The belief of all of these persons that the issues bound up in the book have crucial importance to Americans today added strength to my purpose as I wrote it.

Preface

WHILE IT IS not unusual for college professors to spend decades in university life before retiring, not all that many have had the opportunity to be a teacher and administrator for well over half a century. I am one of those comparatively few. This book comes from those decades of service. I have had many baptisms in university waters ranging in temperature from boiling hot to freezing cold, all resulting from the weighty and often highly charged forces for change. This book is not a tract dealing in abstract issues but emerges from my personal and professional experiences in higher education, including my earlier years. From them I have distilled problems and their causes and venture to express some solutions to them. I have detailed more specifically my university involvements from the end of World War II to the present. During that period I served at every level of academic involvement from lowly teaching assistant to the oft-perceived eminence of a university presidency, which in truth can at times be lowly itself. The assertions I make translate into large and overarching issues and they derive from my participation in specific situations. Clearly they lend themselves to analysis and theory but I approach them and suggest solutions as a result of my "being there," sometimes as an observer but more often as a participant.

Images of lawns, trees, period buildings, and privileged, upscale students carrying books across quadrangles on golden autumn days no longer capture the characteristic American college scene. All institutions of higher education, but state colleges and universities in particular, have been pressured by forces for change coming from each point on society's compass. Groups from every level of humankind produce the students that now pour onto campuses—from the elite and exclusive "upstairs" of economic and social privilege to the "downstairs" occupied by vast millions. There is no limit to their human diversity. They include welfare mothers who take their babies to class with them, men and women in the eighth and ninth decades of their lives still wanting to learn, released prisoners struggling to acquire the skills that will enable them to get along in society, and throngs of workers intent on improving themselves.

Sweeping shifts in the cultural, economic, racial, and ethnic backgrounds of students and faculty have and continue to take place. The types of individuals identified for campus leadership, along with the goals, policies, and educational environments of institutions have changed. In many ways the dynamics and particulars of elite private colleges and universities have been separated from those of public higher education. Job programs tailored to economic necessity have elbowed to one side the previous, primary concern for historic, humanistic verities unrelated to the job market.

The forces are many. But there are five that have altered the spirit and the face of higher education. They are:

1.) Unprecedented increases in the volume and availability of raw and unsorted information along with commensurate increases in the technology leading to its applications.

2.) Global issues increasing the importance of workforce education to achieve economic competitiveness coupled with a broad expansion of public higher education.

3.)   Emphasis on human diversity, especially issues of race, culture, class, and gender.

4.)   Societal attitudes veering away from moral certainties and substituting in their place relative values extracted from the brew of diverse cultures, races, and societies which sometimes focus on equality of rewards in contrast to equality of opportunity.

5.)   The ever increasing bureaucratizing and politicizing of public higher education, where costs have escalated at a rate higher than the economy as a whole.

As a result, higher education today bears little resemblance to what existed on the campuses of colleges and universities of yesteryear. While the outlines of these differences apply to all types of institutions, they relate primarily to state colleges and universities and to the many liberal arts colleges that are not selective in enrollments. The topmost few private and flagship state institutions possessing billions of endowment dollars are less susceptible to these forces. They control their own futures. But most campuses serving the mass market do not have that autonomy. We speak of higher education in America but it should be *higher educations*, which sometimes are not all that high. We have placed *training* in skills and crafts to obtain jobs in changing marketplaces alongside *educating* in ideas and concepts in order to improve minds (and, it is hoped, morality and character). Sometimes this is like trying to mix oil and water.

THE DOWNSTAIRS, UPSTAIRS OF AMERICAN CAMPUSES

When I taught and even moreso during my twenty-five years in the trenches of administration, I never paid much attention to the caste system among colleges and universities. It was not until recently, during my wife's recuperation from surgery, when we watched home videos of the famous British TV series "Upstairs, Downstairs" that I reflected upon a similar condition in American higher education. We have definable castes rooted in culture, race, gender, and economic status. The next time you are at a reception or neighborhood gathering, listen to the proud anecdotes of parents of students who attend private, prestigious universities. At the same time listen to the silence of those whose kids had their choices narrowed to anonymous regional state universities or community colleges. Visit the campus of Swarthmore compared to the University of the District of Columbia, or Vassar compared to Chicago State and "feel" the differences. Talk to admissions officers. You will grasp the reality of collegiate upstairs-downstairs. Congressional Black Caucus members talk about leveling playing fields, but they send their kids to the best private schools.

In the mass market of higher education the level of academic quality in the academic undergraduate experience from every region has decreased by almost all qualitative measures at the same time that streams of students have increased. The rate of appropriations of tax dollars for higher education has soared. Campuses are held captive to narrow and differing special interest groups running the gamut: sports fans, unions, ethnic and racial groups, civic activists, politicians, and job seekers to name but a few. Changes in policy are desperately needed to balance the bizarre range of interests now represented.

My purpose in what follows is to identify society's forces affecting American higher education and how these forces have brought about changes in college life. I look at a number of the problems generated by these changes and suggest solutions. The book cannot be separated from my own experiences during well over half a century in the classrooms and corridors of higher education, which have included students, parents, faculty, staff, alumni, trustees, community activists, and politicians.

The late Nobel laureate Isaac Bashevis Singer reiterated throughout his writing life that while an author should strive for universal significance beyond the personal, this is best achieved through cognizance derived from one's own experiences. In what follows I have not hesitated to dip into my personal experiences. But even though the observations and discussions come from my own awareness and perceptions, this book is more than an anecdotal memoir. It describes and evaluates today's realities. A wake-up call is embodied in its message. I hope I have done it justice.

Introduction

> *It is no longer clear what the place of the University is within society nor what the exact nature of that society is.*
>
> Bill Readings, from *The University in Ruins*

EDUCATING STUDENTS BY immersing them in the classics had always been the major part of "ivory tower" university curricula. These studies were separate from the external world of day-to-day practical pursuits. *Educating* the mind was kept apart from *training* in the skills required to make a living. Training had not been the responsibility of universities. It belonged in apprenticeship systems, trade schools, and in family traditions carried on from father to son. Today we include both in our public and private universities.

During my years as provost and president of Cleveland State University, I presided at faculty meetings where teachers in fields of applied technologies whose careers began with pliers and screwdrivers (and who later joined the faculty because they possessed technical skills necessary for vocational programs) sat next to literature and philosophy professors who were vintage yields of humanist scholarship at research universities. To meld the discussions of the two types of faculty members—those engaged in training stu-

dents for practical pursuits in the job market and those educating students in concepts and ideas—was a challenge I had
not anticipated at the start of my career. This dramatic vocational and academic diversity contrasts vividly with the essential homogeneity of faculty members in the past.

A CASTE SYSTEM

Today in American higher education we have definable
castes even though educators need considerable inducement
to talk about them.[1] They relate to economic status, cultural
differences, and race. There is also a differing outlook toward those higher-education institutions seen as lower status
(translated as working class) for the purpose of serving students from the mass market. They are in stark comparison to
upper-tier campuses serving carefully selected students. The
upper-tier campuses are predominantly private but not entirely. In most American urban areas, particularly in the east
and south, but to an extent elsewhere there are side-by-side
examples of these dissimilar institutions. The elitist institutions are historic while the mass-market campuses came into
prominence after World War II.

The differing positions of mainstream business community
leaders toward the two types of institutions have been dramatic.
These leaders lend their weight to efforts, both organizational
and philanthropic, to buttress community projects and institutions. During the fifties and sixties these leaders were helpful,
often instrumental, in the formulation of public colleges and
universities in their areas. The institutions operate under the
purview of the state legislature or, in the case of community
colleges, both the legislature and local districts. However, in
the decades since, community business leadership has not offered the same energy and help, nor has it translated into fiscal
support. (There has been some "bricks and mortar" support,
but in those examples people get their names on buildings.)

The corporate leaders, themselves mostly graduates of Ivy League and other upper-tier schools rather than those from the mass market, have not had their hearts and minds in support of programs and endowment for these public institutions. They have been uncomfortable. To an extent it has been a "high-class, low-class" thing. Also, the reiterated mantra has been that it is the legislature's responsibility to provide operating dollars to higher education. "After all, we pay taxes." Everyone knows, however, that the legislatures are not going to "support" public institutions. They provide "assistance."

A STACKED DECK

Regional public universities which are owned and assisted but in no way supported totally by the state find themselves struggling against a stacked deck in the development of external, private, and corporate giving. There are a number of reasons for this. To begin with, trustee backing is crucial. If board of trustees members themselves don't provide donations to the university, others cannot be expected to. Board members appointed by governors, often tapped for politically partisan reasons, don't usually have a philanthropic bent and, in my experience, are not often capable of significant giving. Secondly, new universities serving large numbers of students who are the first members of their families to go to college have not had the time to build a loyal and emotionally committed alumni base. Loyal alumni comprise the foundation for private giving. A third reason exists in the fact that most academic and administrative officers of mass-market, public institutions are not very good at hobnobbing with upper-crust society, a source of important giving, both from individuals and family foundations. These officers, like many of their students, often come from backgrounds where they never learned how to handle behaviors within the

"high-class" networks they need to deal with in money raising. It may not be sociologically palatable for them to culti-
vate the elites but that is beside the point. In fundraising you
have to go where the money is.

   The solutions to this problem of money raising in non-
elite, public universities are simple in context but plenty difficult to implement. First, board members' giving has to be
worked on and worked on hard. This task falls upon the
shoulders of the president and board chair. Having done it, I
know how difficult it can be. If a politically-appointed board
member does not have the resources to give important
amounts of money—often the case—then he or she should at
least contribute something, even a modest sum. The problem here often derives from a board member's ego—not
wanting to be seen giving a small amount. The president and
board chair simply have to convince individual board members who are not wealthy that their participation in providing gifts, even though unpretentious in amount, is important
to the larger university effort. For truly successful fundraising 100 percent board participation in giving is requisite.
The same should hold true for administrative officers and
for the faculty. It is seldom if ever possible to achieve 100
percent participation from faculty, but from the board and
university officers it is a must. With the demonstrated commitment of the university family, i.e., board, officers, and
faculty, development officials can go to other sources with a
strong justification for their "asks." Second, the construction
of a solid and loyal alumni base takes place only with the passage of time. It will occur (for example it continues to grow
stronger at Cleveland State, where I served) but it will not
happen overnight. To relate to alumni requires professional
know-how—up-to-date mailing lists and knowledge of the
professional accomplishments of individual alums. It is important that they be kept informed about campus affairs, and

that they understand "their" university values them as daughters and sons. Third, the president, officers, and board members must not be hesitant to make themselves known to the community movers and shakers who hold the keys to private fiscal power. University leadership must get to know these people, demonstrate confidence and savvy, and get beyond uncertainty and caution. One of the most effective portals into this world is through presentations by faculty members or students with tangible accomplishments and something worthwhile to say.

Before coming to Kent State University as a dean in 1966, where my specific intent was to serve in a context where enrollees were mostly first-generation college students, I had spent almost twenty years as a young teacher, an administrator, and tenured professor at the University of Michigan. There I dealt with and taught echelons of third and fourth generation UM legacy students. I was proud to consider myself a "Michigan Man" myself. But my idealism propelled me into another arena that, in a human sense, was broader and represented the democratic ideals of the nation.

Michigan, as a public flagship institution with massive private support, belongs in the upper-tier of universities— not as high as Harvard, Princeton, Yale, or Columbia—but close. The most difficult adjustment between Ann Arbor, Michigan, where we were very comfortable, and Portage County, Ohio (which at that time seemed to have some aspects not unrelated to the middle ages), was the difference in faculty self-assurance between Kent State and Michigan. There was a palpable sense of professional security on the part of Michigan faculty members which at that time did not exist in the faculty at Kent State. (But that was thirty-five years ago. Kent State is now a different place with vastly bettered faculty achievements and self-perceptions.) One of the reasons for KSU's self-doubt lay in a certain tentativeness on the part of the university's officers. Without forcefulness on their part a university will languish.

LESSENED ACADEMIC QUALITY

In the year 1900 most American college campuses were private enclaves. They enrolled over 80 percent of students then attending college. Public institutions, mostly land grant colleges and normal schools, served the remainder. At that time, the total number of college students in America was 237,600 out of the nation's population of 76,212,160. This adds up to about three-tenths of 1 percent. Today the ratio of public to private campuses is reversed and the number of enrolled students is beyond 15,000,000 out of a U.S. population of approximately 281,000,000. This approaches 5.5 percent of the total population. Counting enrollments in continuing education and in corporate universities would add more percentage points. As far back as the early 1950s at the University of Michigan I remember the president, Harlan Hatcher, asking rhetorically, "Why not give every child at birth a bachelor's degree? This would save endless wasted efforts and mountains of money."

It was a damning statement by which Dr. Hatcher meant that the quality of undergraduate education had diminished sufficiently that degrees might as well be given away. The forces leading to this have not lessened. However you view it, his point was well taken. It is not politically correct, given today's rhetoric about race, class, and gender, to say that the masses of students funneled into college both from the GI Bill and subsequently through open admissions to public universities resulted in lowering the academic standards required for the bachelor's degree. But this did happen. On the other hand, it can be argued that the social and vocational good of millions more citizens partaking of higher education outweighs its qualitatively lowered level. This greater blessing is a "feel-good" issue. It would seem to indicate a zero-sum game in higher education, where increasing numbers are offset by diminishing academic quality. It says that if increased numbers of American citizens are to enjoy higher education, it is inevitably diluted. I disagree that this should have to happen, even though my disagreement is not matched by facts. During the last fifty years academic quality has in fact been diluted, especially in undergraduate programs at public institutions.

INCREASE OF STUDENTS AT PUBLIC CAMPUSES

The vast increase in students during the fifties and sixties due to the GI Bill was absorbed by public universities through unprecedented expansion. Upper-tier private colleges and universities simply did not admit these hordes of students, even though the government would have paid the tuition. The quality of their degree programs would have been lowered were their campus doors to be opened wide. It is worth noting that in the upper tier of private, American campuses, the number of students enrolled as a percentage of the U.S. population now is dramatically less than it was in 1900. But this elite group of private research and liberal arts-oriented institutions that are generations old possesses most of the resources. Endowments of the nearly 3,900 U.S. institutions of higher education recognized by the U.S. Department of Education total approximately $197 billion. This number fluctuates with the rise and fall of the stock market. twenty-five institutions (twenty private, five public flagships which include three systems) comprising less than 1 percent of U.S. colleges and universities, control approximately $113 billion of this approximately $197 billion.

This means that less than 1 percent of U.S. universities control approximately 60 percent of the total endowment wealth of the nation's universities and colleges.

The unequal distribution of resources, essentially between the upper class, mostly privates, and the egalitarian publics—the haves and the have nots—continues to grow.[2] In terms of money, star faculty members, and gifted students, the relatively few prestigious, selective-admission campuses dominate the higher education landscape. But it is the extensive group of middle- to lower-tier state universities, community colleges, and less selective private campuses (in total well over three thousand) that have democratized higher education in America.

Out of approximately three thousand nine hundred public, private, and proprietary colleges and universities listed in the *Higher Education Directory* there is such a concentration of human talent and financial endowment in the relatively few at the top that by comparison to "mass-market" and "niche" campuses, those in the top tier have power and prerogative kindred to city states. Because these "medallion" campuses control a predominant share of higher education's wealth they can control their own futures, in contrast to the mass-market institutions which must deal, sleeves rolled up and hard hat in place, with the grit, grime, and untidiness of an egalitarian academic world.

Of the more than 15,000,000 college students in the nation (not counting those attending unaccredited proprietary schools) the sixty top-tier campuses enroll about 720,000. The remaining students, 14,280,000, are served by 3,800-plus institutions possessing far less in fiscal resources and faculty excellence. These fiscally much thinner institutions cannot carve out their futures with the same degree of autonomy that the well-endowed, upper-tier campuses have, and thus must be responsive to the educational market forces within the populace.

During the last century the Ivy League campuses and other elite private universities placed increasing emphasis on research and graduate programs. This came from the strong influence of the nineteenth-century German research university; today major components of student enrollment in these institutions are in their affiliated graduate schools. Their billions of dollars in endowments, to say nothing of their high rates of annual tuition and ancillary fees—in some examples beyond $40,000 (plus federal, state, foundation, and private grants)—concentrate on the support of research and graduate education. It is the graduate programming in the private and public flagship group that has made American higher education the wonder of the world. But at the same time that private institutions expanded research and graduate education, they maintained tight control of the growth in their undergraduate enrollments. This was in stark contrast to the profligate expansion of undergraduate enrollments in state colleges and universities, which accommodated millions of new, first-generation students. These students were not acceptable upstairs.

Upstairs, downstairs was then and continues to be a reality.

FROM CARDINAL NEWMAN TO ARTHUR LOVEJOY

In 1873, in Dublin, Ireland, John Henry Newman brought together a collection of lectures and essays he had published during the 1850s and presented them under the title *The Idea of a University Defined and Illustrated, I. In Nine Discourses delivered to the Catholics of Dublin, II. In Occasional Lectures and Essays addressed to members of the Catholic Church*. Educated at Oxford University, he was ordained as a minister in the Church of England and served the church until he was forty-three, at which time—after his controversial identity with the Oxford Movement[3]—he resigned and was received into the Catholic Church. Shortly thereafter he was ordained as a Roman Catholic priest and years later became a Cardinal.

Recognized as one of the finest contributions of the nineteenth century in explaining the place of universities in the advancement of humankind, John Henry Newman's *The Idea of a University* identified the ideal of "what ought to be."[4] It could be summed up by saying that a university education should be instrumental in creating moral persons. This contrasts sharply with the opinions of many today who question whether or not moral instruction should be a concern of universities. Let me say at the outset that I come down on the side of Cardinal Newman. This does not mean that universities should indoctrinate students in narrow morality. It does mean, I think, that faculty members should profess and exemplify to their students standards of human conduct representing the responsibilities and duties of citizens to the society of which they are a part. Exemplifying and teaching these principles transcends the boundaries of particular academic disciplines.

Forty-two years later, in 1915, the role and responsibility of university faculty members was embodied in the *Declaration of Principles*, published by an eminent group of scholars, including Arthur O. Lovejoy, who founded the American Association of University Professors. This statement, which manifests the rationale for academic freedom, reverberates to this day. Its expression of ideals remains unsurpassed. Holding true to them remains a challenge in our more complex world of higher education, where the cultural homogeneity that was a base for their formulation has been supplanted by diversity. The extent to which this challenge is being met currently remains problematic.

CHANGES

Since World War II American higher education has changed at a rate faster and to an extent greater than during its entire evolution since the seventeenth century. These changes, which have occurred in eight broad areas of higher education, have emerged out of the five societal forces I outlined in the Preface. These forces have brought about alterations not only in the context and mission of campuses, but in how college life proceeds.

The first force comes from the wide-ranging wash of unsystematized information. Like rain, it falls practically anywhere and everywhere. As the raw information becomes better understood and organized, new knowledge emerges. The societal velocity with which this happens continues to increase. It necessitates constant adjustment of curriculums and operations. Being extremely change-resistant and conservative in structure when compared to other establishments in society, universities are at a disadvantage in a rapidly changing world.

The second force mirrors the U.S. citizenry at large as it becomes more diversified. Within this diversity the historic white majority has had to cede its hegemony in many different ways, just as men have had to recognize that they cannot lock women out of professional opportunity, privilege, and prerogative. University campuses are highly visible arenas of contention—sometimes battlegrounds—in this process. The most refractory and intractable of all issues has been attitudes toward race, which in the U.S. is most visibly directed toward African Americans and other people of color. While overt forms of racism have been outlawed through federal, state, and local statutes, beginning with civil rights legislation in the early sixties, this has by no means eliminated prejudicial conditioning on the part of individuals and groups toward people of color. These ingrained, often subjective attitudes, result in behaviors of racial prejudice or bigotry far beyond the reach of statute. Conversely, the demagogic reactions to racial prejudice on the part of not a few highly visible and influential persons of color exacerbate the contentions. While individual civil rights are now protected by law and overt racism such as housing and job discrimination is illegal, covert prejudice and discrimination in a thousand forms continue to exist. This takes the form of individual body language and pervasive negative insinuations.

The third force emerges from consumerism and customer orientation on the part of students. It brings a marketplace orientation to the campus. This has caused a rotation in perception of the lofty role of the professor dedicated to the search for truth, to a merchandizing identity where the professor markets and serves as vendor for his or her particular skills and knowhow, which students perceive themselves to be purchasing.

The fourth force derives from costs related to college operations. They have risen faster than consumer price indices. Government programs to increase college opportunities for a broadening range of citizens have led to increased dependence of both public and private colleges upon government as a source for funding. This results in the bureaucracy and politics (real politics, not just amateurish academic politics) that accompanies increased government involvement when money is appropriated to campuses. It is exerted by both federal and state governments. The bureaucracy tends to segment the campus into fiefdoms of procedures, rules, and policy manuals. Political considerations, like the tentacles of an octopus, creep into campus operations. The brooding omnipresence of bureaucratic and political oversight overlays the learning community.

The fifth force is found in a national shift from the acceptance of moral certainties to that of a relativistic approach in personal and group behavior. This derives from the increasing cultural diversity of our population, within which personal beliefs and community standards vary dramatically, although in the aftermath of September 11, 2001, a renewal of unifying patriotism has taken place. Even so, racial and ethnic diversity will continue to be celebrated, elevating the values of belonging to distinct and separated, cultural, ethnic, or racial groups. When applied to the college experience this has tended to dilute previously defined basic principles. Moral certainty is replaced by a variety of opinions.

These five, broad forces taken together have given rise to specific changes altering the warp and woof of the campus experience. Although there are scores of different changes, I have organized them under eight major headings.

1.) Exponential increases in knowledge and the technologies to profess it.

Through the unprecedented growth of knowledge and the technology of its distribution, curriculums and methods of academic operations need readjustment.

2.) Diversities in race, culture, class, and affirmative action.

A more varied human palette is welcome, but political correctness has appeared, while racial preferences spawn legal battles.

3.) Students as customers.

They come from a broader demographic base than heretofore, and now consume academic products rather than serve as novices in the learning community. Job credentials assume more importance to students as consumers, than learning.

4.) Vulgarities and disrespect on campuses, lowered academic standards, corruption in athletics, and how about tenure?

This resonates as lessening respect for knowledge, and lowered academic standards, especially in non-selective institutions. It also shows up in the ways faculty rights, academic freedom, and tenure are now treated in the academy.

5.) Professional politics and bureaucracy.

They permeate the operations of public campuses.

6.) Problems in shared governance: how they relate to detached professors and their disconnects in teaching students.

Noble processes misused.

7.) Rising college costs, less support, outdated management, and the dilemma of part-time faculty.

Outdated management prevails, along with disconnections between faculty members and campus roles and missions.

8.) Morality.

The replacement of basic principles by relative values.

THE CHANGES SPREAD UNEVENLY

As in society at large, change on campuses will occur because of advances in knowledge. (Of course, advances in knowledge are not the only forces resulting in societal change. The opposite side of the coin, e.g., the suppression of knowledge, can be seen in what happened in Stalinist Russia, and the Cambodia of Pol Pot.) But at universities, advancing knowledges are spread unevenly through the academic disciplines. Mathematics and physics accrete knowledge and technology at such rapid rates that physicists or mathematicians will be hopelessly out of date if they do not constantly replace their knowledge and techniques with new developments as they occur month by month. I have known physics and mathematics professors who moved from their teaching and research work into positions as deans or other administrative positions. Then, after stints of a few years, they wanted to move back into the harness in their disciplinary fields but to their dismay found it impossible to catch up and master the new knowledge and technique they missed while serving as administrators. This provides an interesting contrast to my own discipline—performing pianist—and illustrates the extent of the differences of campus disciplines. The performance techniques at the piano keyboard, in contrast to the techniques of doing astrophysics, haven't changed all that much since the days of Mozart, Beethoven, or Liszt. My own technique at the keyboard was set before I was ten. Today, in the performance of nineteenth-century repertory, pianists often use fingerings at the keyboard that come down from Beethoven or Chopin.[5] When I slipped out of harness as president I was able to resume performing at the keyboard (obviously only after weeks and months of humbling practice) because the technical requisites had not changed. But had I been a particle physicist, because of constant changes in the discipline, it would not have been possible to pick up where I left off.

This illustrates the enormous differences in rates of change between disciplines embodied in the performing arts, sciences, and humanities. I hasten to reiterate, however, that taken altogether human knowledge in today's world develops exponentially. It is one of the largest and toughest issues confronting campuses. The amount of change since 1950 dwarfs that which took place during the preceding two and a half centuries of American higher education. And it continues to change at an even faster rate. Twenty-five years from now most universities will have unrecognizable aspects when compared to campuses of today.[6] The reasons are two-fold and are related to new and developing information and knowledge and to monumental changes in the historic function of colleges and universities.[7]

INSUFFICIENT MANAGEMENT ADAPTABILITY

Sadly, the management structures of most universities are not all that well equipped to adapt to changes in their new environments and roles. Among the main reasons is out-of-date "shared governance." This foggy term describes management practices essentially shared between tenured faculty and administrative leadership.

The sharing of university management responsibility is a lofty concept. But for our fast-paced world, and in particular when the cast of faculty participants turns intransigent, its practice is often a distressing anachronism. The unwieldy management process of shared governance usually results in a glacial creep in needed institutional adaptability that by contrast should flow like a river. Academic politics usually determine which faculty members become involved in shared governance. Faculty politicians who are good at getting elected by their colleagues to faculty governance posts (in ways no different from national, state, and local elections) might not be equally good as leaders in shared governance. Also, the most accomplished academics, who are fully occupied with their own teaching and research (with a few but not all that many exceptions), do not make it a habit to get involved in faculty political matters. This leaves a vacuum too often filled by colleagues of lesser stature who have not always made their mark as academics and who, alternatively, seek their recognition through academic politics. Because of the myriad of disconnects in the processes of shared governance, stalemates inevitably occur. Thus most universities are at a competitive disadvantage as management organizations in our pluralistic and rapidly evolving society.[8]

SEGMENTING ROLES

The segmenting of the roles of different units, both academic and non-academic, has become a necessity in complex universities. Businesses embodying different kinds of service and manufacturing functions have been more successful in this management process. This is why the refrain "Why don't you run your university like a business?" is heard so often. Faculty members deplore it. But even though universities have many stakeholders, they do not translate into stockholders. That said, it does not take away from the fact that separate and complicated parts need to function efficiently and well. Shared governance has had the effect of clouding issues of who is responsible for what. Faculties chant the mantra, "We are the University!"—which in an earlier day and age was true. It remains true in essence but is no longer true in its implementation. While faculties remain at the epicenter of campuses, and always will, there exist many other university domains crucial to the operations of universities that go beyond the expected functions and expertise of faculty members. These domains did not previously exist. This has created confusion. It is why Bill Readings, author of *The University in Ruins* could say, "It is no longer clear what the place of the University is within society."[9]

The dilemma remains unresolved. It could be, paraphrasing Winston Churchill, that shared governance is the worst form of university management, except for all the others. Frustrating as it is, it can work internally—I said can work. But in external affairs it no longer suffices. This insufficiency is exacerbated by the increasingly adversarial relationships between faculties and administrations. But a "corporatization" (ugly word that it is) of university management is not the answer. Faculty members despise the term and mobilize against it.

FLAWS IN THE STRUCTURE OF BOARDS OF TRUSTEES

Lest it be inferred from the above that faculty members are the only ones to whom disconnects apply, board members can be no less susceptible. In state colleges and universities, faculty, students, and administrators have to contend with politically appointed trustees whose partisan agendas bear little or no relationship to the role of the university in teaching, research, and community service. I recall a trustee from the ranks of labor union leadership at Cleveland State who rarely ever came to board meetings unless they involved union issues. When he did come he exerted his influence on behalf of unionized maintenance workers or pushed for the formation of a faculty union. Other trustees coming from racial minorities inevitably manifested support at board meetings for the minority groups they represented, whether or not it related to the larger good of the university community.[10]

The system that mandates political appointment by state governors of state college and university trustees is a blemish on state university governance, as is the small number of statutory members usually making up the board. If university trustees number twenty or twenty-five (or more) and a blockhead—or two or three—become board members, they can be surrounded and their negative force diluted by the larger number of trustees. But when the board is small, numbering nine members each appointed for a term of nine years, which is common for state universities with governor-appointed trustees, then two or three appointees who are incompetent or have partisan agendas can enjoy an uninhibited reign. This happens in many states. Much to my disquiet, I have dealt with it in Ohio. I experienced a particularly egregious example of harm done where politics in appointments trumped merit. I had cultivated an experienced and successful corporate CEO who was committed to CSU, had expressed a desire to serve on the board (and who would have performed well), and had informally committed himself to giving a million dollars to the university. The governor was aware of this, and had interacted with the CEO, who had every reason to believe the board appointment would come through. Instead, without prior notice, the governor appointed a member of the Cleveland Black Ministers Conference, presumably repaying a political debt. Black ministers are by far the most influential group within Cleveland's minority communities. The CEO was sufficiently upset by this cavalier treatment that his gift commitment was withdrawn, as was his involvement with the university, which has never been revived. The minister after serving for a period resigned and left for a job in another city.

The solution to the untoward system of political board appointments will involve controversy and conflict in state capitols, where attitudes toward university governance are inevitably political. Legislative action with very strong backing will be required since governors resist having their appointment prerogatives tampered with. As matters stand, governors in many states simply appoint state university trustees. Obviously they receive recommendations but there are usually no statutory screening processes related to merit or suitability of individual candidates. This is where persons of questionable suitability slip through. The remedy is to establish a process where panels of, say, five candidates for each trustee appointment are developed and presented to the governor. She or he will then be required to appoint the trustee from these panels, which could be developed by groups representing various constituencies related to higher education. This is similar to the merit selection used in some states for the appointment of judges. Along with this reform, the size of the board of trustees at public institutions should be increased to not less than twenty. There could be a given number appointed by more than one constituency. For example, if the size of the board were to be twenty, the governor could be authorized to appoint eleven, the alumni association authorized to appoint three, the university faculty authorized to appoint two, the sitting board could appoint two, and the university non-academic staff association two. Variations could easily be introduced. The process contains desirable checks and balances.

FAR-REACHING CHANGES IN STUDENT ATTITUDES AND EXPECTATIONS

Radical change exists in the difference between students of yesteryear as "wards" of deans and faculties, accepting without question the curriculums prescribed for them, as compared to students of today who increasingly see themselves, not as academic captives on campuses but just the opposite, namely customers paying for the education delivered to them and paid for by their tuition. Actually, their tuition by no means pays for the total cost (on average across the nation about 40 percent), but the perception of students who think they are paying customers is stronger than it has ever been. Further, universities are no longer concerned only with education in the liberal arts and classical studies, which had been separate from the oft times gritty process of training students to make a living. Training programs related to the marketplace used to be found only in apprenticeship systems and in trade schools, but colleges and universities now are major players in this realm. Today's non-elite college students, as users picking up what they see as the tab for this training, expect and demand a say in what it is they are paying for and how it is delivered. They want and expect a "user-friendly" campus.

This 180 degree turn in student expectations exists not only because of changed attitudes within society, but also because of an intrinsic difference between college students of generations gone by and those of today. Going to college used to be a privilege reserved mostly for young men from elite families. Sons of the lower classes generally did not have the opportunity even to think about going to college. College was for the purpose of producing better minds and thus better men who could become leaders. Latin, Greek, and classical literature made up the main part of the curriculum that achieved this noble end. Many of the founders of our nation were steeped in these studies.

EGALITARIANISM AND CHANGING UNIVERSITY ROLES

College is now egalitarian. It is not seen just as a privilege, but as a right. Whereas generations ago an exceedingly small cut of the spectrum of the citizenry attended college, nowadays the percentage of the total population that at one time or another has enrolled in some kind of college program pushes 60 percent. Seventy percent of high school graduates go on to college today, compared to 5 percent a century ago. A baccalaureate degree used to be awarded after a student (enrolling at about age eighteen) had lived and studied on campus for four years. The substance of the degree was supposed to last a lifetime. Today the content of college degrees in professional and technical fields, instead of lasting a lifetime, lasts only a few years. For professional and technical people, which in our age of information, is the great majority of economically productive people, learning must continue throughout a career; thus the universal term "lifelong learning." This has brought legions of persons from all segments of society into colleges and universities. They enter so they can adjust themselves technically to an ever-changing world of shifting job requirements. This has changed the historic role of universities. There are some campuses (thank heaven) where "communities of scholars" and students preserve the tradition of the life of the mind. But by contrast the majority of today's campuses serve a mass market of practical students. They minimize pure intellectual values, and instead maximize practical and technical training that will help them obtain jobs.[11]

This pragmatism has had a profound effect upon the values universities emphasize or minimize as they respond to the needs of the nation's workforce. Practical concerns have been placed above concerns about virtue. This might be well and good for curricula crafted for purposes of economic and technical needs of a mass society. But no matter how well equipped in technical values a trained workforce might be, if the people making up this workforce do not accept and adhere to basic principles of ethical and moral values—honesty, a solid work ethic, respect for other people so they can function in teams, (which includes even such fundamentals as getting to work on time)—our human technology will not function properly in its service to the nation. The guidance systems inherent in our millions of worker-technicians at computer keyboards and control panels will falter.

In contrast to the "hard skills" of professional and technical proficiency, these ethical and moral values have been called "soft skills." This is an unfortunate term of jargon but it fits in with the way we talk today. Universities (to say nothing of families and schools from kindergarten through high school) have failed in teaching these ethical principles. The failure can be seen at all levels of our society. We desperately need an infusion of morality and ethics in practical and technical curricula similar to the way such values were earlier infused in liberal arts and humanities curricula.

FORCES OF CHALLENGE AND CHANGE

The preceding sets the stage upon which forces militating against conventional higher education will assault, feint, and parry throughout the next quarter century. They are discussed in greater detail in what follows. These forces, in ways new to higher education, create academic environments alien to the ingrained habits of faculties, administrations, and trustees. How campuses adjust to them will determine not only the future of higher education in the nation, but the future of the nation itself.

But before launching into my reasoning about the changes, along with my solutions for the problems generated by them, I will hearken back to my own growth and maturing. Since this is not an abstract treatise but a book coming out of personal, human experience, only in this way can I make it ring true.

CHAPTER 1

Rain and Shine

We may consider each generation as a distinct nation, with a right, by the will of its majority, to bind themselves, but none to bind the succeeding generation, more than the inhabitants of another country.

Thomas Jefferson

IT RAINS A lot in Aberdeen, Washington. As a boy I remember a year when the rainfall added up to more than one hundred inches. This Pacific Ocean town of sixteen thousand, founded during the heyday of late nineteenth-century lumbering industry, is on Grays Harbor, due west as the crow flies from the southern tip of Puget Sound—fifty miles from the state capital Olympia, and one hundred ten miles from Seattle. Umbrellas and raincoats are standard equipment, even while waiting outside the delivery room in the Grays Harbor Hospital maternity ward. But by contrast, when the sun is shining, with the skies a wonderful blue, the loveliness of the climate more than matches felicitous environments to be found anywhere else in the world. And everything is green; so much so that the local saying, "you have to watch that the fence posts don't sprout," almost has credibility. It is a wonderful region. This is where I was born and reared.

The Flower family has been in America a long time. The proper noun is *Flower*, singular, not Flowers—throughout the eighty-two years of my life I have had no recourse but to learn to tolerate and to accept with equanimity my being called John *Flowers*. Lamrock Flower emigrated from Rutlandshire, England, in the early 1680s and settled and lived out the rest of his life in Hartford, Connecticut. The Flower group seems to have been nicely situated in England at that time. Records show they had prospered (even knighthoods here and there) so I have no idea why Lamrock took off for the colonies. Certainly it was not for the religious reasons that motivated the Puritans to board the Mayflower. Lamrock's fourth child, a son John, was a justice of the peace in Hartford and the progenitor of the branch of the Flower family in America to which I belong, and why I am proud of my name.

Over the years the descendants of Lamrock's son John Flower moved westward (my father was born in Sibley, Iowa) and ultimately my grandfather, Frank Zephron Flower, with his family, settled on a farm in Fairfield, Washington in the wheat-growing country thirty miles outside of Spokane, Washington where family members still live.

My father Lloyd, who had a strong sense of duty and obligation (and whose principles I respect to this day—even revere) worked on the farm with and for his father. But when he was twenty-one, in 1911, he said, in so many words, to his dad that he had fulfilled his obligation and that he intended to move out on his own. Interestingly his chosen profession, of all things in that as yet less than sophisticated western part of the United States (he had not completed high school), was that of portrait photographer. He opened a studio in Rockford, Washington and not long after learned that in Aberdeen, across the Cascade Mountains on the Pacific coast, there was a studio for sale. He bought it, and the Flower Studio came into being.

With his first wife, Jessie Evans, he moved to Aberdeen. Tragically she died in childbirth in Aberdeen, leaving my father with an infant daughter, Barbara. In those days the interactions of neighborly networks provided human support that today is considerably less characteristic. Dad managed.

My mother, Linda Nelson, Dad's second wife, came from Norwegian and Swedish stock. They were blue-eyed and fair (Mother was a redhead) with a firm Lutheran heritage. They could be stubborn, but had a sense of humor. Swedes and Norwegians delight in poking fun at one another, their favorite ripostes being that a Swede is nothing more than a Norwegian with the brains knocked out, or vice versa. Mother's father, Oscar, by his nature should have been an artist. He was an authentic gentleman, but an inept businessman. He and his wife (whom we called Munsie) and four children had moved from eastern Washington to Aberdeen, where he had a general store. He was too good to customers in extending credit, with the result that his business failed. But it was through the family line of Oscar Nelson that my proclivity for art comes. Mother was an instinctive musician and her twin brothers were naturally gifted, if essentially untrained, painters. Her older brother Arnold, whence comes my middle name, was killed in World War I on the day before the Armistice was signed. (Mother never quite got over it. She could not cope with movies in which there was war violence.)

I have never been privy to the dynamics of my mother's and father's courtship, but it was obviously compelling. Mother had graduated from Aberdeen High School in 1914. She wanted to go on to a conservatory of music in Chicago, but the money was not available. In those days student financial aid from the government had not been thought of. She worked as a secretary in Aberdeen, got to know Lloyd, and then went to San Francisco (which in that day for a young, single woman must have been quite an adventure) where she did more clerical and secretarial work. In retrospect I cannot picture what her life would have been like had she stayed in San Francisco and pursued the option of a career (women had yet to achieve suffrage in the U.S.), but the attraction of Lloyd was stronger than that of a potential career. So she returned to Aberdeen, married Lloyd, and by doing so took on the responsibility of his daughter Barbara. What her parents might have thought about the scenario I have no idea. I came along in 1921.

In the 1920s community respect for Dad grew in Aberdeen (the few snippets of newspaper references to him I have seen indicate that) and at the same time his studio business grew. If a single phrase would describe him it would be "steady and dependable." In the lumbermill town of Aberdeen home furnaces were wood burning, the loads of wood being delivered in wagons pulled by horses or sometimes being carried in those unwieldy trucks of World War I vintage that looked like they could carry supplies to Noah's Ark. Our wood was dumped in the alley behind the house. As a small fry I would "help" Dad pile and stack the wood, sometimes piping up that this looked like a pretty big job. I still remember his response: all you had to do was stack one piece on another, keep at it, and in due time the job would be done. He never talked down nor gave his words inflections to make it obvious there was a larger message being conveyed. He simply said things.

It was in 1926 when I was five years old that my parents started me at the piano. Somehow I had learned the notes on the keyboard. One day I identified the pitch of a tugboat whistle across town on the Chehalis River and my parents realized I had perfect pitch. My teacher was Aunt Dagny, tall, regal, of venerable Lutheran heritage who with considerable pride traced her lineage back to Harold I (Harold

Fairhair, Norway's first king in 872). She was the wife of my grandmother Munsie's brother, John Tenwick, for whom I was named. To her, music was inseparable from life. The fact that I was started at the keyboard so young and taught in a regular way has been a boon to me throughout the decades. My keyboard technique was set before I was ten—piano playing is a skill involving the human motor system—and like learning to ride a bike it does not leave you even though, to stay in keyboard trim, you never stop practicing.

This Victorian lady Dagny Tenwick's musical ambit was remarkable given the purism and straightlaced character of her upbringing in a Lutheran minister's household in Christiania (before it became Oslo), Norway. Her family emigrated to the United States, settling in Redwing, Minnesota. After marrying Uncle John, the two of them moved to Aberdeen, Washington, where he was a wholesale grocery supplier. Her knowledge of music came through Lutheran church music, the keyboard repertory of J. S. Bach, and eighteenth- and nineteenth-century piano works up to Sergei Rachmaninoff, including a brace of Debussy. Even though this was less than universal in historic perspective and style it was not limited in spirit. She was authentic. True, this authenticity did not include jazz, which she considered sinful (it took me years to shed that yoke of denial) but the path of music on which she started me never led into a dead end nor veered into the trivial.

Times were good during the twenties. In 1927 and 1928 we had a full-time maid at home, not unusual at the time given that domestic help made up a significant component of the workforce. Then came the Crash of 1929 and the deep depression of the early thirties. Banks and businesses went under but my father held on. Afterward, when times got better, he was proud that he had succeeded in weathering the depression when so many others were engulfed by it. During the depths of that trying period I remember him allocating a dollar a day to my mother to buy food. And she managed.

In corners of my mind a number of vivid memories from those times still exist. Haircuts were twenty-five cents and Saturday afternoon serial cowboy movies at the Weir Theater were a dime. I was sent every two weeks, quarter in hand, to get my hair cut. (Who had even heard of tips?) A barber shop was a gathering place for men. Salons where men's hair could be blow-dried would have confused the entire community. The barber shop where I had my hair cut still had spittoons. On one afternoon during the depression's depths, a voluble, middle-aged lumbermill worker was seated along the wall. With conviction and sincerity he held forth that workers should be satisfied and able to live on wages of a dollar a day. Today's privileged and self-centered students, particularly those of more recent vintage who drive BMWs and live in houses with three- and four-car garages, have no concept of the deprivation visited upon individuals and families during the depression. These young people of today, admirably, are often caught up in larger issues, the environment for example, but these matters are not part of their immediate personal experience, which to a considerable extent is confined due to their self absorption. Sometimes they mistakenly equate this self absorption with sensitivity, to recall what columnist George Will observed in a newspaper column. It is beyond their abilities even to imagine the possibility of family impoverishment, which was a daily fact of life to young people during the depression. It has never occurred to my grandchildren that turning out a light not only saves energy but reduces the electric bill.

Even though the depression affected everyone's lives, my experiences in grade school, junior high, and high school remained positive. My piano lessons with Aunt Dagny continued without interruption. My mother, musician that she was (church organist for over forty years and organist at the local funeral home), kept me at it and I developed very nicely at the keyboard. Her dedication to me, her only child and son, was complete. I remember one occasion during my teens when I was being difficult and uncooperative my dad said to me that Mother's sun rose and set in me and that it would help if I appreciated it.

As a young pianist I was clearly recognized as the best around and was asked regularly to perform at events and gatherings. I performed quite a bit. Mother used to say to me before I got up in front of people, "Now don't forget to be gracious." I recall this admonition as far back as age eight. She herself had considerable presence, including charisma, and expected as much from me—even at age eight. Obviously this piano concentration meant that I didn't do all the things young guys did after school simply because I spent more time practicing than most other kids. However, my parents did want a "normal" life for me and in fact Aberdeen and the schools essentially provided it. I didn't take part in contact sports, although in those days before the drop kick was eliminated from football I learned to do it and could have made an effective kicker. I did play on the golf team and was a reasonably good tennis player, but performing at the piano was what I was given most credit for. At the graduation ceremony of my high school class in 1939 I performed the Second Hungarian Rhapsody of Franz Liszt. In retrospect, given the pyro-techniques of that piece, it was an arrogant thing to do. But I did get away with it.

Even though the depression had waned we were still on a tight budget. I had applied for admission to Juilliard and to the Eastman School of Music. Both institutions indicated I was admissible and that they would be glad to have me, but scholarship help was not available. My mother and I drove to Philadelphia and I auditioned at the Curtis Institute of

Music, where every student was and still is subsidized. I didn't make it. Coming from a town on the ocean out in the Pacific Northwest with no musical heritage in any professional sense, we were naive and innocent of the stratagems for getting into high-profile performance schools. Had we known how to go at it and had experienced guidance, I probably could have made it.

Earlier in my high school years my mother drove me to Seattle each week to take lessons with Silvio Risegari. He was well known in the Seattle musical network and possessed that wonderful Italian musical temperament. (When I got my driver's license I would drive myself with admonitions to "be careful" ringing in my ears.) I paid him at the end of each lesson with a five dollar bill which he accepted with seriousness and folded into his vest pocket. He had studied with the fabled late nineteenth- and early twentieth-century teacher Theodor Leschetizky, a student of Carl Czerny, who himself had been a friend of Beethoven and had taught Franz Liszt. Leschetizky was part of pianism's sturm und drang and belonged to the high, romantic musical life and style of his era, teaching such later luminaries as Paderewski and Artur Schnabel. He had no less than four wives in succession—all his pupils.

As a teacher Risegari did not wander off into abstractions. Playing the piano was practical. The great and good teachers were or had been virtuosos. They taught by demonstration and example. This contrasts lamentably with so many of today's comfortable, tenured university professors of piano who talk nicely about music but would be hard pressed to go before an audience and perform as a credible virtuoso.

Risegari had toured with Ferruccio Busoni, one of the monumental pianists and composers of the late nineteenth and early twentieth centuries. Risegari's style reflected the day and age of charismatic virtuosi and his technique had the flair and seasoning of an experienced performer. He used to say that a pianist had to be so routined that he could rise from a sound sleep in the middle of the night and rattle off his repertory. But somehow his career did not blossom, no doubt in large measure because he was stuck out in the Pacific Northwest, far from where performing careers happened: New York, Boston, Chicago, to say nothing of London, Paris, and Vienna. Despite that, his teaching represented a rare and uncommon window that looked out on immortal nineteenth-century pianists who established traditions that remain with us. These traditions remain valid even though the language of music has now changed. What I learned from him is not available, firsthand, today.

After I graduated from Weatherwax High School in Aberdeen in 1939 and the possibilities of Eastman, Juilliard, and Curtis did not materialize, my father helped me get a job at the Eastman Kodak Company store in Seattle. It paid twelve dollars a week. I moved to Seattle, continued my lessons with Risegari, worked during the day, and was permitted to practice on the pianos in the display rooms at Sherman Clay & Co. at night. This continued through 1940 and 1941. During that period I studied a considerable amount of the standard keyboard repertory including a number of concertos, some of which I performed in studio recitals with Risegari playing the orchestral reduction at the second piano. He believed that my talent at the piano was real, and was convinced that he could bring me to the starting point of a performance career. What he did not recognize, or perhaps could not bring himself to recognize, was that beginning a performance career that involved the networking and the backing of an agent or agents was simply not possible in Seattle at that time—nor is it today more than sixty years later, even though Seattle has developed into a recognized center of music.

During those years of the late thirties and into 1940 and 1941 the events unfolding in Europe hovered over everyone, although I cannot say I was preoccupied with them. One morning in a workroom at the Eastman Kodak Company— May 13, 1940—I vividly remember hearing the live radio broadcast of Winston Churchill delivering his most famous speech, including the words "I have nothing to offer but blood, toil, tears, and sweat." I can still hear the resonance of his voice in that broadcast and the characteristic enunciations of his delivery.

When December 7, 1941, brought Pearl Harbor, in my twenty-first year, things changed.

It was clear that military service obligations would accrue to me in the near future. Simply being drafted was not an appealing way to fulfill them. Men who were enrolled in college had a number of types of training programs available to them so I left the job at Eastman Kodak (but continued with Risegari) and went back to Aberdeen, enrolling in Grays Harbor Junior College. It now exists on an attractive campus as Grays Harbor College and has become a significant force in the community. The war effort had reversed economic conditions and shortly after that Dad and Mother subsidized my enrollment in the University of Washington. In the meantime, as a pilot-training recruit, I had joined the U.S. Army Air Corps, which in those days belonged to the army as a corps, not as a separate branch of the military. I continued at the University of Washington and with Risegari, while awaiting my call to active service.

I was called for a summer program at the University of Minnesota in 1942 (where we were housed, of all places, under the seats at the football stadium) and then went through basic army training camp at Shepherd Field in Texas. Next came primary flight training in open-cockpit Stearman aircraft, which was followed by what was called basic training in BT-13s, culminating in advanced training at Luke Field in single-engine AT-6s. I graduated and was commissioned in the class of 43-E at Luke Field. There followed operational flying training, and my assignment to fly the Douglas A-20, which was elegant in its response to the pilot. It had twin engines, just one set of controls (thus no copilot) and had space in the rear for a gunner to operate fifty-caliber machine guns.

Before being put into an A-20, I spent a period of training in Merced, California, learning to fly a B-25, which was a wonderfully stable, twin engine, medium-altitude bomber with twin controls. (Sixty years later there are still B-25s being flown at U.S. air shows, owned and maintained by private people— I'd like to have one.) On one instrument training flight out of Merced one of my B-25 right engine pistons broke loose, and of all things came out through the surrounding engine housing. It derived, obviously, from a ground maintenance problem. Without any experience in this kind of emergency, I did manage to land it back at the base on one engine. In today's world of flying such an occurrence would generate an involved investigation. At that time, you simply went on to the next day.

I was then transferred to Charlotte, North Carolina, where I was checked out in a Douglas A-20 in preparation for transfer to the Pacific Theater.

CHAPTER 2

The Pacific Theater

The next World War will be fought with stones.

Albert Einstein

WE WERE ASSIGNED to the Fifth Air Force and sent to Hollandia, New Guinea, now Jayapura in today's Indonesian New Guinea. From there we did more training, especially low-level flying practice runs up the Markham Valley, where we flew low, "on the deck," leaving a propeller-wash wake in the swamp grass. (This is scarcely recommended for anyone with a wife and children.) We did four training missions out of Hollandia, one being over famed Rabaul on the Bismarck Archipelago. These were actual combat missions but, even though the territory we flew over was still held by the Japanese, the sorties were not difficult given that by then the areas had been badly beaten up. From Hollandia we transferred to a base in Mindoro, an island directly south of Luzon in the Philippines. I was assigned to a squadron with the colorful name *Sky Lancers*. From the strip on Mindoro we flew mostly to the north of Manila, with the missions being low-level sorties in support of infantry troops still fighting Japanese in the hills and valleys above the Lingayen Gulf around Baguio.

At that time flying techniques were far removed from the

35

sophisticated procedures of today. There were no computers or precision electronic equipment. In the briefing before take off (usually involving six A-20s to fly in "vics" of three aircraft) we were told approximately where the troops we were to support were located. We were given the radio frequency of an infantry officer located with the troops on the ground who was usually in a jeep. When we got within range we contacted the officer who gave us verbal instructions about where the action was and what to hit. The flying was low-level, literally just feet above the ground, and keeping the radio instructions straight could be tricky, particularly since the terrain and hills looked much the same. I remember on one occasion after contacting the officer, getting his instructions, and starting the run, he shouted back over the radio, "Peel off! Peel off! Goddammit! You're aiming for us!!"

I flew twenty of those kinds of missions. Each mission of itself was worth one point which could be accumulated toward your eventual reassignment to the U.S. If your aircraft absorbed a piece of flak you got an extra point. I'll never forget the time I first realized I was being shot at. As you go in on a bombing and strafing run your fifty-caliber machine guns, mounted in the nose of the aircraft, have tracer bullets, i.e., bullets with a substance that glows as they make their trajectories so you can see where they are going. As they move away from you, your tracers obviously get smaller. But all of a sudden I could see tracers in front of me getting bigger. I can still picture them in my mind. It took a second or two—it probably was a split second—"Holy smoke! They're shooting at ME!!" The combat A-20s had a small cast iron, protective shield mounted in front of the pilot just ahead of the controls. I recall trying to shrink myself as much as I could behind that shield.

OKINAWA

Preparations were being made to transfer the squadron to Okinawa. Our understanding was that the larger war strategy involved an invasion of Japan through the southcoast of Kyushu Island, which is south of Honshu, where Tokyo is located. Infantry troops were to establish beachheads, as in Normandy. Once established, metallic mesh landing strips would be laid down. It could be done fast. Our squadron, along with others, would then fly from the north of Okinawa to Kyushu, covering the invading troops. Since A-20s did not have the fuel capacity to fly from Okinawa to Japan and back, the plan involved missions supporting the troops in Kyushu, then landing on the mesh strip, refueling, and going back to Okinawa. This would have been a very high risk and hair-raising assignment.

Before we pulled up stakes on Mindoro and headed for Okinawa, President Franklin Roosevelt died and Harry Truman became president. He then made the never-to-be-forgotten decision to drop atomic bombs on Hiroshima and Nagasaki, precipitating Japan's surrender. It made unnecessary the invasion of Kyushu. Thousands of lives were lost as a result of the atom bombs but who knows how many would have been lost in the land invasion of Japan? But our scheduled transfer to Okinawa went forward anyway. Prior to that, two events took place that remain indelible in my memory, small by comparison to events on the world stage, but significant in my own personal life.

The first occurred before we left Mindoro. There was an A-20 in our squadron that had been flown on two hundred fifty or more missions. It was used up. The Fifth Air Force maintenance people at Clark Field in Manila (which had earlier been retaken from the Japanese) wanted it to salvage parts. I was assigned to fly it up to Clark Field. I took a corporal with me who had some leave coming to him, which he intended to spend in Manila. But the airplane didn't make it. On the way the hydraulic system failed totally. This meant that systems depending on it, the landing gear in particular, didn't function. There was no manual crank-down mechanism for A-20 landing gear, but there was a procedure to use in such an emergency. It involved releasing the two main wheels and the nose wheel, letting gravity take them down, then maneuvering the aircraft sharply, up and down, hopefully, to get them to lock in place. But the wheels absolutely refused to cooperate. They continued to dangle. There was the possibility of a belly landing but the likelihood of only one wheel locking in the process, especially the nose wheel, might precipitate unpredictable aircraft crash behavior. I was in contact with the Clark Field tower during this episode. They didn't think the odds were very good for bringing it in with three dangling wheels. We agreed that I'd fly over the field so the corporal could parachute down, which he did with no problem. Then the tower said, in essence, take the damn thing over Manila Bay and bail yourself out. It's not worth anything anyway. Those were not the precise words but they convey the sense of what was said.

There's a tricky part in bailing out of an A-20. The pilot sits in front of the propellers. If you just jumped out of the cockpit you'd go into the propellers. What you have to do is trim the aircraft so it will fly level, if only briefly; get out on the wing and stay close to the fuselage by holding onto a line, meant for precisely that emergency purpose; and then fall into the air from the trailing edge of the wing between the propeller and the fuselage, going straight down to avoid being hit by the tail assembly. This was one of those carefully worked out emergency procedures drilled into A-20 pilots. It worked for me. The plane hit the water with an explosion. I drifted down into the bay, was picked up first by a native in a sampan, then by a navy PBY Catalina flying boat. They made me go to a field hospital for a physical check, which I felt to be quite unnecessary.

The second event took place out of Apari on the northern coast of the Philippines. We had left Mindoro, and flew to Apari as the jumping off point for the much longer flight to Okinawa. We stayed at the base at Apari for a day or two, then took off as a squadron for Okinawa. When we got into the air, headed north over the water, my right engine began sputtering. Clearly something was wrong. I could not take the chance of flying that distance over the open ocean with an engine out of kilter, so I peeled off from the group and went back to Apari. When the maintenance crew got into the engine they found that the ignition cable that took electricity to the cylinders around the engine was corroded, probably from the humidity, and caused the misfiring. It took another day to replace it, which was no big deal, but left me with the job of flying alone over an expanse of ocean to Okinawa.

In those days the navigation aids in A-20s were primitive compared to current satellite technology which now provides navigation aids everywhere, whether it be for ocean liners, cars, or hikers. What I did was fly north from Apari to Formosa (not yet named Taiwan), followed north along its east coast, then headed northeast for Okinawa. Such a flight today would be routine and perhaps dull. But if you look at a map of the Pacific Ocean you can see that there are considerable stretches of ocean between the Philippines and Taiwan, and Taiwan and Okinawa. No visual reference points are available in the vast stretches of open water. If you flew by dead reckoning and a perverse wind blew you off course, you probably had no way of calculating it. Even though your compass heading might be proper you could easily miss Okinawa and go on out into the vaster stretches of open ocean to the east.

At that time, however, there was a navigation system, limited in extent, but which I still hold dear.

Imagine a circle and divide it into four quadrants by north to south, east to west lines. From the center of the circle, which is your destination, two radio signals originate; one designated by the Morse code letter "A," which is a short signal followed by a longer one (dit dah) and the other for the Morse code letter "N," which is a longer signal followed by a short one (dah dit). These signals are repeated endlessly—dit dah, dit dah, dit dah, or dah dit, dah dit, dah dit.

The dit dah signals cover the two ninety-degree quadrants which were the northeast and the southwest while the dah dit signals cover the two ninety-degree quadrants which were the northwest and the southeast. When your radio is tuned into the frequency of these signals you can tell which of the two sets of quadrants you're in by whether you hear dit dah, or dah dit. If the signal gets louder as you proceed you know that you are flying toward its origination point. If it gets weaker you know you are flying away from it. If you are in a dit dah quadrant and it changes to a dah dit you know that you have slipped over the line into the adjacent quadrant. The elegance of its logic and simplicity makes it a beautiful system (although pilots in that time would scarcely have used the term elegant).

The wattage of the station emitting the signals at Nara in the south of Okinawa was not strong, and I could not pick up a signal until fairly close to Okinawa. Thus I still had to fly over a lot of water, quite alone. But finally I detected a faint dit dah, and keeping on my heading heard it grow stronger. This was about as welcome a sound of the letter "A" in Morse code as one could imagine. I simply followed it in and pretty soon could make out the coast of the island. The airstrip from which we had been assigned to operate was on the northern part of the island so I flew north along the west coast, located the strip, and rejoined the squadron.

SURRENDER

The surrender of Japan brought an end to all of the planning for the invasion but we remained on Okinawa for a while, living in tents. During that time we experienced one of those legendary Pacific typhoons. The weather station for the base was perched on a cliff above the water. Before it blew away the wind velocity indicator read 140 miles per hour. There were a few hours of warning before the typhoon hit head on and somewhere we scrounged lengths of two-by-four lumber and braced the tents from the inside. Miraculously, I'll never know quite how, they did not blow away.

Then we were assigned to Itami, Japan, living in a boys' academy located on a hill, close to an airstrip outside Osaka. Specific local duties for us were not spelled out but obviously a quick occupation of defeated Japan was the larger purpose. Encountering Japanese people in those circumstances engendered confused behaviors. As you passed them on the street they didn't seem to know what to do—salute? bow? stand to the side?

Before long, as a twenty-four-year-old first lieutenant I found myself the commanding officer of a service unit, essentially by default. A service unit is like a holding company that includes different kinds of organizations. The aircraft of this unit included a C-47, a B-25, plus half a dozen Stinson L-5s which were little, single-engine, fixed landing gear aircraft that the infantry used for spotting and which could take off and land practically anywhere. They were called "grasshoppers." In addition there was a laundry unit, an intelligence office, and an infantry unit. The infantry unit consisted of enlisted men only. They didn't have enough to do. One night a couple of them got into trouble with some Japanese girls, were arrested by the Japanese police (quite within the rules of the occupation) and ended up in a jail which turned out to be a sixteenth-century dungeon that hadn't had much improvement since it was built. I went down into the place, extricated them, and got them into the hands of U.S. Military Police. What happened to them ultimately I don't know, but it would not have been all that serious.

The organizational hodgepodge of a service unit was mostly an administrative convenience at a time when coherence and order in the military were severely compromised. Everybody wanted to go home. Hordes of personnel who had the experience and technical skill to provide orderliness to complex military units managed to get themselves on troopships going back to the United States. But I was having new and worthwhile experiences so I decided to remain into 1946; I would return to the University of Washington in the fall.

My assignments regularly included ferry-flying V.I.P. officer types here and there, sometimes to places where landing facilities were less than felicitous. I remember once depositing a colonel at the door of the Emperor's Summer Palace in Kyoto. To do that required landing an L-5 Grasshopper on the palace parade ground, which had a clump of evergreen trees at the end where you had to come in on final approach. I circled it a couple times, then did what was called a "drag in," which means you approach the landing flat, i.e., not a steep approach, and maintain an airspeed just above stalling. When you are over the trees at the end of the parade ground you let yourself settle pretty fast, gunning the engine just before touching the ground to minimize the thump. Timing is everything here. If you gun it too soon, you will run out of parade ground. If too late you'll hit the ground with a resounding thump.

On other assignments, if it meant going to Tokyo for example, I'd take a B-25. I can remember, still with awe, flying above the cloud deck on the way to Tokyo and there to my left was Fujiyama in all its majesty. One Sunday we took a

C-47 loaded with infantry personnel on a "sightseeing" trip around and over Hiroshima, which at that time just months after the bomb was dropped, loomed as another sight I'll not forget. From there we went to the coast and flew over the active volcano, Kagashima, where you could watch at close range boulders and red hot lava course down the side of the mountain into a steaming ocean.

These experiences were the culmination of the necessities and routines of living in a land and culture totally different from what I had known. It was worth the delay in returning home.

As I reflect now upon my sense and feelings as a pilot coming out of the war in the Pacific, I realize how fortunate I was most of the time. It is true, I did get shot at, and every so often brought back flak in my wings, plus experiencing a few close scrapes in operational, non-combat flying, but I didn't begin to go through the awfulness of the Eighth Air Force B-17 crews flying missions over Germany and Europe, or even worse, dealing with the bevy of combat, disease, and sociological problems attendant upon the Vietnam War.

When the time came to return to the U.S. the papers came through for my captaincy (a discharge promotion). After I had spent the first day or two at home with my parents, my mother heaved a sigh of relief and said, "John, you really haven't changed."

CHAPTER 3

Back in the States

Education is not preparation for life; Education is life itself.

John Dewey

FINISHING MY B.A. degree in music composition at Washington was almost routine. But after more than three years of nomadic life in New Guinea, the Philippines, Okinawa, and Japan, readjusting to the academic environment was no small challenge, particularly when it required sitting in front of professors fond of theorizing. During my South Pacific time those with whom I interacted on a daily basis wouldn't have known what serious art music was, much less see it in terms of a vocation.

In Seattle I reconnected with Silvio Risegari. Just months afterward he died of a heart attack. It was a blow. He left a void requiring me to construct my own musical approach to life. He had had more impact on me than the music professors at Washington. It was clear that pursuing an active career as a professional performing pianist was not in the cards. I could have gone to New York, connected with a teacher there (probably at Juilliard) and given it a try. But I was twenty-five years old and would have to traverse the ground that most potentially successful pianists had started on much earlier. Given the realities of that competitive world, the odds against achieving success were formidable.

Without arriving at it by a logical process, I had decided that an academic career was the proper way to go. So before finishing at the University of Washington in 1948, I had to choose a graduate school. What was important to me in a graduate program was the relationship within it between the academic component of music and its performance. How well integrated into the academic curriculum was performance? I had spent years wrapped in keyboard performance. I couldn't abandon it then any more than I could abandon it now. High-profile Ivy League campuses did not have a history of offering degrees or showing much enthusiasm for academic credit for programs in performance (applied music), although there was certainly no lack of performances on their campuses. Rather, they focused upon scholarship and research work in music. To a considerable extent Yale University represented an exception. But it was the midwestern flagship public university campuses such as Michigan, Illinois, and Indiana that were concerned with and pioneered the amalgamation of both performance and scholarship in music. I was interested in both.

I corresponded with Yale and the University of Michigan, both of whom determined me admissible. I selected Michigan in Ann Arbor. I recently described this choice to a friend who is a fifth-generation Yale graduate. He grinned and said to me, "Well, every man is entitled to one mistake." In fact it wasn't. Michigan did combine those aspects of music that I wanted. When I got to Ann Arbor in 1948, I received a teaching fellowship and got started. I did two master's degrees, one in the theory of music and one in piano, and embarked on the Ph.D., all the while teaching harmony and music theory. The term "music theory" sounds a bit stuffy. The Italians have a much better and musical-sounding word, *solfeggio*, which means learning basic musical skills, beginning with sight-singing. I finished the doctorate, was awarded a Rackham School of Graduate Studies grant to spend a summer studying with Nadia Boulanger at Fountainebleau, and was then moved over onto the regular faculty as an instructor.

NUPTIALS

Lanette Sheaffer and I were married in February of 1950. Of Pennsylvania Dutch heritage (Lancaster County), she had transferred to the University of Michigan from Mary Washington College in Virginia. She was a flutist with one of the most discerning abilities to hear instrumental colors I have ever encountered. She had studied with the famous New York Philharmonic flutist, John Wummer. We married before her graduation, which gave me the privilege of accompanying her for her graduation recital. Our daughter Jill was born in 1951 and son John in 1956. We stayed on at Michigan for more than eighteen years, during which I cut my academic teeth, and moved through the ranks to a full professorship and associate deanship of the School of Music.

NICE LIFE

Ann Arbor, Michigan in the late forties and early fifties (where the university dominated the town—it still does) was a nice place to be. Even with the enrollment of platoons of GI Bill students, the university by today's standards was not monumentally large. The exceptions were Saturday afternoon home football games when another 70,000 or 80,000 fans milled about—like those in the Roman Coliseum 2,000 years ago. Ann Arbor had retained the aura of its earlier college town days. The cultural amenities, particularly musical performances, and the relaxed pace of life made it an agreeable location. A significant portion of the townspeople were sophisticated and quite tolerant. It still is and continues to be recognized by municipal surveys as a highly desirable place to live although with today's larger population, more students and the inevitable traffic problems, it has frayed.

The University of Michigan has been able to keep its football prowess in a reasonable perspective. Faculty members are interested in the gladiator sport, but it certainly did not and does not dominate their autumn thinking. We used to say that when archrival Ohio State beats Michigan, the next day Michiganders might end up with a hangover soon gone, but when Michigan beats Ohio State, Columbus has a collective heart attack. The saying still holds.

As could be expected, music dominated my professional life both as a performer myself and as a listener. The myriad of concerts by faculty and students, along with professional concerts coming from New York and other centers of performance kept us busy, often five or six nights a week. We had a small group we called the Baroque Trio in which I played the harpsichord. We would take the legs off the harpsichord, put it in the back of a station wagon, and barnstorm around the region playing concerts sponsored by the continuing education division.

At that time the School of Music was headed by one of the dominant figures in the world of academic music, Earl V. Moore, who was a "Michigan man" himself, having graduated in 1912. Along with Howard Hanson from the Eastman School of Music at the University of Rochester, who was another monumental figure in the building of university music programs, Earl Moore, did more to shape baccalaureate music degree programs as they developed in the United States than any other person.

MUSIC PERFORMANCE IN UNIVERSITY
CURRICULA

Music instruction at the university level, as American institutions inherited it from Europe, dealt essentially with studies in the histories and theories of music—musicology—and not with the practicalities and skills in its performance. The teaching of the performance of music divorced from literary studies was more akin to what went on in trade schools. In fact it was. The Ivy League schools where the famous German research institutions served as academic and research models eschewed the performance of music as a discipline. They would no more have offered instruction leading to a degree in the violin or piano than they would have offered courses in plumbing. To have elevated music performance to academic status would have precipitated cardiac arrest in professors of the classics, despite what Plato had to say about it in the *Republic*. As late as 1944, Harvard's Randall Thompson, in his book *The State of Music in America*, made distinctions between teaching about music abstractly as contrasted to teaching the journeyman skills of making music. Even though he was a distinguished composer—probably nine out of ten small-town protestant church choir directors across America have conducted their Sunday morning volunteer choirs in his *Alleluia*—teaching the skills of music was to him a practical matter like learning to be an electrician. He said, for example, that no trombone player should be promoted above the rank of assistant professor. Great music was always performed at Harvard—after all Leonard Bernstein went there—but earlier tradition placed it outside the realm of academic credit.

EARL MOORE AND MUSIC IN UNIVERSITIES

During Earl Moore's early career at Michigan, the performance of music had not yet been granted unquestioned academic legitimacy. He was the kind of dean that today has passed from the scene—dictatorial but benevolently so. If a dean currently serving a public institution displayed the autocratic, administrative behavior Earl Moore did, today's authority-allergic faculty and staff would tie him/her up in litigation alleging transgressions including the abrogation of due process, academic freedom, and perhaps violating individual civil rights. But Moore understood what it meant to be part of an academic community. It was more to him than just having a job where you were paid for your services. There was a larger commitment. Being a professor meant having accepted a call to high service that possessed a human value and meaning beyond merchandizing one's professional skills. A faculty was more than a collection of employees. It was an assembly with an exalted purpose—to educate. A faculty union would have been as alien to him as a Martian come to earth to teach the clarinet.

The degradation of this call to high service in much of today's academic community brings about a paltriness of attitude, a crabbed spirit, on the part of many faculty members. Not so Earl Moore. To him, being part of a faculty had meaning beyond the job itself. He was single-minded in his lifelong efforts to elevate the study of music and its composition and performance to the level of campus recognition accorded more historic academic pursuits. It was thus inevitable that the values and convictions about academic affairs Earl Moore talked about influenced my personal attitude and thinking about being an academic man.

LEGACY OF GREAT TEACHERS OF THE PAST

Down the years teachers, scholars and administrators of this caliber gave their institutions meaning. They possessed not only disciplinary knowledge, but wisdom and an ethical sense. The greatest colleges and universities today became what they are because of these people. Such men and women still exist on campuses. But given the winds blowing across higher education today, where people want to consider themselves equal regardless of effort and accomplishment, their impact is minimized.

THE BUTTONED-UP COMMUNITY

In that period of the late forties and early fifties the campus community at Michigan reflected the somewhat buttoned-up behavior and attitudes of earlier times. President and Mrs. Ruthven still gave Friday afternoon student teas where coeds wore white gloves and hats and no male student would have dreamed of showing up without a jacket and tie—to say nothing of the dress code for junior faculty members, of which I was one. Standards of dress then were strict by comparison to the relaxed standards of today. But who is to say which era of dress makes that much difference in learning itself. How about Albert Einstein's relaxed habits of dress or the apparent length of time between his haircuts?

Attitudes were different than now. I'll never forget one episode in 1949 involving a faculty member who was my master's degree thesis advisor. It had emerged that his sexual preference was not in conformity with the customs of the campus. Gay rights had not even been heard of, much less legislated. Even though I was in my late twenties and had already been through a war, I was blithely innocent and insensible of his "problem." Within twenty-four hours of the time his proclivities came to the attention of university authorities he was escorted to a train out of Ann Arbor and his job terminated. A hearing was not part of the system. There could have been no such thing as coming out of the closet. The perception of turpitude would have caused the closet to be torn asunder.

GREAT TEACHERS AND MUSIC PERFORMANCE

During my doctoral student and early professional years—first half of the fifties—I mixed being a graduate student studying musicology and a faculty member teaching music theory. Faculty rules were different then. The possibility of a conflict of interest between the two hadn't really occurred to anyone. I performed at the keyboard regularly in all sorts of student and faculty concerts, being publicly on stage perhaps seventy-five or eighty times a year. I learned the forty-eight preludes and fugues from the two volumes of Johann Sebastian Bach's *Well Tempered Clavier* and played them in a series of lecture recitals. (One of the pleasant recollections of that time was practicing for performances as my four-year-old daughter Jill played with her toys under the piano.) As the decades cumulate in my life that particular effort—learning Bach's preludes and fugues—continues to yield provender to the way I think about musical language and its use at the keyboard.

I used the junior faculty Rackham research grant to accomplish the music student's equivalent of a Muslim pilgrimage to Mecca—study with the icon of twentieth-century music pedagogy in France, Nadia Boulanger. The late composer and critic Virgil Thompson opined that every small town in America had its five and dime store and its Boulanger student. There was always a kernel of truth in Thompson's irreverence (read *A Virgil Thompson Reader*); however, the diversity of Boulanger's interactions with students from everywhere in no way diminished the depth and

profundity of her teaching. In all ways—personal, professional, pedagogical—she was the most disciplined person I
have encountered anywhere. This testament is universally
expressed, whether by the best composers and performers
America has produced or by those who studied with her and
subsequently taught in small towns next to the five and dime.

As I crafted my work for the Ph.D., Hans David was my
teacher. He was a leading Bach scholar and professor at
Michigan who followed patterns of research developed by
historical scholars in nineteenth-century German research
universities. A native of the Palatinate in Germany, he was
trained in the still new discipline of *Musikologie*. Two of his
teachers, Friedrich Ludwig and Johannes Wolf were foun-
tainhead figures in the field. Their work, a century after
being published, has been added to, but not been supplanted.

In the world of performance, the milieu of personalities
surrounding Silvio Risegari during his own developing years
were intimately a part of the evolution of modern keyboard
virtuosity. In like manner, the thinkers in the circles from
which Hans David emerged were those responsible for creating the modern field of musicology. If musicology could be
said to have been authenticated as an academic research discipline in America by the establishment of a chair of musicology at Cornell in 1930, then Hans David, along with
others, carried on the second generation of the tradition
with his appointment to the faculty of Michigan in 1950.

He was the chairman of my Ph.D. committee. But his relationship to me and to other students went considerably beyond that. As a musicologist his love of earlier music was
obvious. He collected early published scores from which he
would conduct ensemble performances with student performers. His personal library is now part of the Riemenschneider Library at Baldwin Wallace College. One evening
in his living room we performed six instrumental sonatas by

George Friedrich Handel from original published scores, which we followed by drinking horrible punch from his punchbowl. These scores had "figured basses," which is a seventeenth- and eighteenth-century musical shorthand not dissimilar to the chord designations in today's "fake books" for commercial music and show tunes.

"Realizing" figured basses at the keyboard requires some skill at improvising, which I had learned in a rudimentary way as a church organist. To perform from printed scores that Handel himself had probably proofed was a learning experience not available in conventional music classrooms. (Such experiences remain with you. Much later, at the Maius Museum at Jagiellonian University in Cracow I was permitted to play a piano, still in working condition, that Chopin had owned and used. During that one ten-minute episode in an unheated building, I learned more about what you can and cannot do in a Chopin performance than in months of conventional study.)

PERFORMANCE: PSYCHOMOTOR ACROBATICS, THE MIND, AND THE EMOTIONS

Keyboard performance, along with that of other instruments, is a pursuit of its own kind with tripartite components that embody: 1.) psychomotor digital acrobatics that you develop through "practice-practice-practice" like a monkey (becoming adept at hair-raising jumps from one branch to another); 2.) intellectual understanding of how the notes create a musical form and how they relate to each other; and 3.) a human emotional connection between you and the music. Of the tens of thousand of music teachers across the country, to say nothing of university professors teaching the piano, those who teach these three components of keyboard performance with understanding and coherence are so rare as to be almost nonexistent.

It is possible to perform music at the keyboard without intellectual understanding but through rote repetition of patterns—which is how monkeys and squirrels learn to jump. (When I was in my teens I went through an agonizing period trying to figure out how I was able to execute what I did at the piano keyboard. It tied me up in knots.) There is an added factor of music transcending the three components of the psychomotor, the intellectual, and the emotional. When talking about music we must remind ourselves that it cannot be grasped through words. It truly speaks in its own language which in essence is untranslatable into discursive terminology, i.e., words. Why else would Louis Armstrong say, "Man, if I has to 'splain it you'd never understand anyways?" But because our lives are bound up in words, from our dreams to muddling through the words on jar labels in the supermarket we are captive to them as communicative tools. The next time you go to a symphony orchestra concert observe the number of people reading the program notes while the orchestra is performing. The audience pays more attention to the language of words than the language of music.

For a person to be a true musician, music itself must permeate the consciousness without the intervention of words. Rhythm, melody, and harmony must speak for themselves, along with all of their interactive relationships, unmediated by discursive terminology. The profound meaning of this is too seldom grasped among music teachers but is the starting point for all significant achievement as a musician. When they were early teenagers the sons of J. S. Bach embraced the reality of the language of music in more natural and at the same time more sophisticated ways than the great majority of all music doctorate students in the U.S., who are waterlogged with words. Good jazz players understand musical language better than most concert pianists. On the other hand well-known heavy metal and hard rock stars, most of whom should be consigned to the lowest level of Dante's Inferno, have no grasp of musical language, but base their performances on stupefying repetitions of meaningless patterns, and on lyrics ranging from the inane to the obscene. (I have absolutely no doubt that the proliferation of this debauched and prurient language contributes to a generalized fraying of moral fiber.)

For me it took decades into adult life to grasp the significance and meaning of music in its pure, communicative sense. I had to work it out for myself. No one taught me. Mozart grasped it as a boy.

FACULTY-STUDENT: THEN AND NOW

I was trained in the techniques of scholarship but at the same time became conditioned as a keyboardist. Thus I was prepared to reside in the academic world of music, one foot in performance and the other in teaching and scholarship. Michigan was a first-tier public research-oriented institution, and while Earl Moore had been able to establish the School of Music as performance-based where, for the creative musician, performance and composition stood alongside research as a criteria for promotion, research continued to be the most powerful force in Michigan's academic environment.

During my earlier years, being a teacher and being a student overlapped. I was able to serve as a faculty member teaching keyboard harmony, theory, and counterpoint on the one hand and then move from instructor in one classroom to being a student in another. This was a crossover that not many younger teachers enjoy on today's campuses with their more clearly restrictive and in some examples unionized bureaucracies. The teaching that I did then was no different in its context from that being done by teachers who had been on the faculty for twenty-five years.

To the Regular Faculty

With the completion of the Ph.D., I moved without any slippage into the full time, regular faculty. Given the apparatus of affirmative action at most public institutions that would not be possible today. Job posting, searches, and interviews would be requisite. When Earl Moore retired and Jim Wallace, who had been Moore's assistant dean, became dean, a colleague who was known and respected in music education, Allan Britton, and I became assistant deans. This was perhaps a small example of "administrationitus" creeping into colleges and felt everywhere in academic life. Moore had one assistant dean. Wallace needed two.

However, there may well have been another issue in the appointment of both of us. The music faculty strongly supported Jim Wallace to be Moore's successor but the upper administration had some doubts about him. The university executive vice president might well have felt (although he said nothing) that Al Britton and I would serve as modifiers for Jim. The vice president proved to be more prescient than the faculty when ten years down the road Jim Wallace's leadership disintegrated. Always a heavy drinker, his problem grew worse. By then I had been several years gone to Ohio. I recall that when I told Al Britton I had accepted a deanship at Kent State University he said, "Johnny, you're freed." Just before Wallace's removal Britton had accepted a job in Arizona but was able to extricate himself from the commitment and was appointed dean to replace Jim Wallace. During his incumbency he pulled the disarrayed faculty back together and put in place a fundraising initiative for the University of Michigan School of Music which serves as a model for other music schools in public flagship institutions. Jim Wallace was assigned to teach music literature to non-music majors. He was an excellent teacher. Not long after he died of a heart attack.

The small piece of history involving Jim Wallace was tragic, illustrating a commonplace of repeated human foibles. But his initial appointment as full dean made for stimulating days. I was only an assistant professor and for the times was green, even for the word "assistant dean" to be attached to my title. But because the bureaucratic attitudes creating distinctions between administrative and faculty functions did not exist then, at least to the extent they do today, I continued to teach and perform. I had written a small keyboard harmony workbook, printed and published by a local publishing house—not quite scholarship in its true sense, but it was one of the ways young academics get the feel of creating publishable material. Thus, although I was an administrator, I was able to move through the academic ranks to a tenured full professorship. This was another career factor that would be much more difficult today. Opportunities to mix administrative and academic involvements in an early career are few and far between.

THE OFFER OF A DEANSHIP

In the summer of 1966, while we were at Walloon Lake in Michigan, where I was lecturing at the UM Alumni Camp, I was offered a deanship at Kent State University. It created a dilemma. Even though Kent State did not compare to Michigan in academic depth, heritage, and reputation, the Ohio campus was clearly developing (the growth in substance and spirit being evident during the ensuing thirty-five years) and the position offered some uncommon opportunities. It involved the more pluralistic administrative responsibilities of heading programs that not only included, but went beyond, the historic fine and performing arts, including speech and hearing, home economics, engineering technology, and architecture. I liked the idea. It seemed to me that someone like me, trained in the communicative art of music, could offer leadership from a useful and different perspective. Lanette recognized that it was time for me to have another challenge, even though it would seriously disrupt our lives, particularly hers and the children. The fact that she concurred in my acceptance testified to her devotion. I realized this at the time, but moreso now. When we returned to Ann Arbor from Walloon Lake the die was cast, and the decision to move to Kent in Portage County, Ohio, had been made.

CHAPTER 4

Michigan to Ohio

*There is great danger in reckless change; but
greater danger in blind conservatism.*

Henry George

TOUGH CHANGE

Our roots in Ann Arbor had grown and reached down. The
children, Jill and Kip, were nicely situated in the University
School, which was a kindergarten through high school affiliated with the School of Education at the University. We
had an ample and comfortable house in a good part of town.
My job as a tenured full professor and associate dean had
reasonable status, substantial freedom with essentially no
supervision, and was as secure as any job could be. It could
almost be compared to a sinecure. Lanette loved the community, was active in university women's affairs, and had developed a class of flute students which she taught at home. It
was a lifestyle of satisfying comfort—somehow too much so.
Everything was too easy. I did not feel challenged to the extent my psyche seemed to require. I do not think this was
some version of a mid-life crisis. Rather, I think it came
from a sense of obligation passed on to me by my father,

more by osmosis than formulated precept. I think this imbued in me a feeling that I was not giving back in the same
measure I was receiving. Further, I had tasted some of the
stimulations of academic leadership. It seemed to me that
persons of my background in the musical arts had special
perspectives that would be useful in the realm of broader
university leadership. At that time—in the mid sixties—it
was rare and uncommon for musicians and artists to occupy
central administrative officer posts in universities. It was
persons from the sciences, humanities, and law that filled
these positions.

At first Jim Wallace concurred that the move represented
an appropriate professional challenge, but as the winding
down process went on he became adversary. The last couple
months were extremely difficult. It turned into a personal af-
front to him that, as an associate dean (by then I had been
promoted) on his team, I was leaving for another campus.
But that issue was minimal compared to unsettling Lanette
and the kids. I had a professional stimulus to look forward to,
but they were required to uproot themselves from their
nicely knit neighborhood and campus interactions, and from
the sophisticated environment of the University and Ann
Arbor, to move to the town of Kent, Ohio.

Kent State University had emerged from the heritage
of a teacher-training normal school, later becoming a regional state college and ultimately a state university. Similar evolution has occurred at hundreds of today's regional
state universities. While the campus at large was slowly
shedding itself of the doctrinairisms of the educationist's
mindset, dynamics within the KSU College of Education,
which was the dominant academic unit, were still fettered
by the Procrustean bed of educationism.

The president of Kent State in the sixties, Robert White,
had been the dean of the College of Education and had

moved through the academic vice presidency to the presidency. The university had become multipurpose in its mission and faculty members were moving assertively in the development of graduate programs for a variety of disciplines. Dr. White supported this movement forward, but as a leader he had never been able to move beyond the conditioning of his earlier professional education background. Even though he had a doctorate from the University of Chicago, he was not comfortable in the burgeoning academic arena outside of teacher training. He was even more uncomfortable dealing with the internationally experienced constituencies outside of Kent involving Cleveland-based corporate leaders who moved in circles foreign to Kent State. This came home to me because of a difficult evening where the president botched an interaction with a prominent and wealthy couple. A friend had organized a small dinner party at his home with the purpose of providing an opportunity for the couple to meet Dr. White and give those from the campus who were present a chance to talk informally about what was happening at the university. An affair of this kind is of course standard practice in the early stages of donor cultivation, with the intent down the road of presenting potential donors with a "giving opportunity." People present, including the potential donors themselves, know what is going on and usually enjoy the pace and rhythm of the cultivation. Things were going nicely when all of a sudden Dr. White took the floor. Lo and behold, he asked the couple for over a million dollars. There was no proposal preparation or any specifics, just a bald "ask." The embarrassment in the room was agonizing. Needless to say the episode shattered the chance for further cultivation of the couple.

KENT STATE AND THE BLOSSOM FESTIVAL SCHOOL

At the time that we moved to Kent the Cleveland Orchestra, then still under the direction of the musical titan George Szell, was preparing to build a facility for summer festival performances at the Blossom Music Center (named after an orchestra benefactor), located on unspoiled land in North-field Township between Cleveland and Akron. This paralleled the development of summer venues by orchestras in Boston (Tanglewood), Chicago (Ravinia), Washington, D.C. (Wolf Trap), and others.

Early in the planning phase, Cleveland Orchestra artistic and trustee leadership determined that a summer school for music students in performance would be a proper and desirable corollary to the summer performances scheduled at Blossom, similar to the independent school under the auspices of the Boston Orchestra at Tanglewood. Accordingly, orchestra people talked with a number of the higher education institutions in northeast Ohio about their interest in helping to organize a festival school at Blossom, but could elicit no positive response from them. My deanship appointment to KSU's College of Fine and Professional Arts had been announced, and the late Frank E. Joseph, then president of the Musical Arts Association (parent body of the Cleveland Orchestra) got in touch with me in Ann Arbor. Before I had begun the new job, we set up a meeting on the KSU campus, where we discussed the possibilities of Kent State joining hands with the orchestra in the creation of a summer music school.

Kent State had always taken its music program seriously and the idea of a summer festival school made sense. But for KSU this possibility had ramifications considerably beyond simply setting up a summer music school. There was status and prestige attached to being identified musically with the world-renowned Cleveland Orchestra. Even in the city of

Kent, locals who by years of habit did not venture beyond county borders were aware, even if only vaguely, of the luster of the orchestra from Cleveland. Up to that time the KSU campus, which did not have much recognition as a center of culture, had never been included, even remotely, in the circles of people in the Cleveland area who were patrons of music. Awkward as he was in dealing with these people, Robert White recognized they could be potentially helpful to the university and gave the effort his full support. During the sixties Kent State had emerged with a rush, possessing raw, partially unrefined energy and increasing fiscal subsidies from the state of Ohio. But Kent also was somewhat unsure of itself and didn't quite know how to handle its growing prominence. Orchestra trustees had become initially interested in Kent because of its perceived increasing share of state resources. Private institutions in northeast Ohio at the time were not that flush, which is clearly one of the reasons for their demurrals when they were approached by the orchestra to join in the creation of a school. They simply did not want to commit the resources. Thus Kent, which had not been the top choice to partner with the orchestra in creating a festival school, did have a strong hand in the increasing commitment of state resources to its operating budget. My arrival on the scene, coming from a prestigious flagship university with a recognized music school, probably helped somewhat as far as the orchestra making up its mind was concerned.

Right after I got into harness in Kent I was deputized to carry out the negotiations with the orchestra. A joint committee between the orchestra and Kent State was formed. I was made its chairman. That was in the fall of 1966, two years before the Blossom Music Center opened. Louis Lane, the resident conductor of the orchestra, was also deeply involved, contributing not only his own uncommon insights but also representing the most important musical presence in the enterprise, George Szell. A number of these persons have died since then, but decades after, I still retain friendships and associations that were forged during the negotiations.

The task of putting a curriculum together, figuring out how and where classes and studios were to be located, to say nothing of determining who should comprise the faculty and the students and then recruiting them, was by its nature difficult and complicated. But the dynamics of how these efforts unfolded was made more complex by the differences between the two cultures: the orchestra on the one hand and Kent State University on the other. The stable, privileged, and self-confident elitism of orchestra trustee-leadership contrasted with the quasi-rural egalitarianism of the Portage County Kent campus. Merging these two in the creation of the festival school which, not totally but to a significant degree, was an outreach by the orchestra, presented a significant challenge. As chairman of the joint committee and subsequently the founding dean of the festival school, I think I succeeded in helping to bring the cultures together, by no means 100 percent, but perhaps somewhere between 50 and 75 percent.

PRIDE

All elite institutions, both public and private, have developed a sense of unique institutional pride. Like leaven, this raises consciousness of campus qualities. It warms the various constituencies of the campus itself and radiates outward. It provides a harmonious force of enormous benefits, particularly among alumni. Nor has this institutional pride been confined only to elite, well-off campuses. A good example was the City College of New York which for years had been referred to as "Harvard for the Poor." Its past aura of academic quality and discipline endowed it with a sense of pride and place. But that was before the 1970s, when, in response to political pressures, the leadership of its parent body, the City University of New York, imposed the extremes of open admissions at CCNY. The purpose was to produce an enrollment pattern that matched the minority and ethnic constituencies of the city. Over the years this policy, which turned out to be sadly misbegotten, resulted in thousands of academically unqualified students being admitted. The process severely damaged academic quality, and destroyed the institutional pride held by its sons and daughters. Finally in the late nineties the CUNY board, despite demonstrations and street theater caterwauling to the contrary, imposed measures to restore academic probity and resuscitate CCNY's reputation. Ultimately this will occur, but it takes years.

Certainly pride in the university existed at Michigan in Ann Arbor. During my nearly two decades there I was much aware and fulfilled by the pride permeating most parts of the university—although I tended to take it for granted. Upon moving to Kent one of the first things I noticed was that the sense of institutional pride on the part of students, faculty and constituents generally was much lower. Kent State lacked the institutional dynamic where it was felt to possess particular and unique qualities that, apart from the coursework and degrees offered, made it a place that contributed to the human and emotional coherence of its students and faculty. This minimizing of pride in itself is no longer true of Kent State. Today it possesses a genuine sense of itself and its growing mission.

CULTURAL DIFFERENCES AND "EDUCATIONISM"
VERSUS LEARNING

At the time this lack of an accepted sense of institutional pride derived perhaps from the narrower historic mission of Kent State. The campus had been dominated since its inception in 1910 by the dynamics of teacher training, which increasingly from the twenties and thirties on partook of problematic practices where teaching methodology, intended or not, gained precedence over the various subject disciplines. For the past several decades every campus in the United States with a college or department of education has been affected to some extent by the ideas of the educationist-academic-bureacrats who had gained political control of the certifying of teachers. This is part, but only part, of the cause of today's sorry state of public elementary and secondary schools in the nation. For those campuses with rings of undergraduate and graduate professional schools—such as engineering, medicine, law, fine arts and other disciplines—academic checks and balances existed. But for those with overly dominant colleges of education, which was true of most regional universities that had grown out of earlier normal schools, the trunk of the academic tree leaned toward educationism.

A vivid example of this occurred in an academic skirmish with the dean of Kent State's College of Education during the first year of my deanship of the College of Fine and Professional Arts. I ended up on the losing end. In the music education curriculum at most state universities the responsibility for the so-called code requirements of certifying music teachers for work in the public schools rests with the college of education faculty. But at most established, comprehensive universities, the remainder of the curriculum, in other words that which makes a music teacher a musician, is the responsibility of the music faculty, just as it is vested in the mathematics faculty for math teachers, in the English faculty for

English teachers and so on. But at Kent at that time the responsibility for the total curriculum for all categories of teachers remained in the College of Education, as it did at most regional universities with a teacher-training heritage. To put it anecdotally, for those students intending to be teachers, the subject-matter faculties served the curricular dictates of the teacher-training faculty, rather than the other way around where teacher training would be adjunct to the core of learning contained in music, mathematics, and other subjects. I believed and of course still do that the responsibility for teaching the "what" and "how" of the substance of the several disciplines belongs within the faculties trained in the disciplines themselves, not in education methodology faculties. To that end I advocated that this responsibility belonged in the music faculty.

This had long since been a non-issue at most flagship institutions (if it had ever been one) but at Kent it turned indisputably into turf.

For purposes of discussion I had placed the issue on the agenda of a music faculty meeting. This would probably have been preliminary to a request to the college and to the university curriculum committees for the transfer of curriculum responsibility from the education faculty to that of music. This sent shock waves in the direction of the education faculty and put the dean into a state of paranoia. He scurried across campus complaining to President Robert White that John Flower was plotting the overthrow of the College of Education. Dr. White, as mentioned above, had previously been dean of the college of education. As president he reached down, bypassing the academic vice president and myself, and unilaterally removed from the agenda that item relating to curriculum responsibility being transferred from the College of Education to the music department, muzzling any faculty discussion. It was a defensive maneuver preserving the hegemony of the faculty of the College of Education over the music faculty in matters that the music faculty knew more about than their peers in education—a classic example of educationist politics. Following that administrative scrunch I had two choices; accept it or resign. Before leaving for Kent the executive vice president at Michigan had said to me that if I didn't like it at Kent they "could probably find something for me" if I wanted to return to Ann Arbor. But we had sold the house and gotten the kids settled in new schools. A move back would have been another domestic upheaval. Also, by that time I had developed solid relationships with and commitments to those I was working with at the Cleveland Orchestra. There was no way I could pick up and leave. So I swallowed my pride. Today, such an arbitrary action from a president's office might well precipitate a faculty dustup or a lawsuit involving infringement of academic process by the president. In those days such action could not even be a consideration. The Portage County courts would have been aghast. This episode, minor in the perspective of subsequent events, illustrated the mindset of the leadership of most regional campuses that emerged out of a teacher-training heritage.

That was more than thirty-five years ago. During the intervening decades Kent State has matured institutionally and academically with striking energy. Programatic growth, especially at the graduate level, has immeasurably broadened its horizons.

However, the problem of training teachers for the public schools in America continues to exist on all campuses with teacher training programs. I said earlier that the educationist-academic bureaucrats who had gained control of certifying teachers were only part of the cause of the sorry state of today's public elementary and secondary schools. Indeed, they continue to be a problem. But the larger one is how we, the

American citizenry, have handled the profession of public school teaching. A plethora of polls indicates that the American public views education as a top priority in a hierarchy of issues, even within the renewed sense of patriotism and security consciousness brought about by the horrifying spasms of terrorism on 9/11. Although this public opinion exists, national statistics regarding pay, working conditions, and the professional status of teachers do not at the same time provide evidence that this concern is being translated into effective measures for improvement.

Teachers express discontent over the defects in the system. There exists widespread unhappiness with the generally low quality of the preparation they receive in college. The extent of this malaise is manifested in the figures released by the National Commission on Teaching and America's Future, which reveal that over 30 percent of all teachers and close to 50 percent of those in large urban districts reject the profession by exiting their jobs within five years of their entry into them. Over the decades, having been close to college programs that prepare teachers for the public schools and also regularly interacting with public school administrations and faculty, I can attest to the monumentality of the dilemma.

The problems are so complex and far-reaching that there is absolutely no single solution. Two large dimensions of problems are evident. The first is within the processes of education itself. There are many issues but the three most important ones are: inadequate teacher preparation programs in colleges, flawed and bureaucratic state departments of education where great influence is exerted over the "what-how-who" of teacher licensing, and the politicization and incompetence in the governance and management of local school districts.

The second dimension is sociological. Correcting the

flawed processes of education and its delivery (even though necessary) cannot solve the problems in the public schools as long as the current sea of human troubles surrounding them persists. These troubles afflict inner cities but are by no means confined to them. Suburbs, including upscale gated communities, are not exempt. From elementary schools through high school, today's students contend with drug dealers, knives, and guns. Inner-city minority sixth graders going home from school sometimes wonder if they are going to make it. When they get home, or wherever it is they live, they enter a dysfunctional environment: no knowledge of who the father might be, or where he is; a mother herself struggling with addiction. Grandparents often serve the role of parents by default.

In the predominantly suburban communities or gentri-fied areas of cities where minorities have escaped this vortex of human disintegration another social problem inhibits children from learning, even though they are often econom-ically privileged. Minority blacks harbor deep resentments because of overt discrimination in the past and covert racial prejudice in the present. Privileged blacks in these circum-stances do not inveigh against "whitey," as is common on inner city streets, but they reject much of what whites stand for. This includes educational values derived primarily from white culture, namely the requisites to learning that involve careful reading and study. Black students often do not em-brace the necessity of study, and worse, their parents do not insist upon it. I have observed this at firsthand over the years. Because they are not usually prepared as well, black students as a group consistently score lower on standardized tests than whites or Asians. It is not because their skin happens to be black or brown, but because they have not accepted the intrinsic values of study.

As far as the problems in the educational processes referred to above are concerned, what are the directions I think we must go in order to effect positive change? First, teacher-training programs must be reformed. Many of these programs are disgracefully indolent and passive. The test results of students in colleges of education are below the average of all students enrolled. These standards must be raised. The plethora of required methodology courses must be thinned out and courses with academic discipline reintroduced—hard-nosed grammar, rigorous mathematics, languages, honestly presented history, and literature. Students should have a solid academic major field and at least one minor, and prove their control of these fields by passing requisite examinations. It won't be easy. There are far too many comfortably tenured faculty sitting on their haunches, who will resist through noncooperation. Second, I believe that the dinosaur-hatched and doctrinaire bureaucrats in the many state departments of education distributed in the various state capitals should be tarred and feathered. Over the years inefficient people in these departments have accrued power far beyond their intellectual and rational capacities to wield it intelligently. These boards should be replaced through merit selection similar to that outlined earlier, including representation from the constituencies of universities which provide the programs in teacher training. These merit-selected boards must exert control and direction over their respective professional staff members to an extent far greater than heretofore. All of this will require legislation which will cause minor revolutions, but it is necessary. Third, the governance and management of local school districts requires an alternative to popularly-elected school boards. This is primarily a problem in big cities in disadvantaged districts, where management and governance are beset with self-serving politics and corruption. Popular election of school board members opens the door for hacks and incompetents. In smaller cities and towns where some sense of community remains and where the reputations of the candidates are often known to the voters, popular election works fine. There is no reason to change it. But more often than not, in the big cities it has proved disastrous. An alternative exists which, when implemented, has brought about marked improvement in the public schools. This involves placing the management and governance of the public schools under the mayor's purview. The superintendent, as CEO, is appointed by the mayor, as are members of the school board. Boston, Chicago, Cleveland, and New York are among those who have turned to this system. It has resulted in dramatic change. Inevitably this raises a hue and cry over the disenfranchisement of voters, but the improvements in education cannot be denied.

The sociological dimension of the public education problem—the poverty, crime, and drugs in which it exists—remains one of the toughest problems in the nation today. Educators themselves do not have the power to solve it. Schools will have to continue to cope with it, which means the quality of teaching and learning is diminished. As a result colleges and universities will have to keep on providing remedial instruction. This deflects resources that should go to bona fide college-level courses. The larger solution will have to come from the moral force of the nation's citizens.

ABERRATION

As dean of the College of Fine and Professional Arts at Kent State I also had lessons that taught me about the warp and woof of academic deviousness. We had appointed a chair of the music department who was a highly-skilled musician. He was also highly skilled at rubbing his colleagues the wrong way. People used to say he could walk down the hall, not say anything, and still make people mad. This latter proclivity was separate from the qualities that enabled him to marshal the artistic and educational resources of his department. He was a strong force in the programmatic development of the Blossom Festival School. His strengths outweighed his foibles, but three faculty members took it upon themselves to unseat him peremptorily. No due process or "bill of particulars" was involved. Their obstreperousness generated not logic but protest and pressure. I called a faculty meeting, made sure a parliamentarian was present, and said, in effect, make your case. They weren't able to, such forces as they could muster were present but not effective. The energy behind the contumacy dwindled and soon after fell apart. Subsequently, and of their own volition, two of the three moved to institutions in other states; later on, the third created another campus situation that ended up in federal court and dragged on for years.

UNSETTLING FORCES FOR PROTEST LEADING TO MAY 4, 1970

During the final years of the noisy sixties rising antiestablishment dissent against the Vietnam War spilled onto campuses in every region. Kent State was not the likeliest venue for high-protein protest to take place. The Kent campus, its history and location could not compare to Berkeley, Columbia, and scores of other universities in its response to the vibrations of student protest. But tensions at KSU were palpable. You could feel them as you walked across the campus.

The administration at Kent was ill-prepared to deal with the in-your-face protest dynamics superseding customary student behavior. The university's central executive group remained conventional, administratively conservative, perhaps somewhat more authoritarian than most, but they trod somewhat cautiously recognizing that in the sixties they couldn't get away with the dictatorial practice accepted in the first half of the century. Even so they were not prepared for what was to come. Rallies organized by Vietnam War protest groups were very different than panty raids. The new ingredients of group protest came from techniques learned through civil rights struggles of the fifties and sixties. Activist students possessed no ambivalence. America's involvement in the Vietnam War was 100 percent wrong and the protest against it represented a morally right struggle against that which was morally wrong.

Students themselves represented the principal ingredient of protest. Non-conforming citizens with civil rights battle seasoning did not simply emigrate to campuses and take over mechanisms of protest. However, their knowledge of how to go about organizing rallies and protest marches was used by the activist students on campuses. Beyond the borders of campuses they were usually represented as outside agitators—which was inaccurate and unfair, even though problems did arise in that there were, as always, some unprincipled persons simply making trouble. While all this was going on Kent State continued to function as a growing and maturing university. There was much business to attend to. We were wrapped up in it. We were aware of the presence of police and National Guard troops on campuses in different parts of the country. In the days before the May 4, 1970, tragedy, when National Guard troops along with military vehicles appeared on the Kent campus, the faculty and staff—myself included—grudgingly accepted their presence (even though it was a blatant violation of historic academic independence) as a manifestation of the times we were living in. This laissez-faire attitude on our part was a mistake, although there was not much we could have done about it anyway.

The Ohio governor, James Rhodes, deeply into a re-election campaign, did not hesitate to play the politics of law and order. He made a highly inflammatory speech in which he referred to protesters as worse than "brownshirts." This Nazi reference (which held considerably more currency then than it would today) intensified the resentments. The ROTC building, one of those old, rectangular barracks-type wooden structures left over from World War II, was burned down by protesters and accompanied by harassment of the firemen fighting the blaze. This was a major escalation. Then, on the beautiful, sunny day of May 4, tired, inadequately trained, and inexperienced National Guard troops collided with a melee of students. What followed became history—shooting that resulted in four deaths and nine persons wounded. It occurred just a few paces outside my office in Taylor Hall. The worldwide reaction generated hundreds of millions of words of commentary, which continued for months and years. For many of those close to that drama of disaster, its impact has remained through the decades. My personal reaction was embodied in the comments I made as dean, to the faculty of my college (fine and professional arts) a week afterward. I excerpt from them below.

> *The tragedy on our campus a week and a day ago changed our lives. Each of us lost something of himself. None escapes blame—neither gown nor town, and in the larger sense, neither state nor nation.*

> *Our world is changing and we must change with it. We recognize that Kent State University cannot be the same nor should it. . . .*

> *As a community of teachers, thinkers, and artisans we form a crucible. We need to create a new alloy of understanding. The older alloys have not proved sufficient. We have not recognized this nor have our constituencies.*

We call ourselves teachers, but have we totally identified our personal accountability? Have we used our own teaching skills to explain what we are? Perhaps part of our large credibility problem that exists between us and more than one of our constituencies, derives not so much from the validity and honesty of our belief, but from the way in which we present them. We have been on one wave length, students on another, the community on still another. . . .

We need to consider how good a job we have done of exemplifying the meaning of a faculty. Have we sold that birthright to other agencies? Is it surprising that statehouses and the public view us not as a faculty, but merely as a collection of paid instructors, poorly supervising a collection of unruly trainees? . . . We have assumed the prerogatives of faculty, but have we consistently worn the gown of accountability? . . .

The current mode of campus operation under the modified injunction is difficult and onerous. The injunction itself shows that a mutuality of trust and respect has not existed between the university community and city and county community. . . .

Many of the pursuits of this college are of precisely the sort that symbolize man's higher worth and motivation. These are especially found in the visual arts, music, rhetorical effort, the theater, and the techniques of craftsmanship. Through these and other efforts this college is a repository of creative energy, thinking, and doing. We need, as a faculty and students, to focus this energy in such a way that it humanizes and removes us from our own prejudices, fears, and preconceptions. . . .[1]

The university closed for the remainder of the academic year, with classes being held in church basements, in faculty homes, and elsewhere throughout the community. An injunction against Kent State greatly inhibited instruction and university management. It illustrated resentments of a significant portion of local people, who perceived Kent State as a breeding ground for troublemakers. Many locals believed that the students who were killed put themselves in the position to be shot and had only themselves to blame. In the eyes of politically conservative segments of Northeast Ohio's citizenry, a person identified as part of Kent State was classified as a potential agitator. We lived in Hudson, Ohio, at the time, a charming transplant into the Western Reserve of a New England-style village. Much political thought in Hudson at the time fell slightly to the right of Genghis Khan. Socially liberal thought was practically nonexistent. Many meetings on the subject of Kent State took place, some of which I attended, and I was pressed hard, sometimes with disparagement, to justify my being part of the KSU administration and faculty.

Some months later I wrote an op-ed piece for the *Akron Beacon Journal*[2] in which I commented about the moral and ethical dichotomies related to the KSU tragedy and in some detail about the current clash of values between older and younger generations. I mentioned the sad fact that Christian women in a local church's ladies' aid society were pouring tea for a circle meeting one day, and justifying students being shot the next. Because some readers perceived it as supporting dissenting students this piece generated a spate of anonymous hate mail wherein I was called just about everything from a communist to the devil's advocate.[3] In the same edition of the *Beacon Journal* a staff writer wrote a news analysis, "Profound Clash of Values," in which he presented something of an exegesis of my piece.[4] After several references to my comments he summed up his own remarks by saying, "No apology should be given, of course, for violent dissent which leads inevitably and irreversibly to the violation of another man's [sic] rights. By the same token, violent and indiscriminate repression is not a just remedy for destructive dissent. The 'eye for an eye' mentality leads straight to a kingdom of sightless brutes where blind force replaces the rule of law as a governing principle."

The Kent State campus paroxysm had reverberated beyond Kent, into the affairs of other campuses and broader U.S. society. Some campuses closed temporarily to thwart circumstances that might beget further violence. In the nice weather throughout that summer of 1970, and into the next academic year, the Kent campus continued to be the site of rallies and assemblages. On October 16, 1970, a state grand jury report exonerated the National Guard and indicted twenty-five persons, mostly students. A noteworthy excerpt from this undeniably biased report reflected much citizen reaction to campus dissent and that of Kent State in particular. The report said that "The administration at Kent State University has fostered an attitude of laxity, overindulgence, and permissiveness with its students and faculty to the extent that it can no longer regulate the activities of either and is particularly vulnerable to any pressure applied from radical elements within the student body or faculty."[5]

On campus there were cadres of faculty members who, through the initiative of the Faculty Senate, were detailed to move about the campus in groups throughout the day and night, not so much as a patrol but a presence. I joined more than one of them and can remember being dog-tired out on the lawn at three o'clock in the morning. Throughout all of this I was impressed by the inherent strength within the KSU faculty itself. Indeed, as always, there were some haywire faculty members here and there (which because of the faculty's refusal to apply self-corrective professional measures to make them accountable has engendered public disapprobation no less now than then) but the consistency and resolve of the KSU faculty maintained the university. It is that strength, along with well-above average board and administrative leadership, especially during the last twenty years, that has brought Kent State University forward until it is now poised, more than most regional state universities, to assume a significant place in the hierarchy of U.S. campuses. This is a remarkable achievement given what the university went through.

Despite the inordinate difficulties of that post-May 4 period Kent State had to proceed with its business. As I review my memos and correspondence throughout those months and the ensuing two years, I am surprised by the amount of routine academic business that transpired. But there were changes. Robert White stepped aside from the presidency into retirement seven months after May 4, to be succeeded by Glenn Olds, and I was moved from the fine and professional arts deanship into the central administration as associate provost. Things were returning to normal patterns, even though they were not the same.

"FATHER" JOSEPH SMITH

During this period there was a professor in the music department, now deceased, who was a philosopher and former Jesuit priest who had left the order and married. He viewed himself as a superior scholar whose role did not include teaching undergraduates. He was, by his own assertion, only meant to teach graduate students. At established research universities with cadres of distinguished scholars, who often integrate graduate students into their research projects, it is standard practice to function only at the graduate level, although frequently—for the pure joy of it—these famous academics teach introductory courses to undergraduates. But

Kent State was not in that mix. Teaching undergraduates comprised a crucial component of the teaching assignments of professors, who were expected to assume their share of the responsibility.

When Joseph Smith refused a departmental assignment to teach an undergraduate survey course in music literature saying, "I decline to accept," he left the students in the class without a professor. The administration had made clear that the assignment was within his contract terms. I had taught similar classes in the past and to maintain the schedule for students I stepped in and taught the course. We waited, expecting his colleagues in music to counsel him that it was an abrogation of his contract to refuse to teach the course, to say nothing of it being an ethical and professional breach. They did talk to him, but throughout the term he refuse to budge. (Down the centuries Jesuits have not exactly been known for their flexibility!) He was given a similar assignment for the next term and advised again about his contractual responsibilities, to no avail. With no recourse left, the administration invoked the requisite due process, and even though tenured, he was dismissed. It was a case, pure and simple, of failure to meet a contractual obligation. The faculty did not spring to his defense. Predictably he sued in federal court. It took many years and tens of thousands of dollars in direct and indirect litigation costs before the suit was finally dismissed. Only a distorted view of academic freedom could allow such a circumstance to arise, where a self-centered individual tried to trump responsibility to the institution. Only in the litigious context of the United States could an egregiously unfitting court action drag on as long as it did before being dismissed.

My practical learning during the six and one-half years incumbency at Kent State was both revealing and broadening. It was also jarring and unsettling. KSU was not an upstairs campus. This broke me out of the protective wrapping of the School of Music at Michigan and provided a tempering which I think helped as I dealt with issues in the years to come.

CHAPTER 5

Vulgarities and Disrespect on Campuses: Lessened Academic Standards

We no longer ask, "How much has student achievement improved?" We ask, "Is everybody happy?"

Albert Shanker

WHERE HAS CIVILITY GONE?

The sixties, especially late in the decade approaching the early seventies, were raucous and noisy. Attitudes and behaviors permeated student bodies on campuses across the country that had not emerged before the reaction against the Vietnam War catalyzed them. The so-called "free speech" movement, beginning in Berkeley and picked up immediately at Columbia, was a shallow misnaming. It was not essentially free—it should have been called the "shock speech" or "dreadful speech" movement—freedom has a much deeper meaning than those individuals who thought they were displaying it in their words realized.

NO COMFORT

I was not comfortable in that melee. I was brought up in a context where appearances were all important. My mother, Linda, manifested the characteristics of the Victorian era, when appearances prevailed. Queen Victoria was still alive when Mother was born in 1896. Mother could never have been expected to shed the drapery of her own upbringing and conditioning. It was an ingredient of her environment. I remember occasions when she visited us in Ann Arbor while I was on the faculty of Michigan. She would walk by the Michigan Union and see unkempt African-American guys hanging out and rapping by the side door of the Union. She would utter declamations of disapproval. There was nothing dishonest in this. It was simply that the appearances to her were all wrong. Thus the lessons I learned about student behaviors during my six and a half years at Kent State (the same would have been true at other campuses) served as preparation for the circumstances I was to confront later in direct contravention to my childhood conditioning.

THE DECLINE IN CIVILITY

When the subject of the decline of civility on campuses comes up, those who think the concerns are overstated usually relate the long history of less than well-mannered behavior at universities. Reference is made to the famous food fights at Yale in the 1820's or the fisticuffs and boisterous student behavior at medieval universities. Students acted up sometimes merely on general principles, but on other occasions their ire was aimed at faculties for one or another grievances.

After I had joined the Kent State University administration in 1966 the turbulence from campus unrest swelled nationwide. Over the previous four years I had watched the growth of campus incivility, which had become one of the mechanisms of protest. The Free Speech movement characterized the attitudes of some radical and activist students of the sixties. The distemper of words for shock value has now come back, inexorably degenerating into jargonized vulgarity. On campuses the deviate word-fashion reemerges in some student publications such as offbeat pieces, and publications disposed toward protest. For example at Cleveland State University in the fall semester of 1999 the *Vindicator* (a student newspaper) flung verbal violence at the CSU president following a misadventure in a campus-wide computer programming changeover that resulted in bureaucratic complications and delays in processing student aid checks. For a student publication to vociferate stridently against such a turn of events would be natural. What is noteworthy in this example is the violence of the language and the abandonment of even a pretense of civility.[1]

But during the sixties, by contrast, underneath the intemperate and disreputable language, a force had coalesced in protest against the immorality of the Vietnam war. In general terms the protest represented a reaction against the values inherent in the kind of a society that condoned the war and more specifically against the controlling "establishment" seen as promulgating the war. The establishment consisted essentially of any and all authority figures. The administrative role that I fulfilled as a dean and later, after the Kent State shootings, as an associate provost, automatically made me an adversarial authority figure. I remember once agreeing to address a rally sponsored by the SDS (Students for A Democratic Society) in a room overflowing with two hundred people. Given the dynamics of the moment, less than a month after the May 4, 1970 tragic campus events, this was a miscalculation. The SDSers couldn't have cared less about any logic or thought contained in what I might say. What they wanted was to have me there as a target for invective. Before it was over the hyperactive group leading the rally cornered me and let fly with a fusillade of vilifications. It was all I could do to extricate myself. To have called for the police to help would have escalated the potential for violence. Despite the prevalence of this kind of behavior at the time I believed and still do that the student protesters and their supporters in the late sixties were morally right in reviling the conduct of the war. But they were sometimes unprincipled in the methods they used to conduct the protests. One of these methods was the indiscriminate trashing and demeaning of authority figures and leaders they identified with the society responsible for the war.

LACK OF DECORUM

Another component of protest was simply to fulminate against authority on general principles. In its most extreme, anarchistic form, it simply called for "a destruction of what is," which in its expression had little or no connection to the Vietnam War. This kind of protest against authority in the decades since the sixties has had a significant, and negative, social effect. Within it lie the roots of lack of respect for the structures of society which in specific ways shows up today in cynicism, a loss of idealism, and the rise in uncivil student behavior in college classes.

Here I do not necessarily refer to unconventional classroom behaviors, such as welfare mothers desperately trying to extricate themselves from poverty who take their babies to class with them in public, urban universities—but certainly not at upscale, upstairs private colleges and universities. Inevitably the mixing of baby-sitting with that of attending an academic presentation causes disruption. But at least there is a purpose behind the actions, even though it creates difficulties for other class participants. Open admission universities increasingly provide child care services.

Nor do I refer to the tough, no holds barred adversariness of competing ideas that has characterized academic, intellectual debates for centuries. (In this vein, it is revealing to read the diatribes of Jonathan Swift in *Gulliver's Travels*, or encounter the storms of reaction against the revered John Henry Newman in his Oxford Movement days.) Civilized communities where vital minds are at work can be disputatious. This has the appearance of incivility, which in fact it can be, but it also has the redeeming feature of flushing to the surface and placing in relief the issues being debated.

Rather, I refer to unconscionable violations of group courtesies in classes (absent vigorous, intellectual contention) and the infringement of commonly accepted rules of decency and respect of others. While the actual percentage of students displaying this unseemly behavior is relatively small it is more than enough to create problems of increasing dimensions. The *Chronicle of Higher Education* identified it as a national problem in a March 1998 article citing vivid examples from different regions of the country: "Some scholars argue that academe has never been above a good slugfest. But close encounters of the uncivil kind are leaving many professors stunned, even shaken. How, they ask, did the decorous world of academe disintegrate into a free-for-all?" The article goes on to say that, "Undergraduate insolence grew so bad recently at Virginia Tech that the Faculty Senate formed a 'Climate Committee' to look into the situation" which, according to the chairman of the committee, "is much worse than it was—I think the incidence of this in the last ten years has doubled, if not tripled, in terms of the amount and the severity."[2]

CELEBRITY VERSUS DESERVED FAME

Another current example can be found in the lack of willingness or sensibility to recognize and respect heroic persons—
whether the heroism be physical or intellectual. As Stephen
Ambrose from the University of New Orleans wrote in a
New York Times op-ed piece young people used to "want to
know who were our heroes and what did they do?" "Yet
teaching about heroes is scorned today in many academic
circles as 'triumphalism' [whatever that word is intended to
mean] and is not done." To a considerable extent we can
thank the safely ensconced and now academically tenured
children of the sixties for this. It has opened the door to a
preference for celebrity—worshipped for being well known—
in place of earned respect for accomplishment leading to the
betterment of human kind. It cannot be denied that the ma-
chinery of the media can make celebrities out of third-raters
including rock stars and pro athletes with questionable personal habits. But the media celebrity hunters would not succeed were we not willing as a society to buy what they are so
good at writing. Thus, celebrating fame for authentic accomplishments leading to the improvement of society
doesn't happen all that often. The incivility in the sixties did
indeed have some rationale because no matter how crude
and vulgar their actions, many participants thought they
were involved in a movement with a purpose. By contrast,
the improprieties and disrespect now shown on and off campuses have no social purpose. They are simply selfish and
self-centered. It is impossible to extrapolate what today's decline in decorum means for us as a nation. Speaking as one
who grew up as a teenager during the depression it is inevitable that I look upon the world with a perspective formed
during times exceedingly different from today. I cut my professional academic teeth during the fifties and my own children were teenagers during the sixties. Today I watch

baby-boomers' children, the so-called Millennial Generation now in their late teens to very early twenties. These kids tend toward coarseness in language. Their sexual habits in comparison with mine growing up would have made my cohort candidates for Mother Teresa's convent. They show rather little concern for conventional courtesies to others, and largely because of the personal privileges coming out of golden economic times of the nineties are self-centered in their habits—much more so than the children of the depression—and more so than those of the fifties, even the sixties, and the seventies. But does that mean that the Millennial Generation is inherently more selfish when compared with preceding generations? Who knows? Elders have forever complained about flawed younger generations. What counts is the stamina and resilience this generation of kids will show when and if things get tough for them, as for example the citizens of New York showed in the aftermath of September 11, 2001. For the Millennials and the preceding Generation Xers the real testing has not yet come.

DEFAMATION

Inevitably, given our litigious climate, incivility in language directed at someone else on campus will, from time to time be tested in court for defamation. The *Synfax Weekly Report*, which covers issues of the law and policy in higher education, has dealt with this subject in detail, by extracting from court cases and setting forth what kinds of words can be used in the roughness of debate between adversaries.[3] There is considerable ambit in words that can be used to put another person down.

Defamation does not occur if, "[T]erms that are either too vague to be falsifiable or sure to be understood as merely a label for the labeler's underlying assertions; and in the latter case the issue dissolves into whether those assertions are defamatory. If you say simply that a person is a 'rat' you are not saying something definite enough for a jury to determine whether what you are saying is true or false. If you say he is a rat because . . . whether you are defaming him depends on what you say in the because clause."[4]

"Among the terms and epithets that have been held . . . to be incapable of defaming because they are mere hyperbole rather than falsifiable assertions of discreditable fact are 'scab,' 'traitor,' 'amoral,' 'scam,' 'fake,' 'phony,' 'a snake-oil-job,' 'he's dealing with half a deck,' and 'lazy, stupid, crap-shooting, chicken-stealing idiot.' "[5]

As a professor and administrator I have heard much of this and more in the halls, cafeterias, and meeting rooms of the academy. It can be raunchy and deprecating. It also verifies the quips uttered in many quarters that if university-faculty senates were selected by random picks out of the telephone book rather than elected faculty members, university governance would improve. Just because judges have held that uncivil words are not necessarily defamatory does not elevate them to the level of civilized discourse. There is a difference between incivility on the one hand and strong disagreement on the other, expressed with logic but without equivocating. Universities have always provided forums for tough and vigorous interaction. But it is not possible to legislate *civil* discourse. That is the fallacy of politically correct, campus speech codes which time has proven do not work. The remedy can be found in the long, academic history of disciplined and ordered thought given expression by individuals who might have separated themselves from the norms of convention, but did so with reason and forethought. The legacy of the sixties—undisciplined free speech aberrant from the noble meaning of constitutional free speech—has eroded that heritage.

THE GI BILL AND ITS RAMIFICATIONS

Signed by Franklin Delano Roosevelt in 1944, the GI Bill opened doors of higher education to masses of veterans of World War II. They flocked to campuses in every state. Without GI Bill subsidy most veterans would not have had the opportunity to go to college. There were no barriers. As long as a veteran had ninety days of military service he or she received one day of GI benefits for each day of service, regardless of race, gender, or cultural background. One year of service entitled a veteran to one year of benefits and so on. There were no bureaucratic impediments.

Whatever college admitted the student, the U.S. government picked up the tab. These students, over two million strong, bettered their lives by going to college and in the process permanently altered higher education and American society itself. For the most part these GI Bill students valued the opportunity and made the most of it. Over the years I have had hundreds in my classes.

The GI Bill was neutral with respect to types of campuses it paid for students to attend. It was essentially free of bureaucratic and regulatory difficulties. It did not step between the students and their institutions, nor were strings attached to the appropriated funds like those attached to federal programs of today.[6] The result was a supremely successful program that helped millions of students in ways no entity except an enlightened federal government could accomplish. This enlightenment was leavened by the political concern that maybe the American marketplace could not absorb the large numbers of discharged veterans dumped into the economy and therefore it would be a good idea to divert some of them into colleges. Nonetheless, the GI Bill changed the face of America. Seldom, perhaps never, has there been a more felicitous mix of individual initiative and U.S. government programming.

But in subsequent years millions of college enrollees migrated onto campuses from stratas of America that had never before been college-bound. They were bent upon improving their socioeconomic status through college degree programs of vocational *training* so they could get good jobs and earn steady incomes. This contrasted with what had earlier been liberal arts *education* not directly related to the job market but ostensibly possessing value of and for itself. This emphasis upon practical degree programs caused a decline in the liberal arts as a proportion of academic course offerings. The national common denominator of pure academic excellence (at least as academic excellence has been understood historically) became lower and that of vocational training higher. On the one hand, abstract academic excellence has never quite been characteristic of "working people,"—with obvious and wonderful individual exceptions. On the other, job training which is tangible and concrete has been and remains "for the common man." This ascendancy of training over education was especially visible at open admission state colleges and universities, where legislatures of most states mandated that all graduates of accredited high schools within their state be admitted to that state's colleges and universities. The jargon word "access" came into currency years ago to describe the social and economic value of a college education being made available to citizens for whom it had not been available in years past. To this day, no discussion in committees of state legislatures about state-assisted higher education ever takes place without the term "access" being regularly bandied about. During the seventies and eighties in the halls of Ohio's Capitol Building in Columbus, I heard the term repeated *ad infinitum*, but never was it even considered whether or not getting a college education was the right thing for everyone to do.

However, attitudes might now be changing. There is a

growing awareness, even in the face of the universality of aspirations for access, that something has been lost in the decline of academic standards.

DECLINING ACADEMIC STANDARDS

Academic quality in U.S. public schools has plummeted.
Achievement testing of students from kindergarten through
high school, which provides trend lines over the years,
proves this. A random sampling of journals, magazines, and
the print media turns up an abundance of articles, charts, and
quoted studies documenting this decline. "Average U.S. high
school students lag behind their peers in France, Germany
and Scotland in academic skills, says a report by the American Federation of Teachers."[7] Inevitably, a deterioration has
followed at colleges and universities, particularly those with
open admissions. A bar graph of high school graduation rates
in 1996 as a ratio to the population at the typical age of graduation, from selected countries, published in the *Chronicle of
Higher Education*, showed the United States with a 72 percent high school graduation rate, falling behind twenty-
three other countries. Norway and Belgium, for example,
have 100 percent rates, Japan 99 percent. Only ten countries
surveyed were below the United States, all of them being developing nations.[8] In an op-ed piece in the *Wall Street Journal* in 1998 entitled "The World's Least Efficient Schools,"
Chester Finn and Herbert Walberg provide devastating
commentary about U.S. schools being the least efficient in
the industrial world. "This country spends more per pupil
than almost any other nation, yet its year-to year gains are
among the smallest." "Thanks to the OECD (Organization
for Economic Cooperation and Development) it is possible
to compare gains [in reading] made by students between the
ages of nine and fourteen across many nations. It turns out
that U.S. students gain the least; on average they make just

78 percent of the progress of students in 15 other lands." "The news is similar in math and science." "So the U.S. is near the top in educational spending, but close to last in achievement gains."[9] This deficiency in acquiring knowledge characterizes not only public school students, but the U.S. population at large. The Chicago Academy of Sciences, at the behest of the National Science Foundation, surveyed 2006 adults about the extent of their knowledge. This was done through random telephone interviews. According to the NSF, only 25 percent would get passing grades. Less than half understood that the earth orbits the sun every year. Just 9 percent knew what a molecule is.

In my own teaching and counseling relationships with college students I have consistently had to deal with a general decline in levels of student academic standards. In academic record-keeping this has been masked by grade inflation. For example, when Cs used to be given they have now become Bs, and Bs turn into As. Grade inflation is universal. It occurs on the very best campuses. In 1996 a report from Princeton University indicated that "83 percent of the grades between 1992 and 1995 were As or Bs, compared with 69 percent between 1973 and 1975." The College Board confirmed the same phenomenon at the high-school level. They said "[T]hat test takers with A averages grew from 28 percent of the total to 38 percent in the last ten years, but the SAT (Scholarship Aptitude Test) scores of those students fell an average of twelve points on the verbal portion and three points on math."[10] Obviously an A at an upper-tier campus serving a highly selective student population, even though it might be inflated, has more currency than an A at an open admissions, public university serving an inner city population. So the better graduate schools do what they have always done in evaluating applications for admission (but not talking about it and sedulously avoiding any documentation) namely, "index" grades according to perceptions of the quality of the institutions giving the grades.

AN INAUSPICIOUS EXAMPLE OF A DECLINE IN STANDARDS

Perhaps the worst example in the decline of standards through open admissions occurred at City University of New York. At the end of the 1990s no system of higher education took it on the chin for deteriorating standards as much as did CUNY, particularly its flagship campus, City College of New York. During the 1970s, the increased enrollment that resulted from expansion during the fifties and sixties was augmented through the active recruitment of minority students who were academically ill prepared. The stated purpose was to ensure these groups were represented as students at CUNY by their percentage of the city's population.

City College of CUNY had always been known and respected as being among the best, if not the best, U.S. public campuses offering opportunity for qualified applicants who were poor. It used to be called "the Harvard of the Poor." The education was free, but students had to qualify academically to enroll and maintain high standards once there. No less than eleven Nobel Laureates, to say nothing of astonishing numbers of CEOs and distinguished business and professional people emerged from CCNY. But in the mid-sixties City College (which dates from 1847), along with the other campuses of City University of New York, began to soften entrance requirements. In 1970 CUNY Trustees opened admissions to four-year colleges to anyone in the upper half of a high school graduating class and opened community college admissions to anyone who graduated from a New York City high school. In one year this doubled the size of the entering freshman class at CUNY. The students simply were not prepared for college academic work. Enrollments in remedial classes soared, bleeding money away from the departments of regular instruction, and because remedial work, as contrasted to regular college-level instruction, was seen as stigmatizing to students this distinction was minimized. The results were academic disasters. "Students could take remedial and non-remedial courses at the same time, and the distinction between the two often became hard to perceive."[11] The course work at CUNY campuses, especially CCNY, was "dumbed down" to a common denominator to fit the lower academic accomplishments of the students it was getting. This went on for almost thirty years.

Finally at a May 1998 Trustee meeting, the Board reversed the open admissions policy and voted to restrict the admission of students to CUNY four-year campuses. Those who could not demonstrate proficiency in reading, writing, and mathematics requisite for college-level work would not be admitted. The removal of remedial courses from the eleven CUNY senior colleges by the year 2001 took place. Responsibility for remediation was placed in the community colleges. This was a first step in academic rehabilitation. But it came amidst demonstrations, with squawks and howls that disenfranchised citizens were being denied their rights to higher education. Protesters did not recognize the fact that remediation was still provided at community colleges, from which students could transfer to four-year institutions. In December of 1998 a coalition of civil rights groups filed an action against CUNY Trustees seeking to overturn the decision to remove remedial courses from the system's eleven four-year colleges. Other actions followed. The Board of Regents of New York State became involved by planning to assess the impact of the trustee action. It was suggested to the U.S. Department of Education that, on the basis of discrimination, minority students did not have comparable opportunities to prepare for college as other students, and therefore, by law CUNY should provide remedial education in its four-year institutions. In the meantime the Regents commissioned an independent panel of five experts outside the state. The panel concluded that taking remediation out of the senior colleges would not "diminish affordable and equitable access to higher education in the city," and, "that the remediation plan was likely to increase the quality of academic programs throughout CUNY." The panel wryly observed that the debate had involved "invasive political theater in which outrageous claims are the norm."[12]

Problems had also emerged in the six community colleges of CUNY over the test determining proficiency in English writing. For many of the students at these campuses, English is a second language. The CUNY system had always required a proficiency test in writing as a condition of graduation, even though coursework had been completed. Before the graduation ceremonies in 1997 questions were raised as to whether or not all prospective graduates had taken or passed the test. A flap ensued, with some students being informed at the last minute that they could not receive their associate degrees because they either had not taken the test or had failed it. Predictably this generated student protest. The mayor of New York and the governor of the state entered the fray, vowing that standards must be upheld, which no doubt helped the majority of CUNY trustees who held firm. Circumstances like this also highlight another fact, namely that the credential represented by a degree has much more importance to protesting students than the value represented by learning. Students were upset by the danger of being denied a credential. Nothing was ever said about the inherent value of learning to speak and write English creditably.

But the emotional and political discussions about access

to a college education, at least in the sense of what higher education has meant through its history (which certainly was the meaning of CCNY), have not characteristically been connected to the issue of whether or not a college degree is appropriate for all groups of citizens.

A CLASH OF VALUES

A dramatic clash of values, distinctive to the American character, emerges here. Providing access to a college education for citizens previously closed out of higher education, even though they may not possess the qualifications for admission, has become an enunciated value. This is buttressed by the verity from the Declaration of Independence: "We hold these truths to be self evident, that all men are created equal, that they are endowed by their Creator with certain unalienable rights . . ." But it is also true that the context of these words is broader than their literal meaning. In fact we are not all equal. In the words of a sometimes dyspeptic and politically incorrect columnist from Cleveland, Dick Feagler, "What the Founding Fathers must have meant . . . was that all men deserve the dignity of an equal chance. We're not all the same. But we should all be allowed an even shot at the standard of achievement."[13]

It cannot be denied that in the nation's public colleges and universities the highest possible level of quality in academic integrity and substance is a crucial civic value. Developing knowledge and converting it into wisdom (which is what universities should be all about) is what moves a civilization forward. The common denominator component of a society does not move it forward. It is the geniuses and the dedicated men and women of uncommon accomplishment that provide the motive power for progress. Since the rise of universities in the middle ages most of these persons of intellectual genius in science, literature and philosophy (not all, certainly, but most) went through universities. Today it is undeniable that providing access to university programs to large numbers of individuals unready for the programs has had the effect of qualitatively depreciating them, and thereby penalizing those others who are prepared for higher education. The integrity of the academy has been compromised by providing entitlements to it for citizens unready to grasp and absorb it.

The solution is not all that complicated. Other educational institutions, especially community colleges, can and do provide remedial education so that those who are unready for a university education can make themselves ready. This is where remedial education belongs. There are practically no barriers, economic or social, to entrance into public community colleges. Educational functions should be segmented. Four-year institutions are not and cannot be all things to all people. It might make previously disenfranchised individuals and groups feel better to be admitted to a four-year, senior college, but the "feel-good" syndrome does not provide knowledge and intellectual skills requisite to enter bona fide degree programs. Programs for the purpose of providing these skills are readily available in community colleges and should be used.

Reaction Against Academic Decline in Teacher Education

There is some evidence of a reaction against the decline in academic standards. This comes as a result of public disillusionment over public, tax-assisted university budgets being depleted to fund classes covering what should have been learned in high school. The CUNY controversy exemplifies this. The disillusionment is also directed toward teacher education programs as the source of teachers for public schools. Through teacher-certification code requirements, which have the force of state law, these programs are, to a consider-able extent, indentured chattels of state departments of education, held in line through their onerous civil service bureaucracies. To cleanse the bureaucracies within the state departments of education involves doing political battle in state capitals. But attacking retrograde professional educa-tion curricula on college campuses (often derogated with the term educationist) is more direct and represents the initial phase of the campaign.

The predictably outspoken John Silber, who retired from the presidency of Boston University but who is president once again, minced no words in saying,

> This spring [1998] Massachusetts administered its first statewide test for candidates hoping to teach in the public schools. The announcement of the results has provoked astonishment and outrage. Almost 60 percent of the candidates failed . . . 30 percent failed a basic test in reading and writing, and the failure rate on subject-matter tests varied from 63 percent in mathematics to 18 percent in physical education . . . Reactions were predictable: approval from those appalled by the decline in quality of the public schools and howls of complaint from education professionals, including college profes-sors and deans. . . . The controversy over the test has obscured the real story, which is that so many prospec-tive public school teachers failed a test that a bright 10th grader could pass without difficulty. . . . Nowhere are standards lower than in schools of education. In 1997, the average combined SAT score for all students was 1016. But those hoping to become teachers scored only 964, 5.1 percent below the national average.[14]

It might be that Massachusetts sparked an effort, picked up by other states, to improve teacher education. In state after state measures are being taken to toughen standards. To accomplish this there are threats of probation and potential closure of college and university teaching programs where a significant portion of graduates do not pass certification exams which, concurrently, are also being made more stringent. A few months after the Massachusetts candidate test debacle, Texas, New Hampshire, Georgia, and the California State University system were identified as moving forward on new initiatives to strengthen teacher education. In addition, the two systems in California, CSU (California State University) and UC (University of California) have agreed to require the same high school work for admission. This will simplify procedures but will not alter the intrinsic academic differences in admissions between the two systems: where UC considers only the top one-eighth of the state's high school seniors, while CSU will take the top third.

Of all the states, New York has taken the most adamant position in the move to improve teacher education. As of September 1999, the New York State Board of Regents, "set up procedures to penalize teaching schools where students routinely fail the state's licensing examination which itself is being made more rigorous. . . . Beginning in the current school year, at least 80 percent of the students who graduate from New York State teaching programs must pass the state licensing exam for teachers or that teaching school can be put on probation for three years and then shut down." If the 80 percent rule were in effect today, state officials said, at least two dozen of New York's 113 teacher education programs could lose their accreditation, including several at the City University of New York.[15] The new standards place more emphasis on the need for coursework in the subject that a given public school faculty member teaches. All of this is heartening to those of us who believe in the centrality of disciplinary substance as contrasted to the dominance of methodology.

The American Federation of Teachers, which is the nation's second largest teacher's union, added its voice to the chorus demanding improvement in the quality of public school teachers. In April 2000 the AFT, after acknowledging that the public school teaching profession has suffered losses of professional esteem, advocated national testing and the establishment of "rigorous new standards for those who want to become teachers."[16] This was a groundbreaking announcement from a union that traditionally has opposed such tests and adds impetus to the movement for reform.

In addition to converging efforts on college-level teacher training, the state of New York inaugurated proficiency tests in mathematics and English for eighth graders. The tests were more rigorous than those previously given students. The results, announced on November 5, 1999 by the State Board of Education and the Regents, were dismaying: in New York City a *77 percent failure rate* in mathematics along with a *65 percent failure rate* in English. New York City has districts with high percentages of ethnic minorities and poor students and, given the chronic social problems of public school students, would be expected to fare poorly, but the remainder of the state, outside of the city, did not do that much better—*a 46 percent failure rate* in English reading for eighth graders, and a *54 percent failure rate* in math. If these tests were to be administered nationally in junior high or middle schools there is little reason to believe the results would be that much better.

But a problem exists in the implementation of standardized tests at state, to say nothing of national, levels. In contrast to other nations, the U.S. does not have a national system of education. On the contrary, there are approximately 15,000 school districts nationwide. Separate districts have broad autonomy in matters of teaching and curriculum, subject to supervision by the departments of education in each state. This supervision has developed into a more bureaucratic than substantive oversight. The overweening problem in standardized tests exists in the broad differences between academically low-performing and high-performing schools, which cannot be separated from wide socioeconomic differences in their geographic locations. No state or national test, yet devised, bridges the gap. High-performance schools complain bitterly about the tests dumbing down expected student achievement, and low-performance schools complain that the tests discriminate against large numbers of minority students within their enrollments.

Instead of concentrating upon improving student achievement, school systems, as contrasted to state officialdom, seem to be pulling back and relaxing their own standards. One reason is that parents don't seem to be committed to requiring their children to perform at higher levels. The complaints are legion about the "pressures on kids." This leads to attitudes of indulgence. In Wisconsin, for example, the state caved in to parent demands that it "[W]ithdraw a test that every student would have had to pass to graduate from high school. At least half a dozen other states and large districts are also moving to soften the expectations for students that have been drafted, in every state except Iowa, in at least some form and in some grades."[17] But the national resolve to elevate standards exists in the echelons of educational leadership. This resolve was evident in the $26.5 billion K-12 education bill signed by President Bush on January 8, 2002. Among many provisions, it requires state tests in reading and math for every child from grades three through eight and requires schools to raise the proficiency levels in reading and math during the next twelve years. The bill is a remarkable example of bipartisanship along with the penchant in Washington D.C. to throw money at problems. But it is also an example of a laudable intent to improve education. Time only will tell whether or not this intent coalesces around kitchen tables.

CHAPTER 6

Academic Freedom, Tenure, and Corruption in Intercollegiate Athletics

> *Tenure is an extremely emotional issue for many faculty members, and it may be impossible to change the system without tremendous upheaval.*

> Donald A. Farber, *Trusteeship*

> *I think it's an important statement that the [NCAA] chose [as its president] a college president, a sitting president . . . The statement is that intercollegiate athletics is integral to higher education and the success of higher education.*

> Myles Brand, Indiana University, upon becoming NCAA president

OF ALL THE debates over higher education the hue and huff about academic freedom and tenure is the most emotional. Arguments have been heating up through the 1990s and, as is characteristic of emotional debates, the wrong issues usually take precedence. Libraries have shelves weighted down with disquisitions on the issues of tenure. The purpose of the following brief discussion is not to propound yet another disquisition, but to highlight the crux of the problem: accountability on the part of tenured professors regarding their individual performances. If the academic profession (especially the AAUP) were to focus on the issue of a tenured professor's responsibility of individual performance, and monitoring it credibly rather than decrying attacks upon tenure, the contention would abate. Tenure of and for itself is not the problem. Rather, it can be found in the lack of adequate mechanisms to deal with circumstances when tenure is abused.

ACADEMIC FREEDOM

The concept of academic freedom—the freedom to inquire, experiment, and speak out regardless of whether or not it conforms to the dogmas of reigning authority—goes back to Classical Greece. Socrates drank hemlock rather than compromise this freedom. But it wasn't until the early 1600s that speaking freely and conducting objective, unbiased scientific experiments, upon which academic freedom is based, began to be codified. The Englishman Francis Bacon, in his *Advancement of Learning* (published in 1605), clearly identified the need for freedom in order for experiments to have validity. This new appearance of tolerance, slow in coming, followed on the heels of sectarian, religious wars that had wasted and wearied the people of western Europe—the same forces that caused the Pilgrims to set sail for America. Today, all free nations both in East and West recognize academic freedom as the bedrock upon which integrity in teaching and research work rests.[1]

TENURE

Systematized faculty tenure is not European. It is uniquely American. We inherited the ideas that engendered academic freedom from European thinkers, but they never attached tenure to it simply because university teachers were government employees and possessed the same entitlements as other government employees. It is still that way in Europe. There, the social compact between worker and state is stronger than in the United States. Today's French railroad workers, for example, who can retire in their early fifties and be taken care of for the rest of their lives, or German workers who have lengthy vacations and very generous health care and other benefits, expect more and receive more in publicly-funded benefits than U.S. workers. As European governments now find it increasingly difficult to sustain the high cost of these benefits and are attempting to scale them back in order to balance budgets, it is no wonder that worker actions increase. As I write this, unemployment in the United States hovers slightly above 6 percent, but in Europe it is between 8 and 9 percent. Within this scene professors are just as likely to mobilize and tie up street corner traffic in Frankfurt am Main as transportation workers are in Paris.

In America the professor's social compact for security and professional freedom has existed within the tenure system. When the 1915 *Declaration of Principles* was drafted by the distinguished historian Arthur Lovejoy and other founding members of the American Association of University Professors, responsibility and accountability were manifest throughout the document. To be a professor meant responding to a high calling. Professors should not, for example, be considered as employees of the president and trustees, in the sense of a business establishment, but appointees fulfilling professional functions of teaching and research, which are the foundations of a university. In the words of the AAUP founders who drafted the *Declaration*, "A university is a great and indispensable organ of the higher life of a civilized community, in which the work of the trustees holds an essential and highly honored place, but in which the faculties hold an independent place, with quite equal responsibilities—and in relation to purely scientific and educational questions, the primary responsibility." The *Declaration* goes on to say that, "[I]f education is the cornerstone of the structure of society, and if scientific knowledge is essential to civilization, few things can be more important than to enhance the dignity of the scholar's profession, with a view to attracting to its ranks men of the highest ability, of sound learning, and of strong and independent character."[2] Tenure was an inextricable part of this magisterial concept, relating the university to the higher life of a "civilized community," and had in part the function of guaranteeing a professor's employment in order for academic freedom to be exercised.

Tenure was developed during the first quarter of the twentieth century, in part because research work in the sciences (requiring experimentation) and in the social sciences (still new and requiring analytic techniques in clinical work in social settings) were growing by leaps and bounds. Professors carrying out these research initiatives simply had to be free. They were backed to the hilt by the early AAUP. Universities were then dominant centers of research work. Universities continue to be primary research centers where basic research (which may or may not have an immediate, practical application) can be freely pursued, but today, in addition, various other kinds of research centers sponsored through foundations, by instruments of government, or by corporations have emerged. For example, one of the largest and certainly most significant scientific projects of all time, mapping the human genome (over three billion chemical letters spread out on lengthy strands of DNA, literally the "Book of Life") has been and continues to be carried out jointly by a private company, Celera, and a consortium of publicly-financed institutions under the aegis of the National Institutes of Health. By contrast, at the turn of the nineteenth

into the twentieth century, for a private, for profit company
to have undertaken basic research of this magnitude would
have been unthinkable, both financially and scientifically.
(True, John D. Rockefeller's Standard Oil did its own research work, but it was scarcely comparable to mapping the
human genome.)

By the first quarter of the twentieth century university
research was becoming important to the economic growth
and development of the nation. Sometimes this research ran
counter to the special interests of large businesses. A classic
example, cited time and again, occurred in Wisconsin, where
research by university professors that developed margarine
clearly ran counter to the capital investments and strategies
of the dairy products industry, basic to the state's economy.
Given the influence of this industry upon the University of
Wisconsin, the professors who carried out this research
would have been left twisting in the wind had they not been
protected by tenure.

Today of course the context is quite different. Civil rights
statutes crafted from the 1960s on, and based upon the freedoms set forth by judicial interpretations of the First Amendment, preclude punitive action against professors pursuing
free inquiry in bona fide research, regardless of where it
might lead or whether or not it might go counter to the views
of university governing authority.[3] If the current web of
statutory provisions both federal and state had existed during
the earlier days of the century tenure would probably not
have developed as it did.

During the second and third quarters of the twentieth
century greater coherence in matters of tenure emerged,
along with the crafting of specific procedures protecting
professors against arbitrary actions against them by presidents and trustees. The AAUP's 1940 *Statement of Principles*
contains these procedures. They have had far-reaching influ-

ence within the ranks of faculties, administrations and trustees. By 1966 the ideas of faculty-administrative shared governance, initially predicated by the concepts in the 1915 *Declaration of Principles*, took shape in a joint statement of the American Council on Education (ACE), the AAUP, and the Association of Governing Boards of Colleges and Universities (AGB), entitled *Statement on Government of Colleges and Universities*. This statement identifies the shared responsibility of governance in academic institutions on the part of faculties, administrators, students and governing boards. The three-way statement makes clear that "the variety and complexity of tasks performed by institutions of higher education produce an inescapable interdependence." In 1967 a further joint effort of the AAUP, the U.S. National Student Association (NSA), plus other associations and civil rights groups, drafted a *Joint statement on Rights and Freedoms of Students*, thereby codifying the role of students in the mix of academic freedom and institutional governance. The document defines freedoms for students in the affairs of institutions. Due process and procedural standards concerning disciplinary matters are spelled out in detail.

Thus within a short span of little more than fifty years, thinkers and leaders in American higher education had forged these concepts and with brilliant phraseology organized them into a corpus of principles that placed university faculties as both foundation and vanguard of American civilization. The breathtaking sweep of their belief in the function of knowledge emerging from university faculties and its integration into our society was unique in the history of higher education. It was a mix of elitism and egalitarianism; of the status quo and entrepreneurialism; of conceptualizing and doing. It helped make the professoriate into one of the most respected and privileged classes of professionals in America.

WHAT IS HAPPENING TODAY?

This heritage is being changed beyond recognition by a significant component of "proletarianized" academics located mostly at mass-market institutions. Academic traditionalists use words like tarnishing and squandering to describe what is happening to the profession. The unalluring word proletarian means a class of industrial workers who lack their own means of production and thus sell their labor to live. When weighed against the professoriate in the early days of the 20th century, compared to the professoriate in mass-market higher education today, this definition has profound implications. It denigrates the call to high service of professors enunciated in the 1915 *Declaration*. Could Professor Lovejoy have conceived of selling his labor in order to live? Hardly. But it is taking place today in various sectors of the higher education mass market. Reasons are to be found in the magnitude of social change in the nation's citizenry between then and now.

It must be kept in mind that Professor Lovejoy's world of academic professionals was profoundly different from the mass-market, academic world of today. Broad and extensive differences in functions, types and clienteles of American institutions of higher education were not in the mix. Taken altogether they were more similar in characteristics than they were different. The culturally confrontatory, racially dissonant, class conflicting, and sociologically segmented professoriate did not exist in his day—at least anywhere near to the extent it does now. A Dean could expel a young man if he did not fit in. There was no ACLU (American Civil Liberties Union founded in 1920) to take up the cudgel against violation of the individual rights of students by campus authorities. Arthur Lovejoy's academic world consisted of males from white, Caucasian backgrounds. The same was true of students who came essentially from white families of privilege. His constituency of higher education was neither multicolored nor culturally multidimensional. It was upper crust and culturally single dimensional.

DIFFERENT SIDES OF THE TRACKS

By contrast a significant portion of today's faculty members who teach in mass-market institutions, come from the other side of the tracks or close to them. Since World War II many college teachers have ratcheted themselves, intellectually, upward from the working-class environments where they were born and reared. But they carry with them nonintellectual, emotional ties to the first-generation college students whom they teach. Many emerged from families that struggled to extricate themselves from worker servitude to the elite few—those few who controlled the industrial empires where working-class husbands toiled ten and twelve hours a day—and as often as not died early. It is no wonder that a significant component of today's mass-market professoriate, steeped in these proletarian principles, don't pay much attention to the meritocracy and historic academic values that Professor Lovejoy espoused. Their identity with the AAUP is not with its exalted history of enunciating the call to high service represented by an elite professoriat, but as a union that promulgates their special interests of salaries and working conditions in ways essentially no different from the Teamsters or the AFL-CIO.

In 1910 the number of students enrolled in American colleges and universities was 355,200.[4] Out of a U.S. population at the time of 92,228,496, that enrollment comprised less than four-tenths of 1 percent. As the twentieth century turned into the twenty-first, the number of college students in the nation exceeded 15,000,000 out of a population of more than 281,000,000. This pushes five and a half percent. In less than a century the increase in percentages and in gross numbers is awesome. The impact and implications of this growth are turning today's higher education inside out and upside down.

EXPANDING ENROLLMENTS IN PUBLIC CAMPUSES

The growing network of public land grant colleges and regional normal schools (developed in the nineteenth century to train teachers to staff the expanding systems of public schools and which evolved into single purpose teachers' colleges in the twentieth century) were not within the orbit of the class-conscious private liberal arts colleges and universities. Land grant colleges sometimes had the modifying terms "agricultural and mechanical" appended to their state college titles, referring to their vocational purposes.[5] But even on these public campuses, which occupied a somewhat lower social stratum, faculties were conditioned to behave in "a fitting manner." While land grant colleges were meant to concentrate on techniques of agriculture, their curricula included dollops of Plato, Latin, and Greek. Faculties often lived in college-supplied houses, and interacted with their students outside of the classroom. Often they joined them at Wednesday and Sunday services in the campus chapel. Being a professor was more than a job. It was a calling. The descriptive term "ivory tower" was relevant even though land grant colleges reached out through extension services to help farmers master new agricultural techniques (which over the decades resulted in U.S. food production being the wonder of the world). This was the beginning of the "campus-community involvement", now heralded by every urban campus in the nation, in contrast to the ivory tower. But professors were still not known for their "community involvements" or "social consciences" as we understand them today. The social sciences did not emerge as academic disciplines until the twentieth century. There were exceptions, Oberlin College being a noteworthy example in its commitments to women and to black people. For the most part, however, attitudes and actions of faculty members were circumscribed. In campus governance presidents were strong and faculties weak. Academic communities were self contained and subject to oversight by authorities who were not always even handed.

Times have changed dramatically. Higher education is now diverse—economically, socially, and culturally. "[B]y the fall of 1994, the proportion [of racial or ethnic minority groups] had increased to 24 percent. African Americans made up the largest share of this figure in 1994 (10.1%), followed by Hispanics (7.4%), Asian Americans (5.4%), and American Indians (0.9%)."[6] Accompanying this shift in demographics has been a shift of student enrollments from private to public institutions. Early in the century private institutions enrolled the great majority of students. By 1950 "[H]alf of all students were enrolled in public institutions, while half attended private colleges or universities. By 1960, the share attending public institutions had increased to 59 percent. This figure continued to grow to 75 percent in 1970 and 78 percent in 1980 and has remained steady at 78 percent in recent years."[7]

It is no wonder that the difference in the higher education landscape between 1915 and 2003 has changed the attitudes, and the principles and values of the professoriate.

The regional public university and community college professoriate (staffing approximately 2,200 out of roughly 3,900 U.S. institutions of higher education) no longer thinks of itself primarily as being indispensable to "the higher life of a civilized community" as the 1915 AAUP *Declaration* reminded us. Rather, the professoriate sells its services—technical expertise and current knowledge—and lobbies for increases in its compensation and benefits for doing so. The purpose of tenure is not seen primarily as a safeguard for the free search for truth, but more often simply as a mechanism for job preservation.

Professor Lovejoy and his colleagues are turning over in their graves.

The dramatic changes in the attitudes and points of view of the mass-market professoriate, and the emphasis on campus-community interaction, have opened doors through which politicians have streamed. It has introduced components of political partisanship on campus.

INTERCOLLEGIATE ATHLETICS

Any woman or man who has served as a president, provost, or vice president for student affairs on a campus involved in Division I NCAA (National Collegiate Athletic Association) sports will attest to the merry-go-round created by the sports-addicted public and alumni booster clubs. One side of the athletically minted coin is stimulation and emotional highs. The other side is depression and emotional lows. More than one president has referred to the love-hate relationships engendered in administrations and faculties through intercollegiate involvement in football and basketball. Problems caused by other sports such as golf, tennis, swimming, and track and field do not approach the magnitude of those created by basketball and football.

There are three major problems in intercollegiate athletics. Firstly, graduation rates are lower for athletes than for other students in Division I programs, particularly for black males in football and basketball, but whites also graduate at lower rates than other students. Secondly, athletes participating in intercollegiate competitions are treated differently and more leniently than other students. Similarly, big-time coaches receive preferential treatment with respect to perquisites and salary, to say nothing of some being able to get away with patterns of personal behavior which, for regular staff or faculty would close out careers—recall that Bobby Knight at Indiana University flaunted his unconstrained bad behavior, including thuggish physical assaults that were publicly reported for years, until his president, Myles Brand (now president of the NCAA), finally dismissed him. There is also my own experience as a president whose well-known basketball coach was arrested in the company of a prostitute in front of a suspected crackhouse. Thirdly, big money does have a corrupting effect.

In September of 1999 the NCAA released statistics that indicated graduation rates were at the lowest level in seven years.[8] On the top teams the academic records of basketball players have been getting worse. The *Wall Street Journal* reported that "According to the NCAA's recent figures, twelve of the last sixteen schools in this year's [2002] men's tournament—a Dirty Dozen of the Sweet Sixteen, if you will—had basketball graduation rates of 50 percent or lower."[9] In the Final Four the University of Maryland had a graduation rate of 19 percent and the University of Oklahoma a graduation rate of zero—that's right, an unadulterated zero.

Back in 1989 the NCAA had adopted a standard known as Proposition 16 that imposed minimum academic standards for student athletes on scholarship, namely that admittees score at least an 820 on the SAT or a composite 16 on the ACT. That level is not even close to excellence, but at least it was an acknowledgment by the NCAA that an academic problem existed; that something needed to be done about student athletes playing on college teams, using up their eligibility, and then leaving the campus, perhaps scarcely being able to read. They have been referred to as "throwaway" athletes. The issue of Proposition 16 wended its way into the Philadelphia courtroom of Federal Judge Ronald Buckwalter, who ruled in March of 1999 that the freshmen eligibility rules of the proposition had an "[U]njustified impact against African Americans." The judge ignored the fact that since 1989 some progress—not dramatic improvement but some—took place in the graduation rates of black athletes because of Proposition 16. His ruling set the issue of improving the academic achievement of student athletes back to square one. "Buckwalter's ruling is an insult to black athletes. His logic is an insult to everyone. This bad decision should be overturned."[10]

Examples of misconduct rising to the level of criminal acts, while certainly not unique to college football and basketball players, nonetheless have been a troubling phenomenon during the nineties. From state university campuses in state after state examples have emerged of violent acts both on and off campus by football and basketball players, mostly charges of physical aggression or sexual assault. If the college football or basketball teams are winning ones and the accused or arrested players crucial to the teams' good fortune, coaches all too often wink. Losing good players they recruited wastes their time. There does not seem to be a sufficient base of facts to prove that athletes get into criminal trouble more than other students, although there has been some evidence submitted by a few NCAA Division I campuses that athletes "[H]ad committed a disproportionate share of sexual assaults reported to campus judicial boards."[11]

The corrupting effect of the big money coming from big-time competition is obvious, not only in student athletes who, against the rules, often benefit from the under-the-table largesse from from high-powered boosters, but more significantly in the spin that athletic departments put on the meaning of college athletics. They represent sports as having an equalizing function that smoothes out differences of race and class, as well as teaching discipline and teamwork. I believe this, absolutely, in club sports and in NCAA Division 3 sports. However, the mammoth overhead costs of Division I football and basketball, particularly for the major university competitors under the influence of millions of spectators and millions more listeners and viewers, puts the classical ideas of sportsmanship into the background. Sportsmanship is not what counts. Winning is. Winning teams cost money; thus, winning coaches garner contracts worth millions of dollars in pay and other perquisites, and players who are flunking academically, are propped up.

Players themselves are not known for having clear ideas of what a college education means. If they are excellent football or basketball players they often leave college for professional teams and the potential of astronomical incomes after two years on campus, which amounted to a farm club. Sports paid off for them. But how about the rest? Spectator sports are inextricably a part of America, as they are elsewhere around the world. David Holahan, who played baseball and football at Yale and is a freelance writer, observed for *USA Today* that each year there are about four and a half million high school students playing football; of that number 39,000 make it onto college teams; of that number just 500 will be drafted by the pros; and only a hundred can expect a pro career.

A significant proportion of the tens of thousands of others, unready for college and not good enough for the top echelons of football and basketball, fall by the wayside and end up with neither a college education nor a sports career. Society at large, with its insatiable appetite for spectator sports is largely at fault. So are most of the universities that are caught up in the maelstrom of big-time sports.

A variety of commissions motivated by different educational organizations, including the American Council on Education, have proposed steps to correct the problems related to big-time intercollegiate athletics. In June of 2001, the Knight Foundation Commission on Intercollegiate Athletics released a report containing many recommendations, the most important being that college presidents must reassert themselves in order to control intercollegiate sports. Among the ways to accomplish this would be through a coalition of presidents who would have a measure of independence from the committee structure of the NCAA The cochairman of the commission, the Reverend Theodore M. Hesburgh (president emeritus of Notre Dame University) said that "In football we are not educating half of the young men we are responsible for."[12] Over the years, other organizations, plus presidential and blue-ribbon committees, have recommended corrective actions such as improving rates of graduation and reducing the length of practice seasons, but these corrective measures have been ineffective. "The commission called for the NCAA to require teams to graduate at least 50 percent of their athletes to be eligible for conference and national championships, beginning in 2007. Of the 321 colleges with Division I basketball teams, 180 failed to meet that standard in 2000."[13]

There exists considerable skepticism that the recommendations in the carefully-crafted report will work any better than previous recommendations. The reason is that there is too much money involved and too much vested interest on the part of the presidents who are part of the structure of the NCAA, even though the organization now has a new president (Myles Brand, former president of Indiana University and prior to that, the University of Oregon), an authentic academic, but one who has been part of the system of big-time, big-money college sports for years.

It is a measure of the frustrations of coping with the behemoths of big-time college sports that President Emeritus of the American Council on Education Robert Atwell said this: "We should finally acknowledge that, when it comes to big-time sports, many universities are in the entertainment business, not the education business."[14] Mr. Atwell goes so far as to say that universities might as well "move toward acknowledged professionalism, in which athletes need not be students but rather may be employees hired by the entertainment wing of the university. . . . Coaches could hire football and basketball players who would be students only if they wished to be; there would be no special admissions requirements or arrangements. The athletes would be paid a market wage. . . . If the program ran surpluses, the excess revenues would be paid to the institution's general funds and used for academic purposes or to support other athletic programs."[15] This stand, with which I agree, and which cuts through the maze of hypocrisies within universities and big-time sports, will be in contention for years.

CHAPTER 7

Exponential Increases in Knowledge and the Technology Developed to Teach and Communicate It

One cannot step into the same river twice.

Heraclitus

IN MY ROLE as associate provost at Kent State I dealt with university-wide curriculum issues and related budgeting. I interacted with the various academic departments as they struggled to incorporate their expanding knowledge into the curriculum. The dimensions of this world of growing knowledge, only a minute part of which I could control intellectually, pervaded my thinking. Its boundlessness inspires both awe and humility. For departments to succeed in managing the totality of the new knowledge and bring it all into the curriculum is impossible due to constraints on budgets available for purchase of sophisticated equipment and the limited availability of professors on the cutting edge. Confronting this new knowledge explosion is one of the greater challenges universities face.

THE ETHICS AND MORALITY OF KNOWLEDGE

Pure education, in order to profess ethics and morality, requires the involvement of two basic realms of mind and spirit. The first looks inward into self inquiry: "who am I? For what purpose did I come into being? How should I relate to our world and the universe?" Einstein said "Religion without science is blind. Science without religion is lame." His frequent references to God and religion,[1] and Stephen Hawking's memorable closing phrase in *A Brief History of Time* "[F]or then we would know the mind of God,"[2] both emerge from a desire to achieve self knowledge and then relate it to the universe. When Socrates said, "the unexamined life is not worth living," he uttered the noblest realization of a moral being in striving to know himself.

PHYSICAL AND MATERIAL REALITY

The second realm of inquiry looks outward. Its provinces are the boundless physical realities about us. The spiritual, intellectual, and artistic achievements that have come to us from the great men and women throughout history derive from this inquiring and receptive spirit. It is from this second realm that colleges and universities construct curricula. Mathematics, the physical and natural sciences, the social sciences, the practical world of engineering and computers, health and human help sciences, humanities and the arts, all represent forms of inquiry into the nature and spirit of our world, our bodies and minds. But how one should go about trying to achieve self knowledge has not been a curricular priority. It makes people nervous in ways no different today than for the fellow citizens of Socrates, who sentenced him to death in fifth century B.C.E. Athens. Therefore professorial committees that build curricula tend to neglect that aspect of education that is concerned with self knowledge.

They are not always so sure about their own selves. Instead they concentrate on the analysis of the outside world, concentrating on getting more facts about nature, life on earth, and the universe beyond. It has always turned out be more than we could handle anyway, and because of the increases in knowledge of the world about us, it becomes more difficult to cope with year by year.

FUNCTIONS OF NEW KNOWLEDGE

New knowledge has two functions: to replace old knowledge proven to have defects, and to add to and expand the store of existing knowledge. On the one hand, Ptolemy's theories of a spherical earth replaced the flawed, older theories of a flat earth. Later, Copernicus' and Galileo's efforts showed that the earth was not the center of the universe, but that earth revolved about the sun, which was the center of our solar system. This landed Galileo into deep trouble with Church authorities, who could not stomach the idea that the earth was not the center of the universe. The work of Copernicus and Galileo displaced earlier beliefs. On the other hand, Einstein's discovery and explanations of relativity supplemented, but did not supplant, classical, Newtonian mechanics, which still work in the practicalities of moving about on the earth, swimming, and flying. But Newtonian laws do not function in the sped up cosmic and microcosmic realms where objects travel at speeds approaching that of light— 186,000 miles per second. Einstein's proofs added to the store of knowledge, rather than supplanting our previous understanding.

Campuses today are dominated by new knowledge, both in curriculum and in campus operations. Any desktop computer and commercial software user knows the rapidity with which new products replace the old. This is also true of most subjects within curricula. Knowledge develops so rapidly, and prodigious amounts of information are communicated with such speed, that teaching and research disciplines, in order to remain coherent, must be broken down into sub-disciplines, sub-sub-disciplines, and so on almost *ad infinitum*. The subsets within a particular discipline can become so specialized that even research professors have difficulty communicating from one subset to another. But at the other end of the disciplinary spectrum an opposite trend is emerging. A number of thinkers, both in theology and science (astrophysics and particle-physics in particular), are jointly looking into where and how concepts in their separate fields might interfuse with themes of inquiry common to both. Certainly there seems to be some merging of thought in similar directions at the cutting edges of research in theology and physics: theologians and research-oriented scientists now hold joint conferences. This intersection of thought identified with religious faith and objective, proof-oriented science is a development which began in the last decade of the twentieth century. It hearkens back to the methods of the early medieval philosophers, to whom it did not occur to carve up their inquiries into what now seems to be an infinite number of discrete and separate boxes of thought.[3]

TEAMWORK

Advances in scientific knowledge and technology are now accomplished primarily by teams. This contrasts to earlier advances accomplished primarily by individuals. This is not to say that individual genius in the advancement of knowledge is lessened, but simply that the logistics of technical apparatus supporting scientific research today is so complex as to require management teams. In itself this multibillion dollar national investment in complex university research equipment (to establish an electron microscope laboratory for a biology department can cost millions) changes the mix and greatly complicates departmental staffing. Departmentally tenured professors themselves (in contrast to the *Herrn Doktors Professoren* of the nineteenth-century German research universities) are no longer the sole arbiters of their research work. Not all professors have the skill to control the enormously technical and complex workings of their own sophisticated research equipment. Even though they must grasp the functions they do not always have a technical knowledge of the workings. Technicians (who themselves are not likely to be scholars or tenured professors) commonly know more about the equipment, and what it can and cannot do, than the professors. This means that research professors in the sciences depend on technicians' skills for the functioning of the equipment necessary for their research work. In turn this alters departmental staffing in scientific research departments.

Computer imaging techniques have revolutionized and increased the speed of the perception and understanding of discoveries. For example, astronomers using the Hubble telescope (which functions through teamwork) "see" cosmic events and in so doing have challenged well-established concepts of cosmology. Einstein's achievements also challenged established concepts. But they were accomplished through the abstruse language of mathematics and took years to be disseminated and the concepts grasped. Today, through current computer enhancement processes, the realities reflected in the Hubble can be viewed almost immediately. Images have been fed into the nightly news. The Hubble's revelations, although certainly not always understood, can be seen with rather little delay through computer imaging.

The technology can now be brought into the classroom. Whether it is modeling atoms for viewing in a physics classroom or rendering different interpretations of a Beethoven score for music students, newly developed ways of picturing realities provide powerful accessories to help students learn.

Electronic communications, websites, and interactive audio-visual hookups have added effective methods of teaching and learning.

THEN AND NOW

Up to the latter part of the twentieth century, university teaching for the most part was bundled up in packages and delivered by professors to groups of students. Students sat in front of professors who untied the bundles (courses) and released the contents to the group (lectures). Courses were professor-based, meaning that professors determined content. It was the students' job to absorb it. For generations this kind of professor-based instruction at the undergraduate level was the way that the academic subjects in colleges had been taught. It did not occur to professors, deans and presidents that this method (so-called "chalk and talk") was only one potential way to teach. But today, although lecture-type instruction will always have its place, educational needs are much greater than can be satisfied only with this mode.

In the institutions serving the mass market of students, the need for practical training in technical subjects, in contrast to educating in theories and concepts, is greater than it has ever been. As we go about our daily routines, we cannot manage without some degree of technical expertise. This might mean negotiating the intricacies of superhighway exchanges, while driving fifty or sixty miles an hour, at the same time keeping out of the way of other drivers, or figuring out how to work your way through a series of answering "prompts" to get to a real person at the telephone company—sometimes an impossibility but always worth trying.

As university undergraduate curricula proliferated in the post-World War II era, courses that presented training in practical subjects accounted for most of the growth. They added to the discomfiture of died-in-the-wool professors of the humanities who believed their role was to educate young minds, not train workers for practical vocations. These disparate training programs fit into the growing needs of society for a workforce trained in practical knowledge skills. While most American professors of liberal arts courses at state universities and less selective private colleges tried to model themselves at the undergraduate level as "communities of scholars," under their very noses the transformation of their academic realm into a polytechnic training ground was beginning. The trend illustrated a contradictory force. Not uncommonly, liberal arts and humanities faculty at the expanding mass-market schools had unrealistic and unfulfilled desires to be like the faculty at the elite institutions where the students are carefully selected, possessing minds already prepared for study in the realm of ideas. But by contrast, students in the mass-market institutions come from backgrounds where the need for practical training in skills that would prepare them to earn a living was the first priority, rather than reflecting upon the great ideas of western civilization. Today the current demand for practical courses far exceeds the student market for the liberal arts.

MERGING TRAINING AND EDUCATION

My own background, buttressed by personal experience in teaching, taught me that we tend to overemphasize the dichotomy between educating and training. I have probably been guilty of oversimplification as I have discussed both. There is an obvious difference between the two, but in some instances they do come together. For example, as a pianist I have to be highly trained—there is not much pure educating involved in training your fingers to play rapid runs and arpeggios—but the merging of digital skill with profound musical literature is educating in a lofty sense. What could be more digitally and practically technical than a Pablo Casals performance of an unaccompanied Bach cello sonata, but at the same time, what could be more transcendent than the realization of such a great and noble composition? What could be more humanistic in educating human sensibilities? The answer is found in where you draw the line between what is educating and what is training. Can the digital or technical skill be put to use in creating a noble human experience? I do not have the skill to repair carburetors or fuel injectors, but even if I did, could I put that skill to direct human experience of noble ends comparable to Casals' applying his skill in realizing what Bach wrote?

The needs of the democratized "knowledge society," a term coined by Peter Drucker, demand the production of trained *and* educated workers, even if that education is somewhat narrowly defined. (It is oxymoronic to apply a narrow definition to a true education, but unfortunately so too have other aspects of our society become self-contradictory.) It is different at the highly selective campuses. Compared to the throngs of students in mass-market campuses, the relatively few at these campuses have leverage and ambit because of the highly selective venue of their enrollments. This leverage comes from the greater power of these medallion campuses to propel their graduates forward into leadership roles in society. A parallel exists here to the leader-training function of mid-nineteenth century graduates of Eton, Harrow, Oxford, and Cambridge. (Remember the saying? "England's battles are won on the playing fields of Eton.") But the workers required to maintain the knowledge society can only com from the millions of middle class and so-called working-cla students served by mass-market institutions.

URBAN FOOTPRINTS

The fourth quarter of the twentieth century brought attention to another vector in the growth of knowledge, namely, information about what is happening to the environment due to the expansion of the world's larger cities. Here is where most significant universities are located. At the close of the twentieth century, three billion people crowded into the cities on earth and, according to the United Nations, another 2.1 billion will be in cities by 2025.[4] This shift from an agrarian to an urban population has a profound impact upon the environment. The consumption (food, energy, clothing, etc.) of city dwellers cannot come from production within the boundaries of the city itself. On the contrary, an urban population on one continent will be sustained by the products of land, forests, and oceans perhaps halfway around the globe. Patterns of consumption of city dwellers grow larger and larger in country after country, while the sustainable land and water needed diminishes.

Methods of analysis used in ecological studies now enable researchers to estimate the amounts of land needed to maintain the lifestyles and ingrained habits of citizens living in developed countries. "[T]he ecological footprint of a population is the total area of land and water required to produce the resources that the population consumes, and to assimilate the wastes that the population generates, wherever on earth that land is located."[5] This superbly descriptive metaphor, "footprint," that architects have long used to describe the shape and extent of the land area of a building, graphically captures the relationship of productive land to populations. In their book *Our Ecological Footprint*, William E. Rees and Mathis Wackernagel indicate that populations of "high income countries typically need four to nine hectares (ten to twenty-two acres) per capita to support their consumer life styles." In a *Chronicle of Higher Education* article, Rees goes on to say that this figure assumes that the land use is "sustainable," in other words can continue to produce at the level required by the consumption, but that in fact this rarely happens. Pollution and overuse continue to deplete otherwise productive land and water. Sustainability requires knowledge and judicious use of productive methods.

> Thus, it is easy to see that cities typically impose an ecological footprint on earth several hundred times larger than their political or geographic area. . . . The ecological footprint of London, for example, is larger than the entire United Kingdom. . . . While the citizens of urban industrial societies use up to nine hectares [twenty-two acres] of land and water, the earth contains only about two hectares [4.94 acres] of such ecosystems per capita. The consumer life styles of rich countries cannot be extended sustainably to the entire human population, using existing technologies. . . . In a world of rapid change, no city can be truly sustainable unless the lands in its footprint are secure from ecological change and international hostilities.[6]

The ever larger problem is that as the clock ticks and the areas of sustainably productive land and water are reduced in per capita ratio to the world's growing population, a twenty-first-century crisis looms. This issue will become more crucial than nuclear warheads. *Today it does not yet register on most peoples' screens.* This lack of general sensitivity about environmental concerns became clear to me in 1989 when a prominent and very civic-minded individual came to me (as president of Cleveland State University) with a proposal for an environmental institute for which he would have taken the responsibility for initial funding. He had previously been turned down by two other institutions. I was unable to muster the support necessary to put such an institute in place.

But universities, which are increasingly in harmony with

their particular locations and which for the most part are situated in cities, are becoming more sensitive to environmental issues both in faculty scholarship and in curriculum. There is no doubt that universities will assume more and more of a leadership role in environmental research and academic programming. Campus communities and advocacy groups for improvement of the environment will grow closer together. The federal and state government will continue to *regulate*, but it is university faculties and students that can *educate* the larger citizenry about the increasing danger to the world's population of environmental degradation.

TECHNOLOGICAL ADVANCES IN TEACHING TECHNIQUES

Teaching methods cannot be the same today as they were yesterday. They require more flexibility. It is understandable that professors who have spent their lives in the traditional systems of professor-based college teaching are uncomfortable in this newer environment. Many shun it. But students' needs in society's marketplace now take precedence. It is an obvious assumption that professors know more than their students in the subjects they teach, but that does not mean they automatically understand, in a functional and applied sense, the patterns of what students need as they prepare for and adjust to a changing world.

This is where the revolution in electronic technology opens doors to learning so that instruction can become student-based as well as professor-based. It has enormous flexibility. Through this technology nontraditional students (who are rapidly becoming America's "traditional" students) can fit available instruction to their particular needs and to their own work schedules. Part-time students can pursue degrees through "distance learning" programs using the internet. E-mail can be used by students and teachers either locally or at a distance. Students can pursue their studies through one-way television instruction, or through interactive TV hookups. This releases students from the shackles of campus-only-based degree programs. With increasing insistence, students are demanding instruction that is different from that presented in the traditional academic setting.

Even so, some of the regular, tenured professoriate have resisted the new technology. This occurs partly out of fear of not being able to master it, but mostly because it remains outside familiar teaching habits. The characteristic response is that electronic technology as a "delivery system" dilutes academic quality because personal contact is minimized. "Where is the eyeball to eyeball contact?" This is a catchy observation with obvious grains of truth, but remains unproven. Personal interactions through new technology can and do broaden the contacts traditionally available. CD-ROM, video, and the internet make available worldwide resources from libraries, databases, and museums—to say nothing of e-mail. Taken together they broaden the spectrum of learning possibilities. Fortunately, the negative component of the professoriate does not seem to be the majority (the best faculties embrace technology) but there is enough foot dragging that some obstacles to the use of technology in regular campus degree programs still exist.

DISTANCE LEARNING

By contrast most or all instruction is provided electronically in so-called distance learning programs. In many examples these are added programs at traditional universities but many have been and continue to be launched by organizations separate from traditional campuses. Virtual universities, where all instruction is provided electronically, are springing up. Corporate universities such as American Express Quality University or Motorola University, among many others,

which use technical methods to deliver education, have si-
phoned students away from traditional universities. In these
institutions more and more practicing professionals outside
of academe are being used as part-time teachers. A U.S. Department of Education survey found that between 1995 and
1998 a 72 percent rise in distance education programs occurred, a total of 1190, altogether requiring approximately
54,000 online education courses that were taken by 1.6 million students.[7] Ultimately, unless traditional professors teaching in the new mass market of students adapt to their needs
and embrace the newer technologies, they are in danger of
finding themselves replaced. Tenure will not protect them
from the new meaning of being professors.

BACK TO THE BASIC ISSUE: CURRICULUM

The explosion of knowledge results in a fragmenting of cen-
trally designated, unified curricula. This unity was the raison
d'etre of universities in the first place. President Emeritus of
Cornell Frank H. T. Rhodes points out that "[W]hat constitutes essential knowledge and common discourse, has essentially collapsed. As a result universities in the United States
have a problem," which he compares to "Dante's definition of
hell where nothing connects with nothing." Rhodes goes on
to say that students "rarely receive any overarching, meaning-
ful statement of educational goals and intellectual purpose
within a larger, coherent framework." He believes that faculty
members must "recapture the curriculum."[8]

No authentic academic would argue the point. In the
Chronicle article Rhodes identifies seven needed categories of
"qualities." They include: 1.) openness and an ability to
communicate, 2.) self-confidence and curiosity, 3.) a sense of
proportion and context, 4.) delight in the richness and variety of human experience, 5.) intellectual mastery and passion
in one chosen area, 6.) a commitment to responsible citizen-

ship, and 7.) a sense of direction with self discipline, personal values and moral conviction. He explicates these qualities in some detail, with eloquence and grace. They do not represent a curricular structure such as a regimen of "great books" along with studies of mathematics and science, but instead are desirable characteristics of properly educated individuals. Trips abroad are mentioned, along with rigorous writing requirements at the undergraduate level, and the involvement of mentors with individual students.

This teaching and learning environment would be ideal but expensive. To provide it faculties would not only have to recapture the curriculum, but would have to find the will to recapture themselves and confront issues of values and morality, which for the last half century they have consciously avoided. At upper-tier private residential campuses, where the education of students involves not only the courses offered but also includes being a part of and living in a campus community, the possibility exists for the achievement of Frank Rhodes's perfected model. It would inevitably be an "upstairs" campus, mostly for the relatively few who could afford it, but also including those from lesser-privileged homes able to compete successfully for full scholarships. The cross-section of American students receiving the ideal college education in this best of all possible academic worlds for undergraduates, would be very small. Even if it were implemented at most medallion campuses the enrollment of perhaps 200,000 undergraduates would be less than 1.5 percent of total U.S. college enrollments (more than 15,000,000). As an education it would be an ideal for which to strive—but how about the other more than 14,800,000 U.S. college students?

It would be wildly utopian to expect success with this model in the vastness of the "downstairs" mass market, which embraces millions of students enrolled in U.S. colleges and universities (some of whom do not read beyond the junior high school level). Rhodes's article exemplifies what has not been expressed in the writing of most representatives of contemporary, medallion institutions of American higher education. Think what Derek Bok (Harvard) and William Bowen (Princeton) do not say about the realities of the total U.S. higher educational picture compared to the elite few. Rhodes's hypothesis is superb in its abstraction. But as for the percentage of U.S. citizenry that could experience it, it is extremely limited. If we accept the partitioned validity of his gated community hypothesis, we would need not only to convince faculty members to practice it, but more desperately we would need to work on how it could be implemented in the world of the mass market. The elite educational leaders who promulgate his hypothesis have not done that.

In that world you have to deal with working students who have neither the time nor the money to live as a full-time student in a campus community; in that world you have to deal with students who are mothers and fathers of young children, who, when they should be reading, studying, and preparing themselves for class, must tend to sick kids; in that world you have to deal with students whose economic burdens are horrendous. When their minds should be cleared to contemplate the categorical imperative of Immanuel Kant, they are trying to figure out how they can make the next car payment. It is no wonder that their primary concern for a college education is how it can help them to make a better living.

Leaders in American higher education have not worked toward integrating pure education into the specifics of training programs serving the millions who in our information technology-based society maintain the momentum. The reason for this lack of initiative boils down into an essentially moral base. The first requisite is that the faculty teaching in this world of the many want to educate masses of students in human values and in how to think critically. That commitment does not seem to permeate the faculty establishment. Nor can it be legislated and administered in a collective setting. It has to be embraced and professed by faculty members, one by one, to individual students one by one. The challenge is gargantuan. Let us consider parts of the issue.

CHAPTER 8

Diversity in Race, Culture, Class, and Affirmative Action

All shall equal be
The Earl, the Marquis, and the Dook,
The Groom, the Butler, and the Cook,
The Aristocrat who banks with Coutts,
The Aristocrat who cleans the boots.

W. S. Gilbert
"Iolanthe"

AFTER WORLD WAR II, in the late forties, when I began my career in academia and by the fifties realized it would be life-long, the term "diversity" on campus had not even been con-templated, at least as we diagnose diversity today. This was before the national civil rights victories of the late fifties and early sixties. In the early 1940s I was in tactical flight training at Hunter Field outside of Charlotte, North Carolina. This was preparation for being assigned to the 5th Air Force in the South Pacific. I remember segregated washrooms and water fountains in Charlotte, along with separate entrances to buildings with the signs above them, "for colored." I recall buses on which black people did not even question riding in the back. I recall no integration at any of the Air Corps units in which I served. The idea of a black pilot within the squadron where I served was not even considered. During my early years in Aberdeen there was only one black person in a community then numbering 20,000. He drove a truck for the local power company and, wearing a nice dark suit, taught Sunday School at the Methodist Church. When in 1948 I started as a teaching assistant in the School of Music at the University of Michigan there were no blacks, Asians, or Hispanics in the graduate program of music, much less Native Americans or acknowledged homosexuals.

DIVERSITY

The current emphasis on diversity on campuses is a powerful impulse for good, with one caveat. It must include respect for variations in skin color, religious beliefs, social and cultural backgrounds and the differences shown by people in the ways they look at the world around them. If respect is the context, the changes diversity has wrought on campuses will be for the better. But if difference is introduced only for its own sake, not connected to the intellect and discipline necessary to the learning experience, then diversity will result in a human kaleidoscope that is interesting but does not further the essential aims of a university.

Achieving diversity in students and faculties has now been an orthodox administrative policy and procedure for well over a quarter of a century. The policies were generated by federal and state statute and prodded into being by federal regulatory agencies as conditions for the receipt of federal dollars. University presidents (whatever their inner feelings might have been) and student affairs staffers with a variety of campus mantras (doctrinaire or otherwise) overwhelmingly endorsed efforts to achieve diversity. But this lofty purpose hasn't always been realized. Sometimes diversity has had the effect (intentionally or not) of focusing upon human differences simply because they are different, without regard to intrinsic educational value. Students from diverse backgrounds, divided not only by race but by class and economics, have not mixed all that well together, especially blacks and whites. If they integrated effectively, why would there have been the efforts for separate dorms, separate commencements, and separate racial and ethnic units?

Actually it is not diversity itself that generates the dissension. If diversity among individual students and faculty creates an authentic intellectual diversity, i.e., respect for genuine differences in ways of looking at things, then the logic of achieving it is unassailable. But there is a rub. The methods used to achieve diversity on campuses (affirmative action, for example) have not always been consistent with individualized, intellectual diversity, which can only be achieved one by one, person by person. Instead, those methods have involved group rights as contrasted to individual rights. Group rights are not necessarily educational rights. In contrast to most mass-market colleges and universities where affirmative action in student admissions is unnecessary simply because of open admissions, selective campuses espouse three reasons justifying its use: 1.) to be inclusive, which translates into the recognition of a need for representation of different groups; 2.) to avoid discrimination; and 3.) to achieve authentic differences between students enrolled, which offers opportunities for authentic differences in intellectual perspectives, thereby making the educational experience broader and better. The first two are social, not educational, reasons. The third is educational, provided that individual diversities are transferred into intellectual diversities.

The impact upon the learning experience is where the

core of the issue lies. From this perspective, diversity has been a mixed bag in more ways than one. The reason for a racially, culturally, and ethnically diverse student body is so that students will mix and interact in order to acquire varying human perspectives and to learn from these perspectives as they depart from or collide with one's own perceptions of values and realities. Billions of words in reams of books, articles, news stories and op-ed pieces have been written about campus diversity, both pro and con. Disagreement as to its intrinsic educational value abounds. There continue to be calls for solid research work, in contrast to anecdotal, constituent satisfaction with it, which proves that campus diversity actually does improve the academic experience. This is extremely difficult to come by.

THE SHAKE-UP

Campuses have experienced a gender shake-up and diversification of students and faculties, which changed white-male-Protestant domination. Jew, Catholic, Protestant, Buddhist, Muslim, Hindu, black, brown, white, beige, rich, poor, privileged, deprived, highborn, lowborn—now enter through open admissions doors. But they have not united in the melting pot of shared values that had described America. Rather, their cultural gravity has tended to hold them within their own cultural, ethnic, and racial boundaries. This has in turn led to pressure for the addition of many kinds of curricula designed to fit the narrowly perceived shapes of diverse groups. Radical feminism disavowed the corpus of literature produced by dead white European males often for no other reason than that they were male, white, and collectively had a history of male domination. Exaggerated Afrocentrism cooked up idealistic histories of achievement of African peoples upon a shaky, or even false basis of fact in order to bolster black student self esteem. I well remember a black student telling me with total sincerity and no animus that he couldn't care less about accounting courses. He wanted to learn Swahili. And why didn't we offer it? His girlfriend said all she wanted was to learn about the kings and queens in Africa who were her ancestors.

Pocket programs have been developed for special groups as opposed to those with a broader outlook. They have tilted into cultural relativism, espousing the view that values cannot be universal. Value is seen by a particular group only as what is appropriate to itself. There is nothing new in this, but its enlargement, brought about by the more complicated mix of students and faculty, has given rise to dogmas fragmenting the unity of the college experience.

STRONG BACKS AND HONESTY

First-generation college students from working class families inundated campuses in the fifties, sixties, and seventies. Their motivations differed from those that went before them. They wanted a piece of the American dream that more privileged students had long since possessed. They wanted to ratchet themselves upward economically. They wanted a better life than that of their parents. The way to do this was through practical college programs, directly related to the workforce, that would fit them for jobs.

When heavy industry dominated America a blue-collar man's strong back and his dependability were crucial. Advanced education of any kind was not important. As the industrial age, with its physically-oriented jobs, changed into today's technology-information age[1] where the ability to handle information is vital, technically-based programs relating to engineering, management, accounting, computers, along with a myriad of other pursuits with a technical undergirding, assumed vastly increased importance. Post-World War II American universities accepted into their curricula practical vocational training programs that previously had been available only in trade schools or apprenticeship systems. Students from working-class backgrounds swarmed onto college campuses. The training courses they sought jostled traditional academic subjects for curricular dominance.

Purely academic subjects had trouble holding their own against job-oriented courses. Credentials in practical fields became the more effective medium of exchange in mass-market campuses, rather than the knowledge gained from the study of great books. Students desired credentials useful in the job market more than knowledge. Training programs that throughout history had been found only in the apprenticeship system or sponsored by guilds and trade schools were incorporated into university degree programs. Because of this it became necessary to introduce into faculties technical people from a variety of trades and crafts.[2] These technical people had different backgrounds. They were average people who worked with their hands in practical pursuits. By contrast, traditional academic types were accustomed to living within privileged academic enclaves. Bringing these two different types together had a profound impact upon the dynamics of faculties. It requires tolerance to understand an argument in a faculty meeting between two participants, one a tenured history professor with a research-oriented PhD from an Ivy League university, and the other an undergraduate teacher of electronic technology who achieved practical knowledge and technical expertise beginning with the use of his hands. I dealt with these complex, human issues, spending years knitting together the diverse teachers who make up a faculty. This is but one aspect of the issue of diversity. Most people, including important politicians, do not understand its ramifications.

EQUALITY OF OUTCOMES

An increasing number of students seek equality of outcomes rather than equality of opportunity. This translates into credentials awarded by the institution. Widespread interpretations of the American founders' ideal of human equality interpreted as equality of opportunity resonate today at a lowered decibel level compared to the past.[3] Rather, the current and widespread attitude toward equality brings with it baggage that has unfortunate side effects, particularly an ethically corrosive ingredient that promotes only the equality of tangible outcomes. Whether or not the efforts to achieve the outcomes were equal is reduced in relevancy. This inevitably exaggerates ingrained sensitivities about race, ethnicity, wealth and privilege. That jealousy and envy is directed toward those possessed of wealth and privilege is an obvious fact.

THE BOWEN AND BOK STUDY

In their book, *The Shape of the River* former Princeton and Harvard Presidents William Bowen and Derek Bok confirm—not only confirm but assume as self evident—the leverage selective admissions schools have as they launch graduates on careers.[4] The opportunities available to most of their graduates are much greater than those available to graduates of mass-market schools. Regional state universities, along with less selective liberal arts colleges and most "niche" institutions, do not have as much leverage. Taken as a whole, their faculties have neither the clout nor the savvy to serve as brokers in political hallways and corporate corridors of power. Their effectiveness cannot approach that of significant numbers of faculty members at prestigious institutions, some of whom have arrived directly from political and business power bases. One of the motivations behind the Bowen-Bok study is the separation of effectiveness between professorial groups at selective, as compared to non-selective, campuses.

Since affirmative action began, after President Lyndon Johnson signed the Civil Rights Act of 1964, criticism has been widespread about the unfairness to qualified whites denied admission because of racial preferences for blacks in selective-admissions institutions. Most of the criticism focussed on a perception that the whites denied admission would in fact do much better academically and in subsequent life than the blacks who were admitted. Further criticism focussed on a stigmatization to blacks admitted under affirmative action, namely, that they were not really good enough and had to have special treatment in order to get in.[5] The purpose of the study was to determine, after sifting through factual data of Himalayan proportions, whether or not the criticism had any validity.

Accomplished with the support of the Andrew W. Mellon Foundation and a "small army" (to quote Bowen and Bok) of helpful research people the work contains survey information on "the college and after-life experiences of tens of thousands of black and white students who entered twenty-eight selective colleges and universities in the fall of 1976 and the fall of 1989."[6] The study does not attempt to picture what happens with respect to academic performance and subsequent life experience of students from the total panorama of U.S. higher education. The writers indicate that the selective schools they included are not characteristic of U.S. higher education as whole and that their purpose was not to make a study-comparison of all minority enrollments, but to concentrate on the performance of blacks. Bowen and Bok go on to say in subsequent comments about their study, "What did we discover? . . . Compared with their extremely high-achieving white classmates, blacks in general received somewhat lower college grades and graduated at moderately lower rates. Still,

75 percent graduated within six years.... Although more than half of the black students attending these schools would have been rejected under a race-neutral admissions regime, they have done extremely well after college.... Far from being demoralized [by affirmative action policies] blacks from the most selective schools are the most satisfied with their college performance."[7]

Opponents of the study surfaced. Abigail Thernstrom (co-author with her husband Stephan Thernstrom of *America in Black and White: One Nation Indivisible*) has researched black admissions patterns in selective schools, and asserted that the progress made by blacks since the 1950s cannot, to any significant extent, be attributed to race-based affirmative action within top-tier elite campuses. She indicated that if affirmative action were ended some black students "would be diverted to good, but less selective schools."[8] This is happening now, particularly in California. The term "cascading" has been coined to describe it. U.C. Berkeley's Martin Trow, in a speech to the Association of American Universities, raised questions about Bowen and Bok's work. He said that Boalt Hall [Berkeley's law school] violated Justice Powell's opinion in *Bakke* (the Justice's U.S. Supreme Court opinion said that race could be *"one element"* in an admissions decision) by giving "whatever weight to race ... in admissions that they needed to achieve the racial mix they were seeking."[9] There can be little question that the Bowen-Bok study verifies that most black students admitted to the select schools in fact performed reasonably and continue to perform even better in life after graduation. But the question has to be asked, what does the study prove that is not essentially common knowledge to those of us who, over the years, have taught, counseled, and interacted on an individual basis with thousands of black students? On the basis of my own experience with black college students (eighteen years at Michigan, which was one of the select schools surveyed, almost seven at Kent State before and after the impossible years following the May 4, 1970 shootings, and twenty years at Cleveland State, where significant community racial issues have affected the university) nothing in the study comes as a surprise or would change my viewpoint. Was it necessary to allocate a considerable sum of foundation money for a study, the results of which would have been self-evident to anyone who has worked in the field? Presidents Bowen and Bok are inextricably part of the world they know best, the upstairs of academe. It is perhaps inevitable that they view the world of historically disenfranchised minority black students from that perspective. That they might have felt a need to justify the results of affirmative action in the upstairs rooms of the academy would be a reasonable assumption. But there is no such need.

Some of the Bowen-Bok perspectives on the function of education can be related to that of the upper classes of Victorian England, where certain schools were meant to produce leaders for the perpetuation of the British Empire. But through higher education's democratization in America, and given the breadth of its availability to all categories of citizens, that view would, or at least should, be an anachronism. What we must strive to achieve is to solve the problem of improving mass-market higher education in the U.S. so that citizens in the larger society are prepared to function effectively in the information society, which desperately requires trained and educated workers, where the particularly gifted and energetic ones are able to rise into leadership. This is happening as America goes down the road.

CIVIL RIGHTS

The civil rights legislation of the sixties had as a high-minded objective leveling the playing fields of life with re-

spect to race, gender, class, physical ability, and other components of the human condition. This resulted in the proliferation of protected groups—for example racial minorities,
women, and the disabled—who by law are protected from
discrimination, especially in the job market and in housing.
Federal, state, and local laws in a nurturing government
promulgate good outcomes for citizens. But as a social assumption, governmental nurture of the individual by picking
up the responsibility for her/his well-being contrasts dramatically with what existed in previous generations. Then,
the responsibility for welfare of individuals was the responsibility of family, the neighborhood, the church, synagogue,
and parish. Sometimes these groups did a good job of helping those less fortunate, and sometimes it was done badly.
But that issue is moot today. The responsibility has been
shifted into the hands of government. Multifarious bureaucracies administer programs whose purpose is the people's
good. But these bureaucracies all too unfortunately replace
direct human interactions between the family and the local
community. When the aging grandmother can no longer
care for herself, it is less likely that she will move into the
home of a son or daughter, surrounded by all the familiar
and immediate circumstances of family. She will more likely
be taken to a nursing home, where her well-being all too
often rests in the hands of a bureaucracy, sometimes faceless,
sometimes even hostile.

AFFIRMATIVE ACTION

Like others who have been around a long time, my professional life has spanned the beginning, middle, and now the
discordant and often visceral reconfiguration of affirmative
action. Officially the term affirmative action goes back to
1961, when it was used as a substitute for the words "racial
preferences" in the text of Executive Order 10925 signed by

President Kennedy. This order called upon federal contractors to hire more minorities. In its essence affirmative action meant that for past discrimination in American life to be rectified, affirmative efforts must be exerted to give preference to minority groups and women in the allocation of jobs, contracts, and college admissions. Its genesis was the Civil Rights Act of 1964, which was passed after contentious debate by southern senators, including Sam Ervin, William Fulbright, and John Tower that reached passionate levels, mostly over quotas and reverse discrimination. After passage of the Act on September 24, 1965, the originating document for affirmative action, Executive Order 11246, was signed by President Johnson. Initially 11246 related only to race. Gender-related preferences came later after pressure from feminists. This little-known fact provides a sidebar of considerable interest since the subsequent boost of affirmative action has benefitted women (for example as they have been appointed to college and university presidencies) more than it has blacks or hispanics. Native Americans continue to be left much further behind.

In a 1995 *New York Times Sunday Magazine* article Nicholas Lehmann wrote about affirmative action as it had been and he predicted with great prescience how the debate about it would proceed. He wrote that "The original, executive-order definition of affirmative action is that it requires employers only to search aggressively for qualified minority applicants—through advertising for instance, or special recruitment efforts. Once found, these new minority applicants would go into the same pool with everybody else and the final selection would be made on a colorblind basis."[10] This was reflected in the masterful maxim of the Rev. Martin Luther King, "the content of our character rather than color of our skin." But it wasn't long before colorblind equality of opportunity for jobs and education ran into difficulties related to meritocracy and how to measure levels of achievement in education. Standardized tests were and continue to be the issue. Lehmann said that, "[I]n a crucial sense, the numerical, education-based meritocracy was bad news for blacks. It rendered the key affirmative-action concept of creating biracial pools of equally qualified applicants meaningless because now everybody was ranked serially. And it apportioned opportunity on the basis of performance in the one area where blacks were the most disadvantaged: education. For as long as there have been standardized tests, blacks have on average scored lower than whites.[11] . . . The history of affirmative action can be seen as a struggle over the fairness of modern meritocracy, with minorities arguing that educational measures shouldn't be the deciding factor in who gets ahead and opponents of affirmative action saying that to bend the criteria for blacks is to discriminate unfairly against more deserving whites."[12]

During the seventies it looked like affirmative action had become a continuing aspect of life in the United States. Federal court decisions, both district and appellate, upheld the concept as a remedy against past discrimination, and preferences based on race along with quotas (not always referred to as such but rather as "goals and timetables") were commonplace. Arguments against affirmative action were few and far between. If a university officer during those years, with or without the vestments of office, were to have argued publicly against it that person would have been drummed out of the administration building. I lived and worked in that environment. But the forces that shaped affirmative action nationally were not democratic: it was not crafted and developed by the Congress or the legislatures as elected by the people. Rather the impetus came from the federal courts and from appointed bureaucrats, particularly from the hallways in the Labor Department such as the Office of Federal Contract Compliance from whence spewed prolific regulations.[13]

But during this period there was some misreading on the part of state and federal judges and doctrinaire bureaucrats who put this vast set of affirmative action forces in motion. They did not recognize the perceptions of unfairness held by the general public. In the region where I worked—at Cleveland State University in Northeast Ohio—I was aware of the disquiet of citizens in the "silent majority" outside the boundaries of the academy. I never had the feeling that they were against giving minorities and women the same opportunity as mainstream white males—indeed of giving them an extra boost—but doing this at the expense of others through providing opportunity for one group of citizens by taking it away from another group troubled them. This resentment was seldom verbalized on campuses either in department or college faculty meetings. If a faculty member were to have spoken out, he would probably have been shunned. (So much for the vaunted freedom of expression on campus.) This went on for twenty years.

During its first two decades, affirmative action was buttressed by the development of procedures leading to racial preferences, and by the establishment of the procedures for goals and timetables to measure the achievement of more minority and female representation in positions of power. At Cleveland State these took the place of quotas which, while not yet strictly defined as illegal, would have been sure to cause a backlash. During this period as provost and president I was under continuing pressure to establish plentiful goals and timetables for increasing faculty appointments of blacks, awarding contracts to black firms and for continuing to increase the percentage of black student admissions. The same kind of pressure did not exist for hispanics or Native Americans. My experience as a white university officer at a mass-market, downtown, public university was typical of every urban area in the country. But a suit filed by Allan Bakke worked its way up to the U.S. Supreme Court and generated winds of change.

THE *BAKKE* DECISION

At the medical school of the University of California at Davis, Allan Bakke, a white male, had been denied admission, not because he failed to meet admission standards, but because of a quota for minorities at the medical school. The rules were changed by the 1978 U.S. Supreme Court opinions that this case generated. It was *The Regents of The University of California v. Bakke.*[14] The *Bakke* decision set the stage for the next twenty years. The decision had two prongs. First, it outlawed minority quotas. A majority of five justices agreed that the use of race to establish a quota (sixteen places out of a hundred) was unconstitutional, thus Bakke had to be admitted. (He was, he graduated, and today is an anesthesiologist.)

What was the rationale for the determination? First, a divided Court agreed that the Equal Protection Clause of the Fourteenth Amendment[15] as a Constitutional issue (equal protection under the law), and Title VI as a statutory principle (race cannot be the reason for excluding anyone from participation in a federally funded program) meant that U.C. Davis Medical School's quota was both unconstitutional and unlawful. Second, Justice Powell, in his opinion, stated that race could be used as one element in admissions decisions. However, this was only his opinion, not that of the Court.

Obviously this case was a wrenching one for the justices, whose arguments lacked unanimity. It caused confusion at first. But over the years the late Justice Powell's reasoning profoundly influenced affirmative action on campuses with selective admissions programs. "Justice Powell held that racial and ethnic distinctions of any sort are inherently suspect and thus call[ed] for a strict scrutiny review. Applying this standard Justice Powell found that attainment of a diverse student body was a constitutionally permissible goal for an institution of higher learning, however, that state interest was not served by a two-track system with a prescribed number of seats set aside for an identifiable category of applicants. Rather, he . . . [V]iewed racial and ethnic diversity as only one element in a range of factors a university may consider in attaining the goal of a heterogeneous student body. Because the University of California at Davis used race as the sole diversity factor, its admissions program could not withstand constitutional scrutiny."[16]

THE ADARAND CASE

Through the late eighties and nineties, significant judicial decisions and state-level plebiscites gathered momentum in the growing challenges to racial preferences. The 1995 Supreme Court ruling in *Adarand Construction v. Pena* was one of them. In 1990 Adarand Construction company in Colorado, owned by a white family, was passed over in the award of a subcontract to build highway guard rails in favor of a minority firm, Gonzales Construction Company, even though the minority firm's bid was higher. The motivation for awarding the subcontract to a minority firm with the higher bid was not abstract social justice, but what George Will in his syndicated column called a "legal bribe," namely a 1.5 percent bonus if the subcontract was given to a minority firm. Adarand sued, which hundreds of other companies with similar experiences across the country could have done, but did not since they would have to deal with expensive litigation. The case worked its way through the Federal District Court to the Tenth Circuit Court of Appeals, eventually reaching the Supreme Court. Justice Sandra Day O'Connor, who wrote the majority opinion, said that "federal racial classifications, like those of a state, must serve a compelling governmental interest and must be narrowly tailored to further that interest." The case was remanded to the Tenth Circuit.

This was done in the light of the Supreme Court's 1989 ruling in the *Croson* case. The *Croson* decision ruled against the administration of the city of Richmond, Virginia, which had determined that only minority-owned subcontractors should be eligible to install toilets in its municipal jail. The Court decided that public-sector institutions (i.e., Richmond) might, in theory, be permitted to take race into consideration in awarding contracts, but only on a "narrowly-tailored" basis. The racial preference had to fit and remedy past discrimination in specific, documented circumstances where the government had a compelling interest. A general, "societal" bias, past or present, did not justify racial preferences. What is the meaning of the words "compelling governmental interest" and "narrowly tailored?" Many lawyers and pundits did not think the words were clear at all and said so. But administrative and legal opinion has developed that says compelling governmental interest means that, if previous discrimination in the specific workplace or organization involved can be demonstrated, then a racial classification can be used to rectify it, providing the corrective plan is narrowly tailored to fit the particular circumstance. This sent university presidents and admissions directors scurrying to consult with their campus counsel as to whether their affirmative action programs were narrowly tailored enough. There was more than just institutional interest involved here. As legal actions emerged and began to take shape, campus officers and trustees discovered they could be sued personally. This had an effect similar to that described by Dr. Samuel Johnson, who said, "Depend upon it, Sir, when a man knows he is to be hanged in a fortnight, it concentrates his mind wonderfully."

Meanwhile the judges on the bench of the Tenth Circuit in Denver, after reconsidering the *Adarand* case, rendered the opinion that in fact it passed Constitutional muster. Predictably this was again appealed to the Supreme Court. The justices again reversed and remanded the case. When the Court of Appeals considered it for the third time the judges, reversing course, vacated that part of the District Court's opinion which effectively upheld the constitutionality of the award to the minority subcontractor but decided that the contractor (Gonzales) did not have standing to sue. The Supreme Court again granted *certiorari* (meaning the highest court would again accept the appeal). This time justices approved the opinion of the appeals court and dismissed the writ of *certiorari* as "improvidently granted."

THE HOPWOOD CASE

Even though the *Adarand* decision rattled cages in the university world, it did not begin to shake the foundations of racial preference in university admissions to the extent of the holding of the three-judge panel of the U.S. Court of Appeals for the Fifth Circuit in the case of *Cheryl J. Hopwood et. al. v. State of Texas.* (The Supreme Court refused to hear the appeal of the ruling of the Fifth Circuit Appeals Court; thus it stood as law in Texas, Louisiana, and Mississippi, but reverberates in other states.) However with the decision of the U.S. Supreme Court rendered on June 23, 2003 in *Grutter v. Bollinger* involving Law School admissions at the University of Michigan the Court concluded that "student body diversity is a compelling state interest." This assertion came from the position the Court took in the *Croson* and *Adarand* cases.

It nullified the 5th Circuit's *Hopwood* ruling, which as of June 23 ceased to be law.

Hopwood began with a suit filed in 1992 by four white applicants to the Law School of the University of Texas at Austin, who were among those denied admission. They had higher grade point averages and LSAT (Law School Aptitude Test) scores than minority applicants who were accepted. As the suit worked its way through the federal court system, the university's right to use race and ethnicity as criteria in admissions decisions was upheld by a District Court judge in August of 1994. However, this decision was overturned by the Fifth Circuit Court of Appeals in March, 1996. It went directly against the prevailing reliance of campuses upon the *Bakke* decision. The striking aspect of the ruling handed down by the Appeals Court was that it rejected out of hand Justice Powell's opinion (this was possible because Powell was not writing the majority opinion for the Supreme Court) that race could be an element in an admissions decision. The opinion, drafted by Judge Jerry E. Smith, identified a number of Supreme Court opinions since *Bakke* that erected hurdles in the way of using racial preferences. The opinion struck down any use of race, even in an ancillary way, in the process of admitting students.

The reaction to *Hopwood* radiated in waves throughout the academic community which approached seismic proportions. The dean of admissions at the University of Virginia, John A. Blackburn, said, "It's an incredibly stupid decision . . . All of us are dazed, wondering, 'What does it all mean?' "[17] The president of the University of Texas, Robert M. Berdahl, reacted immediately, saying that the decision could lead to "[T]he virtual resegregation of higher education."[18]

MOMENTUM BUILDING

Momentum had grown in the movement against racial preferences built into affirmative action programs in other states. The Regents of the University of California outlawed racial preference in admissions. The First Circuit U.S. Court of Appeals in Boston ruled that the venerable Boston Latin School abridged the constitutional rights of a white student when they admitted black students with lower test scores than hers in order to reach a quota of about 35 percent blacks and Hispanics in the entering class. The state of California voters, by a majority of 54 percent (including a 39 percent positive vote on the part of African Americans), enacted Proposition 209, which amended California's constitution for the purpose of prohibiting institutions of higher education and other state agencies from using racial preferences. A similar initiative, I-200, passed in the state of Washington, and concerted efforts (led by Ward Connerly, the African-American California regent who sparked California's initiative) were taken in Florida. Suits were filed against the University of Michigan and the University of Washington for the use of racial preferences in admitting procedures, and so on across the nation.

These efforts at taking apart racial and ethnic preferences in affirmative action had sizable support from citizens in general, previously unspoken. This support also manifested itself in the quieter components of college and university faculties. A national poll taken in October, 1996 for the National Association of Scholars by the Roper Center for Public Opinion Research at the University of Connecticut determined that group preferences based on race, sex, or ethnicity were opposed by professors at public and private institutions. Rank and file members of faculty and staff don't always speak out, particularly those who are untenured. Even when they do express opinions about emotionally charged issues, they tend to suppress their true feelings or misrepresent them in the face of social pressure. University of California economist Timur Kuran deals with this in the section on affirmative action in his book *Private Truths, Public Lies.* He refers to widespread "preference falsification" wherein manifest public opinion on an issue differs markedly from private opinion.[19] This squares with my own personal experiences as a teacher and administrator at Michigan, Kent State, and Cleveland State. For fear of being labeled racist or insensitive on the issue of affirmative action most faculty members remain quiet. As is often the case in American life, the verbally assertive take over.

It is on the campuses of the fewer, selective, private and public flagship universities where the issue of preferences in admissions provide fodder for litigation. At public community colleges and non-selective four-year institutions, where most students who apply are admitted, preferences are unnecessary.

Preferences have always been predicated on the assumption that they are needed to create a diverse student body. This concept was first articulated by Charles Eliott, who was president of Harvard for forty years (1869–1909) and one of that university's enduring sons. He remains an icon in American higher education. Neil L. Rudenstine, during his presidency at Harvard, wrote about diversity in the *Harvard Magazine*[20] where he discussed Eliot's views, along with those of other Harvard presidents. It is implicit that diversity in the Harvard context applies only to those possessing the intellectual qualifications to be part of a university community. That university education should take place where this diverse student body is resident on campus is stated explicitly. Rudenstine wrote that "residential education has remained the strongest expression of an institution's commitment to educating the 'whole person,' rather than only the intellect."[21]

It would strain the bounds of reason to gainsay this lofty view of diversity, where learning goes beyond the purely cognitive. It encompasses emotional, cultural, psychological, and physical aspects of learning. At Harvard and other selective private campuses, diversity has been sought essentially within highly restricted boundaries, given the pool of students admitted. In peculiar ways this restricted elitism manifests itself in the views about preferences of Bowen and Bok, who straightforwardly state that blacks should receive preferential treatment at selective institutions. The rationale is that these institutions provide the boost for them to have high-level careers, and that society needs this because there are not enough minorities at these levels. Herein a negative and unspoken message comes through. The message is that institutions serving the mass market of students are unable to prepare the minorities for career performance at levels comparable to selective schools. Once again the pathology of upstairs-downstairs shows itself.

THE STORY CONTINUES TO UNFOLD

Where do matters stand in the beginning of the new century? After the *Hopwood* case struck down racial preferences; after the California Regents outlawed preferences in college admissions; and after the California and Washington initiatives struck down race as a criterion, university officials in the upper-tier public institutions, which have used preferences for years, predicted that minorities would be closed out and that universities would become resegregated. Has it happened? No.

What has happened is that alternatives are being crafted that approach the problem of racial and ethnic inclusiveness in admissions through mechanisms other than racial preferences. They use preferences based on percentages of top students. These alternatives cut across racial lines. They guarantee admission to state universities for those in a designated top percentage of high school graduates. The flaw in these programs comes from the disparities in quality of different high schools. The top 10 percent of students who would be guaranteed admission from one school of lower quality, for example, could be much less prepared for college than the next lower 10 percent from a higher quality school who would not be guaranteed admission. There exists much criticism of these percentage plans.[22] However, they do not go counter to the equal protection clause of the Fourteenth Amendment, nor is the new playing field a zero-sum game where providing opportunity for a person who is a racial minority means somebody else must lose it.

Beginning in the year 2001 the Board of Regents of the University of California mandated that the top 4 percent of graduates from each high school in the state be accepted into the system, in Texas the top 10 percent of graduates of public high schools are being admitted to the University of Texas and in Florida a 20 percent plan exists. In Texas black enrollment is already at the same level it was before *Hopwood*. The same thing is happening in California, although the minority enrollments are spread through less selective institutions.

Subsequent to the federal appellate court decision outlawing the use of race in admissions decisions at the University of Texas, federal district courts came down on the other side in cases involving the University of Washington and the University of Michigan, holding that a person's race can be one element in determining an individual's admissibility. The federal judiciary was split on the issue. In Washington the decision is moot because of the passage of Initiative 200, outlawing "preferential treatment" to any individual "on the basis of race," as it is in California resulting from the passage of Initiative 209. In Michigan the court determined that the two-tiered admissions plan for the College of Literature,

Science, and the Arts which operated from 1995 to 1998 and admitted white and minority applicants under different criteria was unconstitutional, but that the subsequent plan in which minority candidates are given the advantage of an added twenty points on the 150-point scale used for everybody was legal. Another suit against the University of Michigan Law School for its use of racial preferences in admissions, litigated before another judge from the same court, was decided precisely opposite. The process was ruled unconstitutional. After hearing an appeal of the law school case, the Sixth Circuit Court of Appeals overturned the district court's decision that Michigan's law school had proceeded unconstitutionally. The court also heard the appeal of the district court's decision relating to the admissions procedures at Michigan for the College of Literature, Science, and the Arts but never rendered a decision. The U.S. Supreme Court was then petitioned to hear both cases, even though the Sixth Circuit had not released a decision in the one case. The high court agreed and heard arguments April 1, 2003.

An earlier Eleventh Federal Circuit Court of Appeals decision in August of 2001 had added fuel to the controversy over minority preferences and the extent to which they enhance diversity on campuses. This court ruled that the University of Georgia's admissions procedures in giving minority applicants preferences were unconstitutional. The Court emphatically and precisely asked what does diversity mean? It said that some white applicants could provide greater contributions to diversity than blacks. The university decided not to appeal this decision to the U.S. Supreme Court. (Concurrently, a state of California appeals court struck down a 1978 state law requiring state community colleges to meet certain goals and timetables for hiring women and minorities.)

To say these contradictory rulings by federal courts and

federal appeals courts created difficulties for campuses administering affirmative action is an understatement.

In a packed courtroom, questions and comments by
Supreme Court Justices during the arguments on April 1,
2003, for and against the University of Michigan affirmative
action procedures, revealed a concern about nuance. They
seemed to be looking for something beyond absolutes. Justices Sandra Day O'Connor and Anthony M. Kennedy both
searched for subtlety in the complex issues of race in college
admissions. As I read the equal protection clause of the Fourteenth Amendment of the U.S. Constitution it seems to me
that the use of race as a preference, clearly to the detriment of
others, is unconstitutional. But the Fourteenth Amendment
was crafted and ratified when blacks remained outside most
U.S. systems. If the clause were written today, after the mid-
twentieth century revolution in civil rights, it would have
different wording. Further, special preferences in college admissions are given other categories of applicants—"legacies,"
athletes, violinists, along with others.

THE MICHIGAN DECISIONS

On June 23, 2003 when the Supreme Court rendered its judgements in the Michigan cases the results were mixed—Justice
Antonin Scalia calling them a "split double header." The admissions programs for the College of Literature, Science, and
the Arts was declared unconstitutional by a 6 to 3 vote, while
the Law School admissions procedure was validated by a 5 to 4
vote. The College of Literature, Science, and the Arts verdict
came as no great surprise because the 20 point bonus, automatically applied on a 150 point scale, given blacks, Hispanics, and
Native Americans, though sanctioned by the district court, was
broadly anticipated to be ruled unconstitutional.

But a 5 to 4 decision upheld the Michigan Law School's
admissions processes where race is only one factor in admis-

sions decisions. It is consistent with the *Bakke* case. The Court made clear that the race issue should be applied on an individual basis in consideration with other components of an applicant's credentials. The validation of the consideration of race and ethnicity has been hailed at selective-admissions campuses as a significant victory for the cause of affirmative action. It can be expected to continue for years to come, even though Justice Sandra Day O'Connor as author of the majority opinion said that, "We expect that 25 years from now the use of racial preferences will no longer be necessary to further the interest approved today." On the other hand those who hold to absolutes in the interpretation of the U.S. Constitution, in this case equal protection, have decried the decision to be improper, because, as George Will said the day after the announcement, "Race-conscious remedies for social problems are going to seem increasingly problemmatic because race and ethnicity are increasingly understood not to be fixed but extremely fluid, hence dubious scientific categories."

THE BOTTOM LINE

Diversity relates to the socialization of students and the uses to which various knowledges are put, not to the essence and particularities of knowledge and skill of and for themselves. Human diversity will not change the essence and substance of calculus regardless of whether taught by competent white, black, or brown persons to students of many races. But diversity will certainly generate changing perceptions of different people to what calculus might be used for in the world we live in.

POLITICAL CORRECTNESS

Throughout the continuing and seemingly endless debates about minority preferences and affirmative action political correctness as a latter day phenomenon cannot be subtracted. Does political correctness degrade language? Yes it does. But for the moment why dwell on it? In 1990 I wrote a piece for the student editors of the Cleveland State daily, the *Cauldron*. What I said follows.

WORDS AND COMMON MEANING

Even though a truism it remains appropriate to say that those who comprise a university—students, faculty, staff, and trustees—should be dedicated to seeking truth. To achieve this is difficult, mostly because words, as the primary instruments through which truth is expressed, are interpreted differently by different individuals and groups. One of the more difficult challenges which at the same time remains intellectually and ethically rewarding, is to try and reach common understanding of the meanings of the words we use. Only by so doing will we arrive at shared values.

To get on the turf of clearly understood and shared meaning is extremely difficult, given the academic and cultural pluralism of our campus. On the one hand words used professionally in different academic departments have particular vectors of meaning unique to a discipline which, for those not acclimatized to the unique expression of the discipline, may be difficult to grasp. On the other hand identical or at least similar words or phrases resonate differently or have quite different meanings within different cultural groups. Those born and reared in white suburbs tend to think and use words in their own characteristic ways; to African-American citizens from impacted inner-city environments the same words can and will have different meanings with a different human context. Similar kinds of cultural disparities with respect to words occur in other citizen groups with heritages as different as Mexican Hispanic, Caribbean Hispanic, or from the divergent cultures of Eastern Europe.

This is simply human nature. "Code" words develop, while other words take on a variety of meanings. This means that in written communicating on a campus such as ours where we try and find common ground of understanding, the pluralism of our different cultural backgrounds makes the use of words with meanings that are commonly understood, an extraordinarily difficult task. But we need to keep trying.

To maintain coherence in a diverse campus world becomes more difficult with passing years. A common understanding of the meanings of words is requisite, but we have not come close to achieving this. It has become more difficult due to differing interpretations of the meaning of a college degree, especially between the pure values of knowledge and the practical values of jobs.

CHAPTER 9

Students as Customers

Students want convenient, no-nonsense academics from their colleges but not much else: student organizations have limited appeal, social life has moved off campus. A college degree, it seems, can mean more to students than college itself.

Arthur Levine and Jeanette Cureton, *Change*

SOMEHOW THE NOTION of customer satisfaction had not entered into the thinking of administrators in higher education when I entered college. Nor did I perceive my education and training on campus in a particular vocational sense. It was true that in 1941, with war imminent, many young men saw college not only as a period of deferral from active service but also as a doorway into officer-training school. It is what led me into the Air Corps. But the idea of college itself being a training ground akin to a trade school simply was not a perception either of students or faculty members. Medical professions, law, accounting, yes, but those were high-status occupations and did not quite fit the mold of vocational training.

In those days there was no such thing as universities advertising practical programs in order to attract students. Nor for that matter did legitimate attorneys or medical doctors market their services. If they had done so, they would have received not only the disapprobation of their colleagues but would have run afoul of professional ethics committees.

To an extent a university education was above the marketplace. Today's world has changed this. The profession of law is now as much a business to be marketed as it is a profession, and universities cannot be separated from the marketplace. High-status law firms market their services as all high-status groups do—through lofty connections. Lesser-status law firms, more and more, are taking to buying advertising space in newspapers and magazines and thirty-second spots on television.

DELIVERING EDUCATIONAL SERVICES

With the democratization of admissions and dramatically increased access to colleges in the public sector and in many non-selective liberal arts colleges, market forces for producing customer satisfaction have been added to the equation of delivering educational services and managing the affairs of campuses. In fact this is not altogether new. In his compelling latest work, *The Seekers*, Daniel Boorstin observes that, "in the early thirteenth century, when the population of Paris was about 150,000, the academic population of the city may have been about 3,500. Students became important to the economic life of the city. . . . The earliest statutes in Bologna aiming to guarantee students their money's worth forbade professors to be absent without leave, and required that a master, who departed the city should give a deposit to ensure his return."[1]

THEN AND NOW

Originally the curriculum at American private colleges and universities descended from that taught in the great European cathedral schools and universities of the middle ages, namely the *trivium* (grammar, rhetoric, and logic) and the *quadrivium* (arithmetic, geometry, astronomy, and music), altogether known as the seven liberal arts. The term liberal in this educational sense means to be liberated from one's prejudices. These subjects were unconnected to crafts, trades and farming, which were part of the apprenticeship system related to guilds, and to what fathers taught sons in providing them with the skills to support wives and children.[2] The seven liberal arts (*artes liberales*) served in part to instruct a man in how to become a gentleman. He did not have to master a craft in order to earn a living and thus had the time to learn what for that period were the gentilities of cultivated life. In that tradition eighteenth- and nineteenth-century college campuses in America were places where upper-class fathers sent privileged sons, who commonly capped their college careers with a grand tour of Europe.

How different the thrust of a college education is today. It is broadly accessible and egalitarian. But an upstairs-downstairs syndrome still exists in American higher education. While elite and selective campuses still show elements of the class system based on economic privilege, most of the 15,000,000 students in the more than 3,900 public and private campuses now come from middle-class and working-class families, including an increasing component from economically deprived backgrounds.

Few people grasp the prodigious complexity of U.S. colleges and universities. It certainly escapes the understanding of most citizens in the general public. The many facets of campus arrangements are illustrated by the Carnegie system of classification for institutions of higher education.[3] First devised and compiled in 1970, revised and updated in 1987, in 1994, and most recently in 2000 with a further update scheduled for 2005, the "Carnegie Classifications" analyze and classify institutions that are degree-granting and are accredited by an agency that is recognized by the U.S. Secretary of Education. Currently over 3,856 institutions are classified by the Carnegie system.

CARNEGIE CLASSIFICATIONS AND TODAY'S MARKETS

The Carnegie Classifications take into account an institution's academic and research functions.[4] The purpose of these classifications is to sort out types of institutions. They include high-powered research and graduate-oriented campuses in both the private and public sectors (exemplified by the Ivy League group and public flagship campuses); doctorate-granting universities; master's-degree-granting universities; baccalaureate degree-granting colleges; associate of arts degree- or certificate-granting colleges which include community, junior and technical colleges; professional schools and specialized institutions. These classifications separate the institutions on a functional basis, namely, what it is that they do and in some examples the extent of what they do, as for example the number of doctoral or master's degrees awarded.

Two respected and widely published academics, William Massy and Robert Zemsky, have suggested, perhaps with more than just tongue in cheek, that a simplified method for classifying the welter of U.S. colleges and universities be devised. It would contain only three categories: "brand-name" (medallion), "mass-provider," and "convenience" (or niche) institutions. This is more in line with the reality of the forces in the present day and age, but were it to be invoked to replace the Carnegie Classifications the hue and cry from traditional institutions would reverberate throughout the land.

When the Carnegie classifications were first devised, market forces within the various open admissions public institutions were not as important to institutions as they are today. The classifications then as now were determined by the missions carried out by campuses. Individual institutions were relatively autonomous in deciding what their missions should be. This is changing through the relationships between campuses and their constituencies, especially state institutions functioning under statewide governing or coordinating boards and agencies. Historically colleges and universities had substantially fewer constituencies than today. In fact campuses shunned the idea of constituencies, instead concentrating themselves in autonomous, academic enclaves of teachers and students. They were ivory towers separated from the communities where they were located, and town and gown did not always get along that well. Technical and professional market forces due to job-related needs and the desires of students seeing themselves as customers of the academy would have been beyond the ken of those responsible for the academic function of an autonomous campus. The autonomy is now diminished and in large measure supplanted by market-driven forces. Constituencies involving campus and community, instead of being shunned, are now cultivated by faculties and administrations. Diversity in the student body is another component in the reconfiguring of campus purposes. In other words, colleges tailor curriculum to fit the needs of students being actively recruited and who are most likely to enroll. Except for profit-making "niche" schools, this was a rarity until the 1970s.

While the Carnegie Classifications take into account an institution's track record in degree programming and in research, today's profound campus changes, including the differing dynamics of individual campuses, are not altogether reflected in the latest classifications. Campuses with the same Carnegie classification can be quite different. Princeton University in New Jersey and Western Michigan University in Kalamazoo are both classified as "Doctoral-Extensive." But walk around both campuses, go into the libraries, attend some meetings, classes or campus events and observe how different these two institutions are from one another. The University of Phoenix, as the country's largest private university which also happens to be a for-profit business, is classified as a "Specialized Business Institution." The designation does not describe its broader function, both onsite and online. Functional differences have altered and expanded the role of campuses and the types of students who are recruited and admitted. Light-hearted jargon now describes other changes taking place. Residential campuses with fixed facilities are referred to as "brick universities." New universities, in many examples developed as private, proprietary businesses making primary use of the internet, are known as "click universities," and the increasing number of traditional universities that have added the new teaching technologies to their quivers of academic-delivery arrows are identified as "bricks and clicks."

The rationale for devising classifications illustrated in the original work done by the Carnegie Foundation for the Advancement of Teaching in 1970 is now changing. This is recognized by principals of the Foundation responsible for the classifications, who have indicated that the changes for the year 2000 are an interim step and that the changes envisioned for the year 2005 will be an overhaul of the entire system. Foundation Senior Scholar Alexander C. McCormick said, "It wouldn't really be hard for someone to get other data to create more relevant distinctions . . . . Our 2005 edition will have a much more flexible system to bring together the different dimensions of institutions."[5] To do this so that campus Carnegie Classifications and campus realities come closer together will be a monumental challenge, both analytically and expressively.

MARKETING

Campuses now engage in marketing campaigns. Given that non-selective admissions institutions for the most part do not have much in the way of endowments, campus operational budgets are largely determined by the number of students admitted and enrolled. In the private sector there is a direct relationship between the budget and the tuition students pay. Fewer students means reduced operational budgets to pay faculty and staff salaries. At public campuses in the state university sector the relationship between student numbers and campus budgets is essentially the same because the subsidy the state pays the institutions is largely determined by the number of FTE (full time equivalent) students enrolled. As a general rule, fewer students, less subsidy. Private, non-selective institutions where campus residency is not required receive no FTE state subsidy, so their tuition is substantially higher (typically varying from about $12,000 to about $19,000), than state institutions (around $4,000 to $7,000). The topmost "medallion" institutions with comprehensive tuition and room and board now charge approximately $40,000 or more.

Non-selective institutions, both public and private, have an enduring interest in maintaining enrollments. They perform various gymnastics to maintain as high an FTE count as possible. They also engage in active marketing, public relations, billboard, radio, TV, and newspaper advertising campaigns to recruit students. Even more important is retaining students already enrolled. FTE counts include all students, not just newly enrolled ones, and as a result many institutions have made serious errors in maintaining academic quality. In order to preserve enrollments to bolster budgets, they have kept students enrolled who should have been academically dismissed. This has contributed to the decline of undergraduate standards at hundreds of institutions. This was especially true at City College in New York. CCNY Professor George McKenna comments in a *New York Times* op-ed piece that, "much of the [CCNY] decline . . . results from bad habits that have become embedded in the college's administrative process over the last thirty years. And the bad habit felt most acutely by faculty members and by the better students is the retention of students who have no business being in college."[6] This shows one of today's dismal contradictions between the way public institutions are funded and the integrity of academic programs. It also exposes the influence on public tax-supported campuses by political groups who lobby on behalf of student constituencies that may or may not belong at an institution of higher learning.

While no institution can be totally autonomous, the high-status, heavily endowed private campuses, and in some cases the public flagship universities, (also well endowed, although within the last few years they have been subject to serious political incursions) are about the only ones that will continue to function with a substantial amount of their autonomy intact. Earlier, I borrowed the term city-states to describe their power. Because of the vast resources they possess, they will continue to function in ways essentially determined by their own boards, faculties, and presidents. They control their futures.

The others, which together serve millions of students, must be concerned with mass-market customer wishes. This is not new. Meagerly-funded "niche" institutions have always had to be market-sensitive with respect to their specialties. If not, they die. They are akin to highly adaptive living creatures that adjust to changing environments. Their faculties, often largely part-time, have no illusions about teaching at medallion campuses. They know who they are and what they are paid to do.

INFLUENCE OF THE MASS MARKET

It is in the extensive group of mass-market campuses enrolling most of today's college students where problems relating to market adaptability exist. There are three categories in this group of problem campuses, with the first category being by far the most significant: regional state colleges and universities; non-selective liberal arts colleges without significant endowments; and to a lesser extent, public community colleges. Faculties in non-selective, private, liberal arts colleges are learning how important market adaptability is to their operating budgets. Some have already closed because they failed to realize this and others who don't adjust soon will be forced to close. Faculties in public community colleges have always been more market sensitive and more tuned in to the citizens in their communities than regional state university faculties. This occurs in part because of the direct support of local tax levies for many community colleges (one's own neighbors pay), in contrast to state universities that receive state tax support through a more impersonal formula.

The problems of adapting to today's market forces, thus, are found primarily in the extensive network of regional state colleges and universities. These institutions came into their own through the influx of students enrolling under the G.I. Bill and continued their growth as the advantages of having a college degree became apparent in the nation's workforce. In egalitarianized regional public institutions the majority of first-generation students (those whose parents never went to college) pursue the credential of a college degree to improve their job prospects, and thus move themselves upward economically. Their primary purpose in going to college is not to acquire learning as a value of and for itself. They are not academically idealistic. These masses of students have individual and practical goals that they want their training to accomplish. They are less and less willing to allow faculties to determination their courses of study.

Today's student bodies show a reshaping of sweeping dimensions from preceding generations of college students. Ted Marchese, as a contributing editor of *Change*, which is published under the auspices of the American Association of Higher Education, identified them as "consumerist, uncivil, demanding, preoccupied."[7] The president of Teacher's College, Columbia University Arthur Levine and his authorial colleague Jeanette S. Cureton, formerly from the Harvard Graduate School of Education, amplify Marchese's observation:

> Students ... want their colleges to be nearby and to operate at the hours most useful to them—preferably around the clock. They want convenience: easy, accessible parking (at the classroom door would not be bad); no lines; they want high-quality education but are eager for low costs.
>
> For the most part they are willing to comparison shop, and they place a premium on time and money. They do not want to pay for activities and programs they do not use. In short, students increasingly are bringing to higher education exactly the same consumer expectations they have for every other commercial establishment with which they deal.[8]

At regional state universities student attitudes differ from those of much of the professoriate, particularly those faculty members holding appointments in humanities and science departments. These teachers received their doctorates from institutions that for the most part are heavily into research. The mentoring they received was not oriented toward college students in the mass market, but was academically specialized. As they worked toward their doctorates within the disciplines of the sciences and humanities, it was instilled in them that their disciplines stand independently and that the power of universal ideas transcends the fickleness of a capricious marketplace. But when they graduated there weren't enough academic positions in research universities where their academic work fit more naturally, so they had to settle for jobs in lower-tier schools geared to the mass market. In these egalitarian regional campuses a conflict has emerged between the faculty who want to provide elite, research-oriented education for their students and the students themselves who want training to get better jobs. Regional public university faculty members who spend their graduate student years studying the ideas of history's great thinkers are usually in no mood to adapt their teaching to the needs of students who came to college thinking that the only purpose of a college education is getting a better job.

The millions of first-generation undergraduates now in mass-market institutions have had little to no exposure to the power of thought within the liberal arts. They have no great interest in the life of the mind. The lack of experience on the part of these students in how to handle ideas, as contrasted to the immediate, hedonistic response of their senses, is both a national disgrace and a disaster. The inherent contradictions are highlighted by the billions spent on their "education" in the public schools. These students desperately need the influence of the proven great thinkers of the past. They are not getting it.

But this inherited thought cannot be presented to these college students in the same way that worked in the past for the select undergraduate students in privileged campus enclaves. As contrasted to yesteryear's full-time students, vast numbers of today's students at mass-market campuses are supporting themselves with outside jobs. They are enrolled part-time and cannot fit themselves into the conventional and conveniently structured (convenient for professors) schedules of academic life.

Unfortunately, liberal arts faculties in mass-market institutions have failed to understand the need to adjust their styles and methods of teaching to accommodate these everyday students who come from tract houses in the suburbs, trailer parks, walkups in urban areas, and public housing projects. There are few books on the shelves of the homes where millions of our citizens live. While mounds of information can be downloaded from PCs either at home or at computer workstations at school, surfing the internet is no substitute for reading Aristotle's *Nicomachean Ethics* and then discussing it with a sensitive and responsive member of the faculty. To connect these students to the power of ideas and to accommodate to their needs should be the primary mission of the liberal arts faculty members of mass-market campuses. But this has not happened.

Current and practical student needs have altered the missions of these campuses to exalted trade schools. The forces motivating most humanities faculties and those motivating students on these campuses are at odds. This conflict, in which the student forces are prevailing, has already changed the face of public regional and urban universities, and nonselective liberal colleges in American higher education.

THE BROKEN MONOPOLY

Unfortunately too many faculty members do not seem to realize that other providers of college courses outside the orbit of public college and university campuses are doing a much better job of adapting to student needs and desires. These decidedly non-traditional institutions have broken the generations-old monopoly of conventional campuses. As more students begin to understand this, they transfer in increasing numbers to nontraditional institutions.

The most vivid example in today's burgeoning group of private, profit-making colleges and universities is the University of Phoenix, accredited by the North Central Association of Colleges and Schools. Established in 1976 and now employing several thousand part-time "practitioner" teachers located at centers throughout the United States and other nations, it is a successful for-profit enterprise listed on the NASDAQ National Market under its parent company, the Apollo Group. It has grown into the largest private university in America. It depends upon non-tenured part-time instructors who usually have full-time jobs in their fields and who use common syllabus material in their teaching. They are paid by the course, teach nights and weekends, and have shown no interest in tenure or unionism. Phoenix operates like a business—which it is. Phoenix presents courses in compressed five-week modules for undergraduate work and six weeks for graduate with four hour classes made available year-round at hours convenient for the work schedules of students. This contrasts with conventional universities, where degree programs are set forth sequentially through leisurely semesters, with many tenured, full-time senior professors teaching one or two days a week, the rest of their time taken up variously with committee meetings, politicking, union activity, or their own research.

Collectively Phoenix and the growing number of its counterparts are user-friendly for their college-student customers. About 80 percent of the offerings are practical, market-driven courses with about 20 percent in general education. Students seem to do reasonably well in passing state licensure examinations, although hard data confirming this has not yet accumulated. However, plenty of criticism from traditional campuses exists. It is because these teaching organizations go against the grain of what colleges and universities have always been. Proprietary institutions without exception cater to students as customers of education and training services. They span the gamut of courses and degrees and are presented by private companies on the internet, audio cassette, and video.

Western Governor's University, which was founded by seventeen governors and fourteen business partners including, among others, AT&T, IBM, and Microsoft, opened in July 1998. What spawned this initiative was a congenital unhappiness on the part of the governors at the unwillingness of regular faculties on conventional campuses to adjust their programs and their own teaching habits to the specific needs of the citizens of their states. All degrees from this virtual university are competency-based. Then there are growing numbers of corporate universities, now adding up to a multibillion-dollar U.S. enterprise. These training centers, many of them accredited, provide instruction in precisely those practical subjects that conventional academics have avoided, but which students in the mass market seek and turn to in increasing numbers. The threat these developments pose to conventional university teaching jobs should be bone chilling to the comfortable professoriate locked in the academic paradigm of the past.

CHAPTER 10

Up Interstate 271 to Cleveland and Cleveland State University

Lookabroad thro' Nature's range,
Nature's mighty law is change

Robert Burns

IN THE FALL of 1973 I was invited to become a professor of music and vice president for academic affairs at Cleveland State University, an invitation I accepted. Cleveland State came into being in the sixties. Before then Cleveland, the largest city in Ohio, located in a metropolitan region with a population somewhat less than two million people, did not have a state university. Metropolitan areas such as Toledo, Columbus and Cincinnati, among others, all had state institutions of higher learning. This lack of a state university was viewed as a civic defect by Cleveland's leadership and by Governor James Rhodes. Together they convinced the state legislature to authorize and charter Cleveland State University in 1964. It was built on the base of Fenn College, a private downtown institution whose roots went back to the early decades of the century in classes offered by the YMCA.

Following its official charter as Cleveland State University, faculty members from established schools were recruited as chairs and senior department members. Their contracts set higher salaries than the Fenn College faculty members, who were carried over into Cleveland State. These differences created a two-tier system. Some resentments became inevitable on the part of former, less well-paid Fenn College faculty members. Among the attractions of joining the new university was that CSU had not yet coalesced and did not carry the baggage of out-of-date tradition.

A unique opportunity to create a new and vital campus existed. But in fact the newly recruited faculty members tended to be traditional in their academic views and brought with them attitudes characteristic of established institutions. In turn they recruited younger, junior faculty members whose doctoral work had also taken place at traditional, research institutions. A clear-cut view of how to craft degree programs and to configure research and service work for a new day and age was not present. The student admissions office shared similar views. The result was that Clevelanders joked that CSU wanted to become Harvard on the Cuyahoga. There did not exist a shared conviction about how best to create a new university.

But by no means was that academic conservatism negative in all respects. A university's meaning to individuals and to society cannot occur without fidelity to knowledge—both past knowledge and that which is developing. On the other hand, a university's relevance to individuals and society emerges in a functional sense, for example in how students are taught to use and to apply their knowledge in a new and changing world. In the past, U.S. universities have not been very good at balancing and combining the purity of knowledge and relating it in practical ways to individuals and to society at large. But such efforts are the hallmark of today's campuses, from the lofty pinnacle of Harvard to the most modest of community colleges.

A Cleveland Mayor's Insouciance

My first official function at CSU had a freakishly humorous twist. A new gymnasium with a state-of-the-art swimming pool had just been completed. Though I was not yet officially on the job, the director of athletics asked me to be master of ceremonies for the convocation opening the facility. The usual collection of dignitaries was present, some to speak and all to be recognized. The late Ralph Perk, then mayor, had been invited. (This was the same Ralph Perk famed for having set his hair on fire with a blowtorch at a welding convention. Earlier his late wife had received her fifteen minutes of notoriety by turning down a White House dinner invitation because, as she explained, it conflicted with her bowling night and she did not want to disappoint her bowling partners.) No word had come from the mayor's office to inform us that he would be late for the ceremonies, and after waiting for fifteen minutes we had to go ahead. About thirty minutes into the festivities, and with considerable flourish, in walked Mayor Perk. The university president, Walter Waetjen, who was sitting next to me on the dais and who had no use for Ralph, told me to continue, that Perk forfeited his time to be recognized. This was scarcely calculated to please the tardy mayor. He bounded to the platform, commandeered the podium, and upbraided me with a near tirade for showing a lack of respect to the office of mayor. What else he may have said that was pertinent to the occasion I do not remember.

Put it in Writing

One of the first noticeable aspects in the life of the new campus was the difference in point of view about routine, mundane matters of academic operation between Cleveland State and Michigan and to a lesser extent Kent State. Michigan had been operating for over a century and a half and Kent State for over half a century. At Michigan especially in the forties and fifties there were many faculty purposes and roles not spelled out in written policy but which, as it were, simply came out of the academic woodwork. (This remains true at many older and upper-tier institutions, albeit procedures are now changing because litigation has created conditions where a faculty member's actions can be challenged if they are not justified in written policy.) In the established institutions of that day faculty members simply did not question their legitimacy. The weight of the institution prevailed. By contrast, at newer institutions such as Cleveland State, that which was not spelled out in written policy somehow did not have legitimacy, even though it might be logical and buttressed by common sense. Things had to be spelled out. This resulted in a somewhat different, perhaps even tentative, set of attitudes on the part of faculty, who at the same time were zealous in protecting their participation in the drafting of policy. It tends to reach extremes in unionized faculties.

In 1973, while I was still adjusting to the contours of the campus, the president assigned me the responsibility of shaping and writing an educational master plan for the university. Now master plans are always problematic documents. I did some preliminary digging about what had been done on other campuses. It was not all that helpful. I learned that at one great and famous university a master plan required fourteen volumes which were put on a shelf to remain and gather dust. We formulated a working committee which turned out to be quite large (and possessed of strong doses of academic politics), given the number of constituencies desiring representation. A pluralistic university comprises units of many different kinds and complexities. They are all involved in one way or another in the governance of the institution. This creates cross purposes. A strong tendency for problem solving to emerge out of the constituent units rather than from the central leadership exists. To bring all this together in a coherent master plan undergirded by consensus takes some heroic effort. It never succeeds 100 percent if for no other reason than change moves faster than committees are able to do their work. Thus the components of a master plan sometimes become dated before the process is completed.

We struggled for a number of months but it was slow. Finally I took the unfinished work, sequestered myself for three days, completed a document, and presented it to the committee. I think they were a bit relieved. They chewed it over, nibbled at it and tinkered here and there but essentially accepted what they received. Implementation then became the next challenge. There is no good way of being accurate about determining the success rate of university master plans, but my observations, as a result of my accrediting work through educational associations tell me it is low, perhaps not even 50 percent. Ours did better than that. About 65 percent.

This was a period of significant academic development at CSU, which continued for a decade and a half. There were ups and downs, just like the lines delineating stock market performance, but the patterns consistently moved upward as students, faculty members, and programs accrued. I do not think any doubt exists that the creation of the Maxine Levin College of Urban Affairs, which was part of the plan, represents the most memorable effort of the late seventies and early eighties.

THE LEVIN COLLEGE OF URBAN AFFAIRS

An institute for urban affairs existed on the campus. It was not an academic unit authorized to award degrees but it did have a minimal staff, without faculty status, and made use of joint faculty appointments from social sciences departments.

Its director was a stalwart of the university, Tom Campbell, who held a professorship in history and who was active on the Cleveland political scene. On one occasion he flirted with the idea of running for mayor. The idea behind the institute was that by channeling professorial expertise from the departments of political science, sociology and economics into the city government and service sectors, there could be worthwhile connections between the university and the community. Then and now the relationship between a downtown, public university and its community is crucial. The connections can be creative and of specific help to municipal governance and operations. (They can also be fraught with intrusive dangers to the institution on the part of those in the city pursuing special interests.) Somehow the Urban Institute at Cleveland State never developed a critical mass of creative relationships with city hall involving professors. They just did not materialize, mostly because the departments of political science, economics, and sociology were not doing their jobs in fostering interactions between the university and the community. So we formulated plans for a full-fledged, academic degree-granting unit that would have the status of a college in the hope and with the expectation that better and more creative connections between the city and university would evolve.

We took the proposal, which had as one crucial ingredient joint appointments from various departments across the campus, to the University Curriculum Committee and to the University Council for approval. That was a battle where I acquired a few scars. Faculty members in the social sciences departments who had not been successful in community relationships (frankly because they never got around to it) suffered some damaged egos because a newly proposed academic unit was pre-empting them. But with the help of forward-looking council members and after protracted debate we managed to prevail, even though the resulting vote was anything but unanimous. CSU Trustee and State University Regental approval did not represent a problem, since the logic and value of such a unit was self evident. It was the dog-in-the-manger politics of entrenched, turf-oriented academic departments that had to be transcended. As I look back on it the internal victory was remarkable, in that we managed to gain approval of a college that had fewer than five core faculty members. We then recruited a dean (now a university president) who over a period of eighteen years built it into a nationally recognized urban affairs unit with several score faculty appointments plus growing sources of external funding. For a very new university, identified in the fourth tier of national universities by *U.S. News and World Report*, to have an urban college named number two in the nation by the same news magazine in the specialty of City Management/Urban Policy represents a noteworthy achievement. As the college was put together I worked with Professor Roberta Steinbacher, a shining light on the CSU faculty, who crafted its covenants. Working with Roberta was one of my lasting professional satisfactions as provost.

In my opinion the basic structure we put in place for the Urban College in the late seventies constituted the principle reason for its success. There were two cardinal principles. We insisted that joint appointments between university academic departments as its faculty was built be the first principal. The reason was simple. During the second half of the twentieth century the world of knowledge came together as it has not done since the middle ages. For example, there is no such thing as an astronomer today being only an astronomer. She must also have a working knowledge of chemistry, geology, physics, and other scientific disciplines. Gone are the days when a truly significant professor could concentrate only on one discipline, all the while getting more and more specialized and removed from other disciplines. This is true in all corners of the world of knowledge. The second principle was that the budget structure of the college be unified. We did not create a multiplicity of departmental budget units which inevitably would turn into fiefdoms, fighting to maintain and extend their domains. The balkanization of colleges through competing, quasi-autonomous departments has grown into one of the larger problems of university organizations. We avoided this in the Urban College. Of course the facts and realities of academic politics were ever-present during the fifteen-year period I remained academic vice president and provost. These realities exist to a greater or lesser degree in all types of academic institutions, but they tend to be more raw in public, urban universities situated cheek by jowl with the real politicians of a city and its wards and precincts. These tendencies can be observed vividly in both new and older public urban campuses in every region of the nation, where examples of political controversies crop up regularly.

THE GROUP OF SIXTEEN

Early in my Cleveland State incumbency there was a cluster of professors on campus who seemed intent on restricting the role of the academic vice presidency. Earlier I had reduced the percentage of salary increases of some of them who were highly paid in comparison to other faculty members. This was a matter of equity. Understandably they did not like it and it may have been a factor in their discontent. In truth, their effort was an unadulterated power play. It was a classic example of the "us versus them" syndrome which flares up from time to time on campuses. A number of reasons exist for these mini-academic insurgencies. In newer institutions the contours of the academic ecology are somewhat different from that which is more traditional. Some faculty members have trouble adapting. This contrasts with older campuses where, as decades have unfolded, institutional roles have solidified on the one hand, along with individual roles on the other. These two categories, new and old, both contain advantages and dangers: the advantage of flexibility exists in the new, whereas stability will usually prevail in the old, but the flip side of the coin shows the danger of noncohesion in the new and ossification in the old.

At lower-tier, pluralistic campuses another factor is present. It consists of the greater central control of budgets, as the president and provost tend to exert more direct control of money allocations to colleges and departments. In the older, private universities and also in historic public flagship institutions, there exists to a greater or lesser degree a budgeting policy often described as "each tub on its own bottom," where much discretion exists for budget decisions within individual units. The collorary to this is that these units to a considerable extent are responsible for raising their own operational funds. This policy is not characteristic of newer public institutions at which there has not been time to develop alumni and other constituencies who offer financial backing. In these institutions operational funds come primarily from state appropriations and tuition. It is the job of the president and provost to allocate them, usually with the help of a budget committee. Naturally, if a given unit feels it is not getting its fair share, contention arises.

The technical logistics of most public university income and expense budgeting can be nightmarish. This is due to the institutional accountability to the state, which technically owns the institution where it is chartered. Clearly there must be necessary checks and balances and protective arrangements to thwart subterfuge and flim-flam by creative budgeteers. For example, medium-sized to large public campuses (10,000 to more than 40,000 students, to say nothing of multi-campus systems) will have anywhere from seventy-five to many hundreds of academic budget units. Each unit normally will have a chart of accounts containing budget lines which are uniform across all units and identify various categories of expenditures or income sources, such as salaries, benefits, office supplies, furniture, travel, etc., etc., almost *ad infinitum*. Many of these lines are themselves subdivided so that the myriad of separate entries can be mind-boggling. Complicated rules and regulations regarding which expenditure should be assigned to what category, whether or not funds can be transferred from an underspent line to an overspent one, combine into a frightening complexity where strict adherence to all rules becomes nigh impossible. This is just one example of overweening bureaucracy afflicting public higher education. That more fraud is not perpetrated speaks to the inherent honesty of the vast majority of public university budget officers.

The cluster of professors identified above pictured themselves as the superior academic group on campus and as such, the arbiters of the academic base of the university. They wanted to position themselves to exert more leverage, particularly in this complex budgeting process, the intricacies of which they did not grasp. They became known as the "Group of Sixteen" which morphed into the "Running Dogs." Pre-eminence, and through that, influence, was their goal. They tried to gain support among other faculty members but failed. They did arrange for an evening meeting with the president at his home, which neither he nor they communicated to me. This challenged the social compact of academic openness which should be the basis for campus communication. When I heard that such a meeting was to occur I immediately sent a memo to the president indicating that were it to take place without my presence fundamental fairness would be breached. There was no choice but to include me. At the meeting it was apparent that the group did not have its facts straight nor did it have a cogent plan. It was not difficult to deal with such issues as they were raised. The group petered out.

Academic mugwumpery of this sort can and does occur simply because the protective umbrella of tenure allows partisans who become adversarial, and are unsuccessful in the attempt, simply to slip back into their protected grooves. If the stakes were higher, as in corporate echelons or in the real world of politics such as the Congress or state legislatures, and the unsuccessful malcontents who disregard or misuse agreed-upon procedure in order to gain their own ends might well lose their jobs or their positions, then there would be more thought and reflection before an untoward initiative is launched. This is why the old saw that academic politics is so vicious because so little is at stake continues to be current.

But another face exists to this kind of circumstance. On a controversial issue it could well be that an administrator is wrong in the position he or she takes. Because of tenure a faculty member or members can take issue with the administrative authority figure without fear of job loss. In today's academic world woe be unto the dean, provost or president who visits arbitrary retribution upon a faculty member for being on the other side of the fence—and saying so. As an aftereffect of the Group of Sixteen's restiveness, the president scheduled a two day off-campus retreat for the vice presidents, deans, directors, and department chairs. Like most such administrative plenums, its purpose was to review process and procedure. The president presided. Halfway through he came down with flu and I took over. Shortly afterward the announcement came that the title provost was added to my academic-administrative portfolio. (The term provost, coming from the Medieval Latin *propositus*, means "person placed over others," but a more beguiling earlier usage was, "the keeper of a prison".)

THE CAAC DIGRESSION

In the decade between 1975 and 1985 I volunteered with a number of civic organizations. I have always enjoyed this kind of activity, although as the seventies, eighties, and nineties moved forward the accountability of individual board members for the actions of staff members within their organizations became more and more apparent. Over the years board members learned they could be sued personally if things went amiss in their associations. Although I did not get involved in any legal action, I learned this the hard way.

I had taken over as president of the board of the Cleveland Area Arts Council (CAAC), which was a nonprofit group that, among other projects, organized programs for inner-city youth that involved activities in the arts. The board of the CAAC was a cross section of recognized Clevelanders who essentially lent their names to the virtuous work of the body. I came into it somewhat late. As its work expanded, local funding for its programs was insufficient so it turned to federal government programs, specifically CETA, for support. Programs to provide work opportunities for young people in order to channel their energies in positive directions were available under CETA. The staff people within the CAAC configured a number of programs that succeeded admirably and helped young people. The federal government provided funding that paid the bills. This was negotiated and established before I came on board.

Unfortunately the CAAC staff was unprepared and not technically trained to fulfill the stringent record-keeping and accounting requisites federal agencies require on the part of organizations receiving government money. CAAC record keeping was woefully inadequate. When called upon to account for its expenditures, the CAAC was unable to do so in the form required by the government, and predictably, the Washington bureaucrats were perturbed. This crisis came to a head in less than a year after I became CAAC president. The *Cleveland Press* (Cleveland's afternoon newspaper, now defunct) got wind of the story, made the most of it, and Mayor Dennis Kucinich of Cleveland made things more difficult. He and the CAAC board members who did not hail from liberal and populist networks lacked affinity for one another.

I had two separate audits done, both of which determined that no fraud had taken place. The problems came from lack of knowledge on the part of staff about what absolutely must be done in accounting when federal funds are involved. I struggled both in maintaining board cohesion and interacting with the regional CETA office in Chicago in search of a solution. Cleveland municipal elections then took place; Dennis Kucinich was defeated and a new city administration with George Voinovich as its head took over. A different attitude prevailed in City Hall. We finally got the various parts of the record-keeping mess aligned, and established communication with all parties involved. They had come to the realization that no deceit had occurred—only inadequacy of performance. This marked the death knell of the CAAC, which we quietly buried.

YEARS OF CAMPUS GROWTH

My functions during the fifteen years as academic vice president and provost involved participating in and presiding over growth within the university. This growth issued forth from all parts of the campus: academic programs, land acquisition, building construction, faculty and staff. A significant part of the growth was in the student body. One of my goals was to serve a student body reaching 20,000 students, not counting continuing education. We did not quite make it, but reached 19,286. Those times were different. Today the enrollment has declined to approximately 15,000 as a result of forces described in this book. One of the forces is the rise of proprietary, profit-making college degree programs that cater to the scheduling needs of potential students. Comfortably tenured faculty members have been unwilling to make the adjustments to meet these needs—therefore, fewer students.

My late wife Lanette went to law school and became a lawyer while we were still at Kent State. Not long after I took the position at Cleveland State she accepted the position as Chief Referee (now called magistrate) in the Court of Common Pleas domestic relations court. We had built our house in Hudson in the late sixties and together commuted twenty-eight miles to downtown Cleveland. (Sometimes late in the afternoon while a trial was going on I'd sit in the back of her courtroom and listen to the freakish arguments in divorce cases before we commuted back to Hudson.) We then took a small apartment twenty-five floors up in a west-side high rise with a spectacular view of the city but kept the Hudson house where we had lived for over a decade and which we liked. We stayed in Cleveland during the week and spent the weekends in Hudson. It was a nice way of life, but I wouldn't recommend it. You can never remember where you left the pair of shoes you need. Lanette was a role model for our daughter Jill, who took her education seriously and earned two master's degrees and a Ph.D. She now has an active psychotherapy practice and an associate professorship on a local campus in Saint Paul. It had looked like our son John (we called him Kip) planned to have an academic career. He was in a comparative literature Ph.D. program at Columbia and had a fellowship in the provost's office. When he saw the inside of academic life he decided it was not for him and took off for Europe. He has been in Frankfurt, Germany for seventeen years with AT&T. He is an authentic citizen of their world.

Toward the end of my fifteen-year stint as academic vice president and provost—certainly, no one in his right mind should remain in that role for a period that extended!—things began to wear a bit thin and I was thinking about stepping aside and finishing my career in the classroom, which I had never really left. But then things changed.

EVENTS PRIOR TO MY BECOMING PRESIDENT

The following events illustrate how public universities, especially state universities in cities of diverse constituencies, are subject to constituent and political pressures. Compromise is a requirement of leadership in an urban, academic environment permeated by politics, but when necessary and push comes to shove over an issue or issues, no matter how difficult it might be for the person in leadership, a stand that is uncompromising with respect to principle must be taken.

In most large cities with populations in the hundreds of thousands or beyond a million, public university campuses are surrounded by political, business, economic and not least, racial forces. Each university is a strong economic influence in its local community. The campus generates hundreds of millions of dollars in contracts and services. While the call to high service of the university is to educate and train students of whatever race and background, a contrasting perception of many local citizens views the university's main function relating to them as the purchase of goods and services and providing staff jobs. To acquire a generous slice of the economic pie deriving from campus operations is a goal of various groups.

At the time these events began (1986), CSU had been in existence for twenty-two years, with an enrollment approaching 20,000 students, a faculty of about 600, with another approximately 700 non-academic staff members housed on a campus covering some eighty downtown acres. I had worked as academic vice president and provost since 1973, the number two position under President Walter Waetjen. He had steadfastly resisted the efforts of local politicians to exert control over the university. Many battles took place, all of which he had won. Unfortunately, at the same time, his non-academic bureaucracy (and I hate to admit it, but to an extent the academic support staff such as secretaries and administrative assistants) were quite deaf to the need to develop good relations with citizens of the city. Obviously this was a defect, since municipal officeholders exert considerable control over such instruments as city support services, bids, contracts, building codes and other matters without which no university can function. The white civil service bureaucracy of the university was viewed as being rude. The groundwork was laid for the offensive that followed.

Storm Clouds

The president of the Cleveland City Council at the time was George Forbes, who now serves as president of the local chapter of the NAACP. A born leader, he has a stormy and impetuous past. During one committee session he threw a chair at another council member. On another occasion a notorious photo (that periodically makes the rounds in Cleveland) was taken, showing him physically ejecting a reporter from a meeting. He is a vivid, controversial, and colorful citizen who works tirelessly to improve conditions for black citizens. He is older now but remains his indomitable self.

One night toward the close of a City Council session (March 23, 1987), he accused Cleveland State University of institutional racism. A reporter from the Cleveland *Plain Dealer* covering City Council wrote a story quoting George Forbes. It appeared on the front page the following morning. This was the beginning of what turned into a lengthy fight.

Cleveland State was unprepared for this conflict. President Waetjen, who had been a Golden Gloves boxer and professional football player (after which he earned his doctorate), shared with George Forbes all the instincts of a fighter. The sparring between them provided stories and headlines. But Forbes, with far more experience in public controversy, won the battle of printer's ink hands down. It was suggested that initially Forbes did not intend more than to capture the attention of CSU's leaders, with the purpose of improving job prospects for his constituents and having more attention paid to black faculty and students. But in fact his allegations released forces of racial resentment that had been present but dormant, awaiting an outlet. Over the years these resentments were not focused upon CSU alone. Because of discrimination against blacks, various malefactors were evident, including some unions along with government echelons. With CSU as the perceived offender, attention was focussed on the campus. Forbes dealt with it skillfully. To this day he continues to be straightforward, and when he deems it necessary, in your face about his involvement in racist matters. In a letter to the editor of the *Plain Dealer* he stated in stark and plain English that the NAACP was in the "race business."

Walter Waetjen was prepared to fight it out with George Forbes because facts and data had not been provided about alleged racism at CSU. He made the logical point that it was manifestly unfair to single out the university when similar allegations could be made about other organizations. Much blood could have been spilled. But the Board of Trustees intervened. Here is what happened.

In Cleveland there is an organization called the Cleveland Roundtable. Formed in the 1970s with a racially diverse membership, it has concerned itself with issues of racial harmony in the community. The Board persuaded the officers of the Roundtable to sponsor a group that was named the CSU Civic Committee on Race Relations to look into issues of racism at CSU. In essence, by invoking a group from outside the university, the Board punted on the issue. Even though the CSU Board's motives in its creation were well intended and honorable, the Civic Committee provided an opportunity for those with special interests, under the banner of a legitimately appointed committee, to inject themselves into university affairs. Obviously Waetjen vigorously opposed such a committee. Coming from the old school, he believed fervently in campus autonomy. He had always thrown himself into battles to protect the fledgling campus. But in this episode he could not prevail against his own board. Since he was not yet ready to retire, he yielded.

The appointment of the Civic Committee turned out to be a miscalculation, though honestly brought about. In effect, the policy-making body of the university, the Board of Trustees, had opened the door to a group that included some members with special interests and put it in a position where its member's views, some quite biased, had to be given official consideration in the policies and management of the university. Pressure of this sort, that can and will be exerted, makes unbiased determination of policy difficult. Determining the policies of the university, any university, belongs only to the Trustees.

The Civic Committee was co-chaired by a prominent white businesswoman and an African-American minister. A young lawyer from the CUNY system in New York joined the committee as a part-time staff person with a large stipend, the appropriateness of which was questioned. She approached her job with biased energy and a complete lack of tact. She was eventually let go but only after bombarding the campus with "lawyer nasty" memos full of impossible demands for information. The faculty could not fathom what was going on.

THE CIVIC COMMITTEE REPORT

When the Civic Committee began preparing its report and the members discussed what constituted racism they could not agree upon a definition of the word. Even though it was supposed to look into the issue of racism at CSU, a definition of what racism is—in defiance of logic—cannot be found in the report. Commonly accepted definitions are in most any dictionary. The one I keep at my desk, the fourth edition of the *American Heritage Dictionary* for example, defines racism as, "The belief that race accounts for differences in human character or ability and that a particular race is superior to others," (something the committee would have found great difficulty in credibly attaching to CSU). By contrast, the preface to the Civic Committee report had this to say about it: "The Committee found a variety of interpretations of the concept of racism. People from different backgrounds tend to see racism differently. Consequently, members of the Committee were unable to agree upon a common definition of racism that would allow us, in one voice, to answer the question of whether or not CSU is a racist institution. However, members of the committee do agree unanimously that many of the incidents and conditions that were examined have their origin in beliefs, and/or actions, that relate to the race of the people involved."

Expressed here is a classic example of a tautology, which is a term from philosophic trade language meaning, in this case, an expression looking back on itself that provides no specifics for what follows. Racism could not be defined by committee members and yet they held that "beliefs" and "actions" "relate to the race of the people involved." This lack of a solid definition of what racism is reduced the credibility of the entire report.

The remainder of the short preface is reasonable, even somewhat graceful. As the report proceeded, the several narrative sections were expressed with an apparent sense of good will, but with an implicit, four-part message: 1.) blacks were unwelcome at CSU; 2.) their poor performance should be helped and ultimately cured by special programs for them focused both on academic and non-academic matters; 3.) the presence of more blacks on campus and in positions of importance would make CSU a better place (that the potential increase in the presence and influence of groups also subject to past discrimination such as Native Americans, Hispanics, the handicapped, women, and Asians, might also make CSU a better place was left unsaid); 4.) repeated references to affirmative action placed it as one of the most important functions of the university.

Examples of low student academic performance by blacks are documented in the report, but there were no tangible remedies for improvement delineated other than numerous reiterations of their need. In the arena of hiring, the thrust of the report was that more blacks needed to be placed in upper-echelon authoritative positions, but nothing was said about defining and measuring levels of qualification in order that requisites of such positions be fulfilled. There were seven chapters or sections with a total of fifty-four recommendations on a variety of issues related to blacks and CSU. These fifty-four recommendations were purposeful and zealous, leavened with unfamiliarity about the nature and dynamics of universities. They illustrate vividly the dangers to even-handedness and the potential for intrusiveness into the operations of a university that can be promulgated by an external, special interest group. The report even included a "Vision Statement" for Cleveland State. Given general acceptance of the value of university autonomy and the need to keep external involvement in its operations at arm's length, this statement carried borrowed chutzpah to an extreme. A reading of the statement shows it to have been confined essentially to minority black issues, saying little about other minority or handicapped groups.

In the light of later federal court decisions about racial preferences, had these recommendations throughout the report which related solely to blacks been implemented, someone down the road would no doubt have sued CSU for unconstitutional use of race in university decision making.

True diversity, both human and intellectual, by common consent, improves the environment for learning through student exposure to different points of view. But an interest in what constitutes diversity is now being explored in federal court opinions. Diversity, it is predicated, goes far beyond matters of race. In August of 2001 a panel of the Eleventh Circuit federal appeals court ruled that the University of Georgia unconstitutionally gave preference to race in admitting students; that minority students could "be admitted or advance further in the process at the expense of white applicants with greater potential to contribute to a diverse student body."

The thrust of the Civic Committee report revealed the continuing influence coming from the beliefs and assertions of W. E. B. DuBois who, as the nineteenth turned into the twentieth century, was an intellectual adversary of Booker T. Washington, who was born of a slave mother and in 1881 founded the Tuskegee Institute. DuBois, who was the first black Ph.D. from Harvard and cofounder of the NAACP believed that the basic problem black people confronted— racism—engendered all the other problems blacks faced. Strong protest and defiance of racism on the part of blacks were what he believed to be the most effective ways of combatting it. On the other hand Booker T. Washington, while not denying the realities of racism and the deprivations it visited upon blacks, insisted that African Americans needed to develop behavior patterns and habits that would enable them to function within the economy on an equal skill basis with whites, and that the responsibility to accomplish this rested on the shoulders of blacks themselves. DuBois believed it was the responsibility of whites to change their attitudes and thereby become helpful to blacks. Washington believed the initiative for self help took precedence and had to come from blacks. As the decades of the twentieth century rolled forward, civil rights leaders, both black and white, emphasized the assertions of DuBois over those of Washington: that the causes of cultural and economic wants of blacks came from whites and that whites had to change their ways in order to correct them. The positive issues of responsibility for blacks themselves were not stressed to the extent of the negative issues of white liability. The Civic Committee report shows this influence. Dozens of examples of campus problems of blacks permeate the report. There are no references to what African Americans themselves might do to make improvements.

WALTER WAETJEN RETIRES

Some months before the report was released in December of 1987, Walter Waetjen announced his retirement effective July 1, 1988. He had consistently given signals that he intended to stay on until mandatory retirement came in 1990. Given what he had been subjected to, his change of mind was understood. During the lame duck period not much happened and shortly before his actual retirement date, I was appointed Interim President, and then confirmed in October. It was not exactly a run-of-the-mill appointment given that I had served fifteen years as academic vice president and provost, and I was then sixty-seven, just a year younger than Waetjen. It was taken for granted that my incumbency would be relatively brief. But as the chief officer on campus it became my responsibility to deal with the report and manage the responses to it.

CHAPTER 11

Professional Politics and Bureaucracy

Man is by nature a political animal.

Aristotle

THE CONTAGION OF PARTISAN POLITICS

ACADEMIC POLITICS AS a diversionary pastime of tenured professors is one thing. (Non-tenured teachers rarely indulge. Not protected by tenure, they're afraid to.) But partisan politics practiced by public officials and some politically selected public university board members is quite another. Three former public university presidents collaborated on an article that appeared in *Trusteeship*.[1] In it they lamented the negative experiences they had as presidents who were required to work with the politically selected trustees responsible for their public institutions. In their new lives as private university presidents, outside the partisan, political atmosphere that can permeate public university boards, they rejoiced in the comparative felicity and civility of private sector interactions between administrations and boards. There are few personal checks and balances on public boards. On the one hand less old boy networking exists, but on the other, individual agendas, some resulting from political connections or constituent pressures, abound. It is not uncommon for pressure to be exerted for a particular slant to university programs, or for a predisposed labor or business practice in the management of the university.

As matters stand public university board members are either direct political appointments, usually by the state governor, or they are elected, as in Michigan, for example. At public community colleges, given both state and local support, the process is somewhat more complicated but similar political forces come into play.

External political incursions at state schools both large and small have become more and more blemished. Increasingly trustees of these institutions have attached political agendas to their responsibilities of overseeing their campuses. If, at the beginning of their terms these agendas do not exist, they can develop. Too often politically appointed trustees do not hold their offices because of their fitness for setting policy and monitoring the affairs of the institution, but because they contributed money, or political knowhow, and displayed loyalty to their governors, and their party. They were rewarded with the personal prestige of university trusteeships. These trusteeships usually last from seven to nine years. During that length of time governorships can change from one party to the other. The new governor will usually appoint university trustees from his or her own political party, which sometimes places political adversaries on the board. This kind of politics has led to disastrous and highly visible controversies at public institutions, not uncommonly involving the process of getting rid of a president, sometimes in very messy ways.

While partisan politics is bad enough on boards of public universities, its ugliness is much worse and more dramatic in urban public school districts, with New York City awarded top honors for this brand of drama. In thirty years New York went through no less than ten chancellors of its system, seven of whom quit under pressure or were fired. Political disputes between board and mayor were the chief cause.[2] These political interventions are now occurring with increasing frequency on public university boards of trustees.

TROUBLE SPOTS IN PUBLIC UNIVERSITY LAY TRUSTEESHIP

As the three former public university presidents testified, increasing concern has surfaced about the functioning of public university, politically appointed or elected trustees. This developed to the point that the need for a sweeping reform of public trusteeship was advocated by the president of the Association of Governing Boards of Universities and Colleges, Richard Ingram, in an article in the 1998 May/June issue of the AGB's journal, *Trusteeship*.[3] A lively debate continues. Ingram's piece identified three basic issues about trusteeships that he believes need serious attention: a call for the boards of trustees of public institutions to be larger, merit selection of the trustees, and greater trustee philanthropy. These three issues of size, merit, and philanthropy are much more characteristic of private institution boards of trustees than in the public sector.

The size of boards, for example, in private institutions is seldom less than twenty and not uncommonly between thirty and forty, sometimes even fifty or more. In about half of all four-year public institutions there are fewer than fifteen trustee members, with nine being a typical number. In community colleges the number is usually smaller—seven or five. Ingram cites a 1989 study done by Clark Kerr and Marian Gade which said, "the size of the board makes a substantial difference. We found more difficulty with boards that are too small than with boards that are too large. . . . a very small board can be a disaster. A single person can become too dominant. . . . There is safety in numbers. A big board can tolerate a few poor members; a small board can tolerate none."[4] Personal experience over the years supports that statement, my having been close to nine-member public boards. One or two problematic trustees with personal agendas create problems.

The lack of merit selection for public university trustees remains a basic defect. This is why politics continues to seep into the trustee oversight role of public universities. But given state capitol politics in most—if not all—states, no surcease from unilateral gubernatorial responsibility for trustee appointment is on the horizon.

Trustee philanthropy is a "hope for." Ingram says "if trustees and regents do not practice personal philanthropy, why should anyone else?" Some do, especially trustees of flagship public institutions. But others don't. As long as the others are politically appointed, they never will.

BUREAUCRACY GOES TO COLLEGE AND GETS TENURED

Excessive bureaucracy is a continuing threat to the management of the academy. The term requires definition. Obviously, any complex organization requires procedures and instruments of management—in a word, bureaucracy. On a pluralistic campus involving multiple constituencies the hip-pocket informality of a village town hall will not work. But procedures of management should be functional and supportive. Individuals as scholars, teachers, researchers and students are what universities are all about and when campus proceduralism preempts the energy that should go into creative work, then excessive bureaucracy exists.

In today's academic world excessive bureaucracy envelops not only the bureaucrats themselves, whose vocation consists of slogging in and out of memos and rules either of their own making or those produced by other bureaucrats.

It includes the paper avalanches (including downloaded emails which are supposed to reduce the paper flow but actually increase it) triggered by governmental reporting requirements. It also comes from faculty committees where there is a surfeit of overlapping policy and procedure work already done by administrators whose job it is to do it so the faculty does not have to. A Sargasso Sea of red tape is created. In part this is the effect of a lack of trust between faculty members and administrators. The human energy expended in this kind of academic bureaucracy and thus subtracted from the energy of teaching and discovering new knowledge is beyond calculation.

Litigation and the threat of litigation are further culprits. During the last twenty-five years, enormous amounts of paperwork issuing forth like the volcanic ash of Vesuvius have been created by faculty, students, and staff, who use legal counsel and the courts to redress alleged grievances. Universities are always placed in a defensive posture in these circumstances, which inevitably generates still more paperwork. Litigation is an American social phenomenon which expanded exponentially during the last quarter of the twentieth century. The blame cannot be placed directly on universities, but they have an indirect responsibility because state university law schools have produced hordes of lawyers who need to earn money. They willingly take cases, and encourage the filing of others, that never should emerge into the light of day. Some law schools (usually the less prestigious ones in big cities) teach students the practical tactics of how to win lawsuits. They have not built into their curricula instruction in ethics that would determine the kinds of cases that should never be accepted and carried forward in the first place.

Faculty members refer to the primacy on campus of education and add that because they are the ones doing the educating they should exert control. Clearly this point of view is understandable. But teachers and researchers on public campuses are paid from money generated elsewhere through tax revenues at both state and federal levels. Since a significant portion of the money paying their salaries comes from taxpayers, there are federal and state agencies to control and monitor its spending. Faculty and staff on university campuses chafe at this, with the exception of the bureaucrats who earn their living doing the university paperwork for the monitoring. Even so, while modern university faculties proudly trace their heritage to the medieval university (which obviously had less bureaucracy than today's large campuses) no knowledgeable faculty member of today would be willing to exchange places with a teacher in a small guild of medieval journeymen scholars who had no supportive services or tax supported subsidies. And they were not all that well off. Some famous scholars could obtain appointments in the retinues of princes or bishops, but in exchange they depended upon their patrons. They were treated with deference and given perquisites and privileges. But concepts such as tenure or academic freedom were not part of the thinking of those who paid the bills. Had these concepts been served up to a prince or bishop, the response would surely have been, in the idiom of the day, "You must be kidding." So despite modern-day bureaucracy, faculty members by comparison remain well off.

Other kinds of pervasive bureaucracy cloud academic leadership roles. Because of increased dependence upon technology in most disciplines, professors have become more dependent upon nonacademic support services. These groups have developed bureaucracies of their own, with staff managers and administrators.

The typical illustration of how public universities are bureaucratized is found in how money is handled. When major operational funding comes from tax support under state statutes and major research support comes from federal appropriations, there are mazes of controlling statutes, regulations, and interpretations of regulations. Bureaucrats are required to administer spending under the rules that make up these mazes. The chances of getting entangled, even inadvertently, and breaking the rules, or even breaking the law, are considerable. When reasonable sensitivity is shown to the values of education, the bureaucracy of rules and procedures can usually be made to work. But this becomes more and more difficult. Government regulations are insensitive to a learning community, and problems thus exist in the process of their implementation. This is done on a daily basis by bureaucrats, who sometimes misinterpret, mangle, and at worst subvert the academic values that the rules are supposed to uphold. Worse, most of the bureaucrats, who tend to be in the civil service, outlast the appointed academic leadership. Academic officers come and go with rapidity. They have high visibility and are seldom praised but often blamed. Support service bureaucrats have lower profiles. They see their roles as defined by formal rules and regulations. They have found their niches and are natural survivors.

ELECTIONEERING

Electioneering has had a strong impact on public institutions. Private higher education, while having plenty of internal academic politics, has been relatively free of political scheming from the outside. It has been the state owned public institutions located in urban areas that, for the most part, have had to deal with its various manifestations. Now, however, it looks like eminent campuses are no longer immune. In 2002, no less an institution than Yale University found itself subject to a political campaign aiming to capture an alumni seat on the Yale Corporation, which is its venerable board of trustees. Unions can take most of the credit for this latest thrust at egalitarianizing what has been essentially a closed circle. The candidate was the Reverend W. David Lee, a Yale Divinity School graduate who is the pastor of a local church in New Haven. According to *New York Times* reporter Karen W. Arenson, Lee drew "$60,000 in backing from Yale's clerical and custodial unions and others, and is aggressively campaigning for a board seat, sending out polished brochures and email messages and speaking to alumni groups in cities like New York and Philadelphia. He is upsetting both the normally insular election process and many of those who run Yale."[5] Arenson reports that Senator Joseph Lieberman, the mayor of New Haven, the attorney general of Connecticut and numerous student groups supported Lee. She further quotes him as saying, "what I promise is that the unions and the community and the students will have access to me. . . . How many students can have access to a trustee at almost any time? How many people from the community can talk to a trustee? How many unions can talk to a trustee?"[6]

He did not win but his campaign injected a component of precinct politics into the ecology of Yale.

CHAPTER 12

What Became Known as the Winbush Affair

Relentless color prejudice is more often a cause than a result of the Negro's degradation. . . . While it is a great truth to say that the Negro must strive and strive mightily to help himself, it is equally true that unless his striving be not simply seconded, but rather aroused and encouraged by the initiative of the richer and wiser environing group, he cannot hope for great success.

W. E. B. DuBois

I have learned that success is to be measured not so much by the position that one has reached in life as by the obstacles which he has overcome while trying to succeed.

Booker T. Washington

PRELUDE

I mentioned earlier that within an environment leavened by the politics of many constituencies the need for compromise in the exertion of leadership exists. I balanced that comment with the assertion that there are times when push comes to shove over an issue that the leader must take an uncompromising stand based on principle. This might be at some career cost. Principle, however, must remain.

This was precisely that kind of situation in the aftermath of the Civic Committee involvement with Cleveland State. I was viewed as the antagonist. As a result, some attached the "racist" label to me.

The basic principle in this case was simple (as most basic principles are): namely, to maintain the integrity of the academic processes at CSU. The efforts of the contending groups and individuals vigorously espousing the empowerment of blacks on the CSU campus (other races, ethnicities, women and handicapped persons were not on the agenda to the extent that blacks were) threatened the fairness of academic processes on campus. I will go into some detail about the specific educational and management processes that were challenged. Extensive coverage in the print and electronic media put these challenges into the public domain, as did Winbush's attorney's demand that memos and documents related to them be released. I document examples in the notes to illustrate what it could have meant for the institution had they been successful. The activists were agitated and wanted to change the basis of CSU operations by altering and replacing processes and procedures through which it operated.

The backdrop was that Cleveland State functioned as a university according to the model of current U.S. public higher education. The model took two centuries to evolve. The success of civil rights initiatives in the fifties and sixties had placed blacks, clearly and irrevocably, into the model. The problem was that blacks as a group did not see themselves being permitted to take part in the affairs of the university to the extent that was their right. It was my responsibility as president to maintain the operational integrity of the university for all who were part of the academic community, including blacks. Some events had yet to unfold before the issues were drawn.

A Brief Respite

In the months that followed Dr. Waetjen's retirement and my confirmation in the presidency, I did not argue details or point out the problematic parts of the ninety-one page Civic Committee report. Given the emotional climate and the external perceptions about race relations at CSU, being argumentative would not only have accomplished nothing but would have caused a reversion to the beginning of the episode. I could have been quite right in what I said and had as little impact as calling Lake Erie to account for assaulting the shoreline. While the Civic Committee Report was civil in its tone, those who had an agenda for black empowerment at CSU were partisan and hard-edged. The downtown business community, which did not want to lose patronage from the black community, was essentially silent on the issue. This did not make things easier. The silence made it seem they agreed with the charges made about racism at CSU.

The thrust of my position was that in U.S. society, racism did in fact exist on the part of individuals and organizations, and that the Civic Committee report represented an effort to highlight it so that positive steps could be taken to ameliorate discrimination. I gave a major presentation to the Roundtable, to which I had been appointed as a board member, and followed this up with presentations and interviews elsewhere. While opinions about racist behavior at CSU were not eliminated, tensions abated somewhat. Given what was to ensue, this turned out to be short-lived.

Many white faculty members professed "white guilt" for slavery and racist attitudes in America. They were not yet challenged by students born in the seventies, not a few of whom say, "We had nothing to do with slavery and racism. Why penalize us for it?" At that time the atmosphere in Cleveland's black community, and in many other cities, remained conducive to steadfast support of its leadership's assertions that the problems encountered by blacks resulted from institutionalized discrimination; that the solution was to attack the root cause, white racism. This was the assertion of W. E. B. DuBois. It was not yet modified by the small corps of black thinkers who say, essentially, "Of course racism exists and given human nature, will probably continue for a long time. But African Americans must also look to themselves for lasting solutions."

CSU trustees debated the appointment of a minority affairs vice presidency. (The Civic Committee had first discussed a vice presidency for black affairs but altered it to minority affairs.) Similar posts existed at other universities, although more commonly they were at the assistant vice president or director level, reporting through the academic affairs office—but not a full vice presidency. Two African-American members of the board strongly backed the vice presidency and prevailed. I agreed to the position at that level, although this was a mistake. The position should have been created as a directorship or assistant V.P. with the condition that after a period of time and performance review it could be made into vice presidency. It was a tacit assumption, never challenged, that such a post would be filled by an African American. In fact, such a race-based condition for appointment today would run up against judicial rulings that foreclose, on constitutional grounds, the use of race as the principal determinant in faculty and staff appointments.

A VICE PRESIDENCY FOR MINORITY AFFAIRS

Following the creation of the V.P. position, a search committee was named. It included a majority of black faculty members and staff. After six months it brought in a slate of four candidates, all black. One of them, to whom I offered the position, was Raymond Winbush, who held a doctorate from the University of Chicago and who was at the time the director of the Black Cultural Center at Vanderbilt University. He accepted. All senior administrators serve at the pleasure of the president (or the trustees in the case of the president) and may be removed from the administrative post at the end of their contractual period.

HEAVY WEATHER

The situation was difficult from the start. Where a need existed to calm tensions and build bridges of trust, aggressive moves aimed at benefitting African Americans escalated these tensions instead.

In July of 1989, with his contract in hand but before he had officially begun at CSU, Winbush gave a speech in Cleveland to the Baptist Minister's Conference at the Greater Abyssinia Baptist Church. The Cleveland-area minority newspaper, *The Call and Post*, covered his appearance. It quoted him as saying, "Many urban universities have made a deliberate effort to recruit unsuccessful students, thus enabling the colleges to add more blacks to their dropout lists." Black people, he said, are not prepared to let whites dictate what goes on in large urban universities and he felt brave enough to deal with racism at CSU. The president of the Conference, the Reverend Theophilus Caviness, was quoted as telling him that the BMC "would support and stand with him . . . You are there [at Cleveland State] for us, and we are here for you."[1] He was seen as an agent of the black community positioned on campus, rather than as an officer of the university, one of whose purposes was to serve the community and region by helping to bridge the gaps between the campus and the minority communities.

Throughout the succeeding months there followed a series of interventions in various parts of university operations by Winbush that, if allowed to continue, would not only have placed him beyond the bounds of university accountability but would have permanently disrupted orderly campus process. There were those who said that was precisely his role—that he was brought to the university on behalf of blacks to shake it up and, by implication, alter or do away with campus policies and procedures to such an extent that things would never be the same. But the question this raises is, how does this relate to issues of fairness and equity to all constituents involved? Did CSU's adversaries in the community reject out of hand the processes whites had put in place for university operations? If this were true, or even partially true, in the longer term, what impact would it have on the problem of bringing the races together on matters of the operations within CSU as a public, mass-market institution?

FOUR PROBLEMATIC INVOLVEMENTS

Winbush disregarded established ways of doing things, built not only into university policy but also into the basic principles of the processes involved. In one instance state law was resisted. Four examples go to the heart of the questions posed above.

The first involved interfering in doctoral-level grade administration. A troubling situation arose in the college of education where three black graduate students in the doctoral program alleged that they were discriminated against in the grading of examinations. When allegations such as these occur, important issues of civil rights, academic freedom, academic quality, and fairness to both students and faculty are involved. It is crucial to invoke the remedies built into the written policies of the college and university. Given the potential for lawsuits, this protects the individual students, faculty members, and administrators; it is the responsibility of the graduate dean and the provost to invoke these remedies. Winbush moved in without regard for academic due process and with scant knowledge of the facts, which had not yet been gathered, and championed the students who had made the allegations. This interference increased the difficulty of resolution, and because it came from an important officer of the university, could not simply be passed off as improper advocacy to be regarded with indulgence. The graduate dean informed Winbush directly that his advocacy of the three students interfered with and interrupted due process and jeopardized fairness for all concerned. Ultimately a fair resolution was achieved, but only after the college of education and the graduate school together forced him to stay out of the situation.

In a second case, Winbush was improperly involved in a union staff grievance. The grievance was filed by a civil service employee represented by the Communications Workers of America (CWA). When grievances are filed in a union workplace there are clearly defined rules spelling out the processes to be followed. Of his own volition Winbush entered the dispute on behalf of the worker. This violated the union rules which were part of the union/university contract. It was seen by the union as disregard for due process on the part of a representative of the administration. Had others not intervened and extricated him from the situation there could have been another grievance filed, this one against the university. Instead, the union and the administration were able to resolve the issue politely.

Winbush also intruded in the search for a law school assistant dean. Among the candidates was an African American. The search committee, which consisted of both whites and minorities, concluded that the African-American candidate was not the person for the job. Winbush intervened, with the apparent purpose of trying to press the African-American candidate into the position. I brought to his attention the disabling effect of his intrusion, this time in a written memo which included the following: "It is manifestly improper for you or [would be] for me to intervene in such a way that there would be an appearance of upper echelon administration substituting their judgment in realms of professional performance potential for that of the professionals in the academic units. If, in your opinion there had been an abrogation of a proper affirmative search then your obligation was to bring it to me and I would have looked into it with the possibility of scrubbing the search and starting over." The affirmative action officer (a white woman married to a black staff member) was aware of the recommendations of the committee and had signed off on them.

Lastly Winbush prepared separate, additional contracts in order to pay already full-time university employees for services that other units of the university were established and responsible for providing. Full-time public employees of the state of Ohio must legally be paid for 100 percent of their time. It is against the law to pay a person more than 100 percent of what is stated in the contract or employment agreement, unless there is a valid exception that is properly authorized, such as a full-time faculty member teaching an overload in the place of a sick colleague. Obviously, the purpose of this constraint is to avoid side contracts that would pile up pay and benefits. Winbush made two such improper contracts. When the university officer responsible for the units that were established to provide the service that Winbush bypassed heard about it, he had no choice but to register strong objections.[2] Winbush did not respond seriously but simply said he had called a person in Columbus who said it was all right. He did not name the person.

These four major lapses in the conduct of university business (there were also other problems) were distracting but remained within the family of faculty and administrative staff. However, they exemplify the dilemma that had emerged. The integrity of a pluralistic university depends upon the fairness and equity of the processes of its operations and fidelity in carrying them out. If these processes are circumvented, subverted or rejected by a highly placed university officer, then a lack of confidence will set in. Clearly the motive for Winbush's spurning the carefully worked out methods of doing things was to advance the well-being of black students and staff. This is documented in the cited examples. But whether the interests might be appropriate or not, or whether their achievement might be unfair to others was not on the screen. This was not just the fault of Winbush himself. He was under pressure from segments of the black community in Cleveland to push the interests of blacks. Whether the means of doing this were right or wrong did not seem to be at issue. The well-being of the university in terms of its totality receded. Winbush was seen as an agent of change not accountable to rules made by a predominantly white organization. This was an extension of the Civic Committee's involvement in university affairs and illustrates the dangers that can emerge when an outside special interest group is permitted to intervene. But as I dealt with the problems generated by his office, I kept thinking that by continuing to work and reason with Winbush I could bring him around to function as a member of the larger university team. In this admittedly idealistic attempt I did not succeed.

THE TRUSTEE HUMAN RELATIONS AND MINORITY
AFFAIRS COMMITTEE REQUESTS A REPORT

During this period trustees on the Human Relations and Minority Affairs Committee of the board instructed Winbush to
"[P]repare data comparing retention rates of minority students at Cleveland State University with those at other universities and to develop quantitative goals in this area, for
presentation at a future meeting."[3] Winbush, along with the
person appointed to be his assistant vice president, Donna
Whyte, prepared a draft report entitled, "Some Goals of the
Office of Minority Affairs and Human Relations" which they
submitted to me to give to the board. It was not responsive to
the directive of the trustees and instead introduced a number
of ancillary issues. Had it been presented as a university document its polemics would have caused spasms. For example, the
parts dealing with affirmative action took issue with customary
methods used to assess the qualifications of candidates for positions at the university. "Veiled racism, narrow standards of
judgment, and inexperience with regard to cultural differences
often lie at the bottom of 'best qualified' arguments," it
claimed. "We believe that objective requirements such as degree status, publications and the like must remain as criteria
for academic appointments. . . . [but] we need to expand the
list of criteria to include factors that would enhance the intellectual strength of our departments, though these criteria are
often viewed as 'subjective'."[4]

This is a dangerous position with respect to maintaining
standards. Experience has shown that if extreme care is not
exerted the subjectivity factor can turn into a slippery slope
where academic standards decline. Intellectual strength is
not separate from discipline of thought. In terms of professional output it is measurable and objective. It is not subjective. In affirmative searches a rub exists between measuring
the cultural and social diversity of individual candidates and

evaluating hard-nosed, uncompromising discipline in subject matter. How is the balance achieved? Is a candidate with a superior professional background in the academic discipline involved passed over in favor of another person who would bring cultural diversity but less achievement in the discipline? In recruitment and assessment of candidates, savvy and sensitivity are required. Here, upper-tier, well-financed campuses have the advantage. They scour the marketplace for minority candidates who possess both accomplishment in their disciplines and diversity of cultural backgrounds. They have the money to outbid low-tier, mass-market campuses. This is another reality of upstairs-downstairs in academic life.

THE INFLUENCE OF AFFIRMATIVE ACTION OFFICERS

During the eighties and nineties affirmative action officers wielded considerable influence. They still do. On most campuses all documents related to searches in academic and non-academic units are sent to the affirmative action office. The widespread practice is that if, in the opinion of the affirmative action officer, sufficient effort has not been made to find qualified minority and female candidates, even if the department has decided on a candidate they want to hire, the affirmative action office can overrule the department and mandate that a new search begin. Ray Winbush wanted to bring the administration of affirmative action under his jurisdiction. He and Donna Whyte wrote in the draft "Goals" report that, "Plans should be to phase in the reporting of the Affirmative Action Office to the Office of Minority Affairs and Human Relations by the fall of 1990. . . . As stated in the CCRR (Civic Committee on Race Relations) on page 46, *The Affirmative Action Officer of the University is not actively involved in the recruitment process. The role is limited to voluntary advisement and certification.'*"[5] He then campaigned on campus to achieve control over the affirmative action office. There was no way I could agree to this, particularly given the bias that had been shown. There are examples elsewhere of a successful affirmative action office being part of a human relations and minority affairs operation. But this depends upon administrators sensitive to and knowledgeable about university affairs at large.

The tone and contentiousness of the report tended to put down the university in the context of racism. Unrealistic minority hiring goals were suggested, which even then, before the intensity of the current national debate and court rulings restricting affirmative action, would have been on shaky ground, for example, "We should set as a goal tripling the presence of African-American tenure-track faculty by fall quarter 1994."[6] Emphasis on African Americans to the exclusion of other minorities characterized many passages in the report. Other heavy-handed statements were scattered throughout the report. The chair of the Trustee Committee on Human Relations and Minority Affairs was the late Ruth Miller, a woman admired throughout Cleveland for her leadership and devotion to community affairs. A copy of the draft found its way to her. She scribbled a pithy note to me that had a touch of incredulity. "Did you authorize this?" I responded with a telephone call, "Are you kidding?" I spent more time than I could afford correcting the report but to no avail. The draft eventually fell by the wayside.

Subsequently the then president of Cleveland NAACP, the Reverend Marvin McMickle, weighed in. (I always admired McMickle for his steadfast involvement in community affairs, and still do.) Winbush's lawyer had demanded release of copies of correspondence and documents related to the Winbush matter. The draft report was included and sent to McMickle, who wrote an op-ed piece for the *Plain Dealer* entitled "What did CSU expect Winbush to do?" In it he took me to task for making corrections and revisions to the draft by saying, "Flower literally rewrote Winbush's long report on the operations of the Office of Minority Affairs and Human Relations and the job description for an assistant to Winbush. Such liberties with the written work of a colleague certainly trample on academic freedom."[7]

To invoke academic freedom in this instance was incorrect. It contradicted the noble meaning of academic freedom, which is meant to protect professors pursuing their scholarship. Winbush was not a professor. The draft report was not independent scholarship to which academic freedom would apply. Trustees asked him to write a report containing information they wanted. The report did not fulfill their charge. I would not have been doing my job unless I pointed this out and made corrections. If academic freedom is used as license to keep a supervisor from requiring that a staff member do his job, then logic and order in the conduct of university administrative affairs would collapse.

Questions can certainly be asked: Why was Winbush permitted to behave as he did? Why was he not taken aside and reasoned with? Why wasn't he told, in so many words, that his actions were unacceptable, that he was obligated to be a member of the administrative team? This is a predictable response from people in white organizations. Of course I told him he was off base, as did others, some of them successful middle-class blacks. But the newly partisan activists in the black community continued to pressure for black empowerment at CSU. They saw themselves as having achieved some success in that they had been instrumental in getting a black vice president installed. Winbush was a willing agent.

After the continuing mishaps between Winbush's office and a variety of CSU faculty and staff units, one of CSU's African-American trustees, the late Walter Burks, said to me that Winbush was not only causing problems on campus, but was speaking negatively against the university in the black community. He advised me to remove him. He said that there would be a brief reactionary flurry but that it would blow over.

TERMINATION

At this point, ten months into his incumbency and with the end of the academic year approaching, I had conducted discussions of their job performances with all the vice presidents, including Winbush. I was still working to achieve the goals we had set for the office of minority affairs. It was a new initiative and along with the trustees and others I wanted it to succeed. But quite apart from Winbush himself, in an environment where the black community's resentments toward CSU showed like exposed nerve endings, dealing with the conflicting issues was like balancing peas on a knife. Negative administrative treatment of a black vice president would be a controversial act whether or not it was justified by cause. This was my dilemma.

In a continuing series of notes, memoranda, and discussions over the preceding months, I had pointed out to Winbush that his actions exacerbated problems in race relations. I went considerably beyond a normal administrative limit in patience and tolerance simply because there was so much at stake. I had indicated that his contract for another year would be renewed ($95,000 plus a 2 percent cost-of-living raise) but without any increase for merit because my evaluation of his performance indicated he had not earned it. The salary was in any case high for someone without previous experience in such a position and higher than that of two other vice presidents with long seniority.

His response to this offer was to refuse it in writing, indicating he deserved a merit increase since the other vice presidents got them. This turned out to be the final straw. I believe it was a negotiating stratagem and that he expected me to come back with a counter offer, but after consulting with the trustees I let his refusal stand and withdrew the original contract offer, effectively terminating his employment. Subsequently I was criticized in the media and elsewhere for not presenting a counter offer and negotiating. What was never mentioned was the fact that I had already been negotiating with him for ten months, and that simply because other vice presidents had earned merit pay increases, he had not automatically earned one. It had become obvious that his termination was inevitable. His own agenda did not come close to matching the requisites of the position as it had been defined.

The conflict that followed was more than the struggle of a dismissed employee against his former employer, charging racism in a now familiar scenario. It was also the struggle of militant black leaders, not only against the predominantly white establishment at CSU, but also against the less militant sector of the black community. Although they did not give public voice to their thinking, many agreed that what Winbush was doing was harming the city, Cleveland State, and the black community itself. But once the polarization had begun, blacks who stood on middle ground, whether on the faculty or in the community, would not speak out against a fellow black.

PROFESSOR MAREYJOYCE GREEN

Following the contract nonrenewal which effected his termination (in some quarters referred to as his unjustified firing by Flower), it was necessary to conduct a search for a replacement. I appointed an interim vice president to serve while the search process went forward. This person was Mareyjoyce Green, a long-term faculty professor of sociology who was and continues to be deeply involved in women's issues on the CSU campus as head of the Women's Comprehensive Program. Green is a tolerant and steadfast member of the faculty who has devoted her professional life to Cleveland State. She is one of the few remaining faculty members who held an appointment at Fenn College before Cleveland State came into being as its successor campus.

She was treated shamefully by Winbush partisans, whose volatility had increased with his non-renewal, identified as "firing." Never one to use conflict to achieve her objectives, she presented an appearance and style which were the opposite of Winbush's combativeness. Parts of the black community acted as if she were a traitor to their cause, alternately sniping and snubbing. That this was not exactly gender-sensitive did not seem to occur to the male belligerents. Some members of the black clergy were not above this sort of response. Through it all Green retained her composure, never once sliding into defensiveness.

When she passes from this life into the next, she will be greeted by Saint Peter and her goodness rewarded by being ushered through the pearly gates with no delay. Similar treatment may not be accorded some of those ordained ministers of the Gospel who forgot the message of the Sermon on the Mount. Saint Peter can be expected to delay their entry for a period of atonement.

THE PROTEST

The actual protest, which came on June 28, 1990, was a summer-long sit-in in a building known as Fenn Tower (the oldest university building), which housed mainly administrative offices, including mine. Eight or ten protesters set upon my office and demanded Winbush's reinstatement. They were willing to negotiate, but Winbush's reinstatement was a non-negotiable prerequisite. This I could not and would not do. The protesters left after two hours of fruitless haranguing and began their sit-in in the lobby.

To avoid additional tension, we chose to let the students

stay in the lobby, since it was during the summer session, when the traffic in the building was much lighter than during the academic year. After some uncomfortable days in the marble lobby, some of the protesters, no longer students only but also some hangers-on, moved to the cafeteria area on the third floor where they created a kind of dormitory. It was my hope that we could defuse the situation with our willingness to discuss any issue, without however yielding on the main one, the reinstatement of Winbush. Winbush also took part in the protest. He must have realized that my decision, endorsed by the trustees, was irrevocable. The participation of Black Muslim organizations was welcomed, including such people as the adherents of Louis Farrakhan. Posters and placards cluttering the lobby and other walls, as well as trucks with loudspeakers up and down Euclid Avenue outside Fenn Tower, called for my removal.

Representatives of the Southern Christian Leadership Conference, a group prominent in civil rights at the time of Dr. Martin Luther King Jr., called a press conference and accused CSU of "institutional racism." I understood that Jesse Jackson was approached about coming to Cleveland. Apparently he was willing but the protest leadership did not have the money to pay his fee. It was useless to point out that what was taking place was injuring the university and the community, and that if a member of any other race had been fired or not reappointed because of unjustified and presumptive job performance, there would not have been a hiccup of objection or notice of it taken in the media. As it was, during the summer of 1990 when this protest reached its climax, all four local television stations carried daily reports on what took place. During three months the *Plain Dealer* carried more than a hundred stories, many on the front page, written by no fewer than twenty-four different reporters, as well as editorials, opinion pieces, letters to the editor and the like.

The media churned out material and treated it as a major racial news story, which in turn magnified the event itself. In such circumstances, reasoned discourse becomes impossible and facts are invented and given currency.

At one point, in what had become more than just an irritating disruption of campus educational activities, I agreed to a meeting presided over by two local U.S. Representatives, Mary Rose Oakar and Louis Stokes. It was agreed that it would take place place among principals only, namely Winbush and his attorney, the University's senior administrators, and the two Congresspersons. Its location (provided by the Cleveland Foundation) was not made public. But Winbush's supporters showed up and contributed only noise and distraction to the proceedings. The meeting took seven hours and accomplished nothing, as could have been predicted.

MAYOR MICHAEL WHITE AND STATE SENATOR JEFFREY JOHNSON

The Winbush episode revealed Mayor Michael White's finger in the political winds.

Right after the decision had been made not to renew Winbush's contract and before the mounds of invective resulting from it piled on, I gave White a call, told him we were not going to renew Winbush's contract and that it could be expected to have repercussions in the black community. I phoned on a Sunday night from our Bratenahl condominium; the call is still fresh in my mind. White responded, somewhat lightly, by saying in essence that sometimes what one has to do will be accompanied with a fight and that this is part of the deal. In our conversation he did not seem to take the issue that seriously.

He had been elected the mayor of Cleveland, not so much because voters possessed that high an opinion of him as city councilman and state senator, but because of the vehemently negative opinion the public held for his opponent, George Forbes. Following his first election as mayor, White served for twelve years—the longest tenure of any mayor in Cleveland's history. There were authentically brilliant moments during his years of service, along with many other less felicitous occasions. What his legacy will be remains to be seen, but he left many messes for his successor, Jane Campbell, to deal with. (Campbell was a CSU student with whom I worked closely when I was provost, twenty-five years ago. I am proud of her.) The way White dealt with the Winbush issue presaged the less desirable aspects of White's mayorality, in my opinion.

After our telephone conversation that Sunday night, the Winbush controversy heated up. Racial and ideological battle lines formed and White began to feel the heat. He was pressured to take a stand. Up to that point he had been very supportive of me in my role as president of CSU, where he made a segment of a public relations video preparatory to the launching of a capital campaign. With eloquence he lauded my leadership.

All of this changed abruptly. As a still newly elected mayor, he had not yet solidified his voter base. Clearly, after surveying the lay of the land, he decided that his political future would benefit more from an alignment on the Winbush side of the fence than the CSU–Flower side. On July 14, 1990 he let loose a blast in the *Plain Dealer.* The article said that "Mayor Michael R. White yesterday charged Cleveland State University officials with being racially insensitive and uncompromising in what he called their unfair and unjustified firing of the university's vice president for minority affairs and human relations. . . . White called for federal and state investigations of the university's handling of the 'Winbush matter' and of its commitment to the inclusion of all of our citizens, regardless of race, creed or color into university activities."[8] Nothing came of this other than gaudy rhetoric from the mayor.

Just the week before, then-State Senator Jeffrey Johnson of Cleveland tried to start a campaign to withhold state funds from CSU. At a news conference he declaimed that "Cleveland State University does not deserve one dollar of taxpayer's money if it cannot represent the 50 percent of this city and 27 percent of this county which is minority."[9] He said he would start a committee of black elected officials from around Cuyahoga County to investigate the release of Winbush and also whether "CSU has begun to implement any of the recommendations of the Greater Cleveland Roundtable [Civic Committee] two-and-a-half years ago."[10]

This was the same Jeffrey Johnson who was later tried, convicted, and served time in prison for three counts of extortion by a public official, which rendered him a convicted felon ineligible to hold elected public office again.

OHIO GOVERNOR RICHARD CELESTE

I was never all that sure whether Dick Celeste did or did not cotton to me. During his years as governor he played the part of the consummate politician, which is code, meaning that political expediencies devour personal loyalties and friendships. Celeste is not unique. He simply belongs to the ranks of thousands of other local, state and national politicians for whom political relationships, as contrasted to friendships, are the principal order of business.

The first time I found myself crosswise with the governor was shortly after I was appointed CSU president and had published a *Plain Dealer* op-ed piece about budget problems in Ohio higher education. I suggested some ways of dealing with the issues (which in fact turned out to be what actually happened) but which did not square with what the governor had in mind at the moment. When he read my piece he called me on the phone and delivered an excoriating riot act. Word of this got around—to the amusement of some and maybe a bit to the embarrassment of others, (the Board of Regents in particular)—that the governor did not show more restraint. However, he did not forget.

My inauguration as president took place not long after. It was a fine affair at the newly renovated Palace Theater and included all manner of people and dignitaries—but conspicuously no governor, who had of course been invited. The much-read *Plain Dealer* gossip columnist, the late Mary Strassmeyer, noted his absence in her column. She speculated that the governor was having lunch with George Forbes because maybe George might give him a job sometime. Actually Forbes was much in evidence at the inauguration and when his time came to speak he called me John "Flower**S**." When my turn came I referred to him as Mr. "For**B**." Those present loved it. Concerning the governor—he was snubbing me.

My next personal encounter with Dick Celeste came during the Winbush affair and was much more serious. More than one group had called for Celeste's intervention in the issue, which had been simmering and actively bubbling for two months. It was the last week in August, 1990. On the late afternoon of August 23, Celeste met with six protesters. Coincidentally this meeting took place just hours after then-Senator Johnson and venerable Cleveland Councilwoman Fannie Lewis, along with nine other protesters, were arrested for violating a court order prohibiting demonstrating inside Cleveland's Tower City Center. (They spent the night in jail.) According to the *Plain Dealer* article the next day the governor "[Issued] a statement that 'racism is a reality' at the university." The article went on to say, "Meanwhile President John Flower, who dismissed Winbush as Vice President for Minority Affairs, issued a '10 point action agenda' to address minority issues at the university."[11]

The next day, in his characteristic straightforward and blunt way, my executive vice president, the redoubtable Jan Muczyk, took issue with Celeste in a *Plain Dealer* interview by saying, "I think any politician stepping in at this point is undue political influence," and, "I firmly believe the autonomy of the university, even a state institution, should be protected from undue political influence."[12] Predictably Muczyk absorbed a personal gubernatorial fusillade.

On the 26th the *Plain Dealer* let fly with a counter-attacking editorial entitled, "Thank you, Gov. Kneecapper." The first paragraph took a verbal bungee jump by saying, "Celeste emerged [after meeting with six protesters] to announce that 'racism is a reality' at Cleveland State, that there are institutional problems, and that the impact of racism is real and oppressive. Having said that, Celeste admitted he hadn't talked to the trustees yet—but added that he planned to. Thanks for the enlightenment Governor. You may now sit down. And while you're sitting there, wait to see from which direction the next political breeze wafts. . . . No one denies that CSU—or any institution here for that matter, doesn't have problems with racism. To say that racism is a reality is like saying that carbon dioxide is an element of the air we breathe."[13]

Celeste did meet with the trustees on August 27th—from which he specifically excluded me—but nothing came of it. (Earlier he had summoned me to meet with him in his office in Columbus. Afterward I could never figure out why. The conversation went nowhere. His only sentence that I remember was that he was worried that someone in one of these demonstrations might carry a lead pipe.) After he finished his term our paths crossed a few times. The interactions were cordial. I think his subsequent role as Ambassador to India during the Clinton administration was a distinguished episode in his public life. He assumed the presidency of Colorado College in July of 2002. He will do well in his role.

THE KEVIN MACKEY AFFAIR

In the meantime another temblor took place from a different direction, but which some connected to the Winbush Affair. CSU's head basketball coach, the colorful and game-winning Kevin Mackey (in the NCAA national championship tournament he had brought the team into the "Sweet Sixteen"), was arrested outside a suspected crackhouse in the company of a woman who had previously been arrested a number of times on prostitution charges. Mackey was subsequently indicted for cocaine use and drunk driving. He pleaded no contest, and received a suspended sentence with a proviso that he undergo treatment for drug and alcohol use, which he did. A week after the arrest and after he had been accorded due process within the university I fired him. The issue was clear. In universities coaches of student athletes are supposed to set examples for their students. His behavior had destroyed his veracity on campus, despite his "run and stun" success on the basketball court. The term used today to describe a dismissal for such behavior is "zero tolerance," which in our lawsuit-oriented world can be a dangerous policy. Like every man in trouble, he deserved a second chance, which friends quite properly helped him get—but not at Cleveland State. Later he sued the university and me personally, contending that under federal statute alcoholism is recognized as a handicap and that he was discriminated against by virtue of his handicap. Ultimately the court dismissed his suit. This turmoil was tangential to the unfolding Winbush issue, but there was a potentially related aspect to it that caused bizarre speculation among kibitzers in Cleveland.

It went this way. It is reasonable to suppose that Mackey's

actions leading to his arrest did not happen only that one time. There would no doubt have been a pattern. It is also a reasonable assumption that given Mackey's visibility in the community, a number of streetwise people were aware of what he was up to. These same people can also be assumed to have known some of the activists in the Winbush affair. The speculation on the street could be paraphrased as follows: *Flower fired a black man (Winbush). He probably would not fire a popular white basketball coach (Mackey). If it could happen that Flower would have reason to fire Mackey, a white, but wouldn't, then this could be compared to the case of Winbush, a black, who already had been fired. There would be further reason to allege racism at the top of CSU. Ergo, Mackey was informed on so he would be arrested and the scenario could play out.*

Such convoluted circumstances fit better into a novel than in a narrative about a university. But the reason behind what happened to Mackey outside the suspected crackhouse fits the pattern of events at that time. It also points to the degradation of the academic missions of universities brought about by problems and pressures within Division I basketball programs.

OPERA BUFFA

At about this same time yet another episode took place, not tragic as with Kevin Mackey, but with elements that could fit into the plot of a comic opera. The late Carl Stokes, the first African American to have been elected mayor of a major American city (and as such a memorable Cleveland son), returned home from a TV anchor job in New York City. He was then elected municipal judge in Cleveland. He and I knew one another casually and had cordial relations. Out of the blue (but in the context of the Winbush affair), Stokes addressed an inflammatory letter to me which blistered my presidency and that of my predecessor, Walter Waetjen. He

demanded his name be removed from a $300 scholarship pro-
vided the law school by the Urban League. The reason, he
offered, using the term "malmanagement," was that the way I
was "running the school," was not responsive to "politicians
and their electorate," and because of "documented findings of
racism in the university's policies and practices." It would not
be unsporting to assume that the letter was more for the benefit of Stokes's electorate than for me. Before it could be delivered to me by mail, he released the letter to the *Plain Dealer*
where a story about it was printed at the top of the metro section and that's where I learned of it.

It so happened that Stokes was going through a divorce
at the time. My late wife Lanette was an attorney and held
the appointment of Chief Magistrate (then called referee) in
the Common Pleas Domestic Relations court. Unknown to
Stokes, his case had been assigned to her, which meant she
would be making determinations about alimony, property
distributions and the myriad disputed matters often part of
divorce cases. The assignment was announced just a few days
after the *Plain Dealer* had printed the story about his letter
lashing out at me. That Stokes was flummoxed by the assignment of his case to my wife is an understatement. The guf-
faws of courthouse lawyers could be heard from one end of
town to the other. Obviously Lanette recused herself.

COMING TO CLOSURE

In the meantime the moment was approaching when students
would be returning for the fall quarter (end of September).
The sit-in at Fenn Tower could not be allowed to continue.
The building held the admissions offices, the bursar, regis-
trar, and other offices central to registering new and returning students and necessary for opening a new academic year.
In addition, unsanitary conditions in the building were no
longer tolerable. Without previous announcement or ultima-

tums (which would only have reinvigorated the protest which, by that time, had dwindled) we decided to evict the protesters from the lobby. On the afternoon of September 25, the few remaining protesters were told by the executive vice president, Jan Muczyk, to leave with their belongings—which they did without incident. Cleaning crews went to work immediately. Their task was somewhat akin to Hercules cleaning out the Augean Stables.

In various places on campus there were some more protests and prayers interspersed with malodorous language and out-of-tune-singing. But we considered any further actions beyond reason and therefore obtained a court order restraining any further attempts to disrupt the orderly flow of business in campus buildings. Some defiant students who had again laid siege to my office were arrested. In the course of obtaining the restraining order, a reporter testified in court on behalf of the protesters—in direct violation of journalistic ethics—but he also revealed that at no time were the protesters even as many as fifty—this from a university community of approximately 20,000 students plus faculty and staff.

The entire episode had been manipulated by a small clique of experts in the art of protest, along with militants, opportunistic politicians, and some black clergymen who marched to a different·drummer. Their efforts were magnified because of the extended media coverage.

Throughout all of this, the CSU Trustees remained constant. The chairman, Henry Goodman, made every effort to be supportive. It certainly could have have been different. The position I took from the beginning—that Winbush had to go—which was followed by incessant and ugly protest, some of it directed at the trustees' places of business, could have motivated them to set me to one side in the hope of bringing about peace. But they did not follow this short-term easier way out. I appreciated their constancy. The trustees did take a practical course of action that usually succeeds in such circumstances, a buyout. They were concerned about the possibility of Winbush filing a lawsuit. For my part I did not participate in the buyout or its terms. Having been named in a variety of lawsuits over twenty years, in which none of the decisions went against me, I had learned not to stay awake at night because of them. Nor was I concerned about losing in this particular matter, but a lawsuit would have consumed inordinate time, energy, and money. The Trustees offered Winbush a year's salary plus $25,000 for his lawyer. To accomplish this it was necessary to get permission from the Attorney General of Ohio, which they did.

Winbush's response was equivocal. He made the offer public and expressed his repugnance, but did not refuse it out of hand. Eventually, however, he took the money and returned to Vanderbilt, which had been persuaded to take him back. (He ultimately left Vanderbilt, but stayed in Nashville and is now at Fisk.)

COMMENTS AT THE CITY CLUB

Before leaving town, Winbush spoke at the Cleveland City Club Forum, which is a venerable and tolerant organization that presents speakers of all backgrounds and views. I had appeared at the Forum the preceding week. I think people were expecting a final blast from Winbush, which did not come. Instead he spoke in somewhat subdued tones and did not mention CSU or me except in response to questions during the question-and-answer period. What made his final comments revealing was the following observation in the prepared text of his remarks: "Everyone knows what happened to me was sanctioned by powerful members of the black community." For those in the black community who he said sanctioned his removal, he used the term *compradores*, defining the term as meaning one who is bought. When asked who they were, he declined to name names. If his analysis was correct, this would imply strongly that a sufficient number of citizens within the black community came to believe that Winbush was damaging both the black community and Cleveland State. They ceased to support him. As a result the more militant cadre of blacks was neutralized by those who were closer to the center.

REFLECTIONS UPON THE WINBUSH AFFAIR

Any person in a high visibility position (being president of a large, urban public university inevitably makes one the focus of attention) learns how to deal with criticism and brickbats. But this racial contention was different from the normal run of adverse reaction and comment. The emotions were engulfing. Like being in a storm, you contend and struggle, but there is nothing you can do to make the storm go away.

And throughout this miscarried series of events with all of its purple rhetoric, my wife of forty-one years, Lanette, was fighting a losing battle with breast cancer. It had continued for five years. She died in September of 1991. As the University's first lady she had affection and respect.

The entire episode ate up endless hours of faculty and administrative staff time, disrupted the normal functioning of the university and did nothing to improve real or imagined racism. It fostered polarization rather than amelioration. It showed more than anything that university communities are not well equipped to deal with aggressive, political rhetoric promulgating racial dissent and grievances. Campuses, by their historic openness, are especially vulnerable to unscrupulous protest. Protest leaders orchestrated what happened at CSU with considerable skill, tapping into the black community's reservoir of emotional energy. A cadre of reporters did what some always have done and will continue to do—seize upon conflicting and contrary circumstances, newsworthy or not, and tabloidize them. I mean no disrespect for other reporters who, when they find suspect situations, do authentic and tough investigative reporting, thereby uncovering and shedding light on corruption. They are a bastion of strength in guaranteeing openness of information. But when reporters and editors, as in this case, sensationalize circumstances for the sake of creating headline stories, it not only becomes a nuisance but magnifies the problems themselves and increases the difficulty of finding solutions.

Winbush is a man with the same range of emotions that make us all human beings. His performance was not totally bad, nor that of the university totally good. But the circumstances made for a lose-lose situation. No one involved was covered with glory. For most mainstream whites, including many white members of the CSU family, coping with accusations of racism is difficult. They see themselves perceived to be guilty simply because of being accused. Most white Americans do whatever they can to avoid such situations. In public, even when they disagree with the behavior of blacks, they will utter palliatives. They would not behave or talk similarly toward others whose behavior they disagree with, if those others are white. Political correctness thrives in this climate.

A GREATER PROBLEM

What I believe to be a much greater problem than this, however, is a clash of cultures wherein actions that most mainstream Americans would label as wrong are deemed tolerable by some contending minorities. Earlier I outlined four situations involving academic operations that in part led to the nonrenewal of Ray Winbush's contract by the university. Whether they had been done by a black person or a white,

these dealings were manifestly unacceptable. They disregarded fairness to all who were involved. However, in these
particular circumstances his actions were upheld and justified by his partisans. For example, the Reverend Marvin
McMickle, in his op-ed piece for the *Plain Dealer*, sanctioned
Winbush's behavior when he said Winbush was "found
guilty of doing his job." Rev. McMickle was not being dishonest. He truly believed that CSU needed to be changed in
order to meet the conditions and recommendation set forth
in the Civic Committee report. The essential question not
answered, however, was: How did ethics relate to the means
put forth to accomplish the changes? The Civic Committee
report was somehow misperceived as a mini Magna Carta on
behalf of blacks versus CSU—which it was far from being. In
today's world, carrying out some of its recommendations in
order to benefit blacks would violate the U.S. Constitution.
Somehow Winbush was seen as having unlimited license.
This posture illustrates a social dilemma in the realm of individual and group behavior attached to racial matters between
blacks and whites in America.

It of course is a moral issue. When the behavior meant to
correct perceived wrongs involves transgressing established
standards, do you condone it in order to create advantage for
a previously disadvantaged group? Classic civil disobedience
identifies accountability, along with a recognition that one
pays the price for wrongdoing even if it is done for the noble
purpose of correcting injustice, or perceived injustice. This
has never been expressed more eloquently than in the letter
Dr. Martin Luther King wrote from the Birmingham jail:
"In no sense do I advocate evading or defying the law as
would the rabid segregationist. That would lead to anarchy.
One who breaks an unjust law must do so openly, lovingly,
and with a willingness to accept the penalty."[14] This accountability was missing in the Winbush matter. His partisans

wanted impunity. The national debate on affirmative action and racial preferences emerges from this clash of cultures. We are not even close to arriving at a national consensus. Actually we may be moving further from it if studies that point to an increasing tendency toward resegregation across the nation are correct. This is why, as the Winbush affair demonstrated, universities are so vulnerable to the intrusion of racial politics. It is why racial politics is a more crucial issue on university campuses today than it was a decade ago.

THE CORNEL WEST AFFAIR AT HARVARD

Nothing illustrates this more pungently than the controversy that erupted in January of 2002 between the African-American Professor Cornel West of Harvard and its president, Lawrence H. Summers. This conflict received wide coverage in newspapers across the country and has denuded hillsides of trees in order to provide necessary newsprint.

West, who taught previously at Princeton (and has now returned), is a well-known scholar who held the exalted title of "University Professor" at Harvard. He has written and contributed to twenty books. In recent years Dr. West diverted his academic energies, advising Al Sharpton in his presidential bid, and recording a rap CD. He had been criticized for "[U]ncritical grading practices (that) have contributed to Harvard's serious grade inflation problem,"[15] where over half of all grades are As. Summers, still relatively new in his presidency, had met periodically with professors in different departments. In conferring with West, the president apparently urged West to, "[E]ngage in more scholarly research and join in the battle against grade inflation,"[16] which of course could be inferred as criticism of his recent performance. Indeed, it was taken by West as disrespect and as an insult. He threatened to leave Harvard and return to Princeton, possibly with a few colleagues. (With Professor

K. Anthony Appiah he has now carried out that threat and departed. Appiah, a highly respected scholar, had previously taught at Princeton, but in returning gave no indication that the West contretemps influenced his decision.)

Along came Messrs. Jesse Jackson and Al Sharpton. In his column "Politics and People," Albert R. Hunt of the *Wall Street Journal* asserted, "Enter the civil rights 'leaders.' Mr. Jackson, charging (that) Professor West felt "violated," (and) demanded to see President Summers. Mr. Sharpton, claiming that Mr. Summers's chastisement of Mr. West could 'intimidate' African Americans, threatened to sue Harvard. Both questioned the commitment of (President) Larry Summers—Treasury Secretary in the Clinton administration—to affirmative action."[17]

After an unsuccessful fence-mending meeting with the president, Cornel West in an interview said that, "even though the conversation had ended in a spirit of 'mutual respect,' he was still considering leaving because 'once you're unsettled, you begin to think about other places.' "[18] Much about the above portrayal of hurt African-American feelings has resonance, particularly as it relates to racial preferences. Gerald L. Early, Professor of English and African-American Studies at Washington University, is quoted in the *New York Times*: "This is precisely the sort of insecurity that plays out around affirmative action: did I get this job, or did I get into this college because of merit or race? Do people see me as an equal, or as an 'affirmative action case?' "[19]

But how about West as a scholar? I have certainly not read all twenty books he has written or collaborated in writing, but I have looked into several and read what should be representative of his thinking and writing. Early on, his writings in philosophy were dialectical and abstruse. More recently he has been partisan. I thought, if these books were not written by Cornel West, an African-American with a great knack (just like Al Sharpton) for becoming well known, would people pay that much attention to them? I am not alone in my reaction. In a *Newsweek* piece generated by the Summers West controversy, Fareed Zakaria quotes Leon Wieseltier writing in the *New Republic* about West's books, "They are almost completely worthless . . . noisy, tedious, slippery . . . sectarian, humorless, pedantic and self endeared."[20]

This opinion leads directly to the crux of the issue which the African-American Shelby Steele set forth in the *Wall Street Journal* op-ed piece, "White Guilt = Black Power." Steele is controversial, but he can never be faulted for his intellectual credentials nor for the impact and clarity of his presentations. Mr. Steele says:

> Harvard's new president, Lawrence Summers is reported to have rebuked arguably the most famous professor in the university's well known, *if undistinguished*, [Italics mine] Afro-American Studies Department—Cornel West. Even on their face, the reported charges behind this rebuke seem screamingly true—that Mr. West is an academic lightweight, that his service to Al Sharpton's presidential campaign and his recording of a rap CD embarrass his professorship, and that his grading practices have contributed to Harvard's serious grading inflation problem. . . .
>
> With this sensible rebuke, there has begun an elaborate, if predictable, choreography of black indignation and white guilt. . . .
>
> The black power brokers have told Mr. Summers that he does not have authority to say what he sees when he looks at Mr. West. . . . The muteness that white guilt imposes on whites undergirds black power. . . . And when whites are silent, black mediocrity is no deterrent to black advancement. . . .
>
> Everywhere that minorities press institutions today as

groups, there is an erosion of excellence. The reason for this is that white guilt allows institutions to respond only with deference—deferring to the greater *moral authority* [italics mine] of minorities by lowering standards, and remaining mute to minority mediocrity, to save the institution from the racist label.[21]

There is another twist. Dr. Summers has been criticized because he took it upon himself, as the president of Harvard University, to advise and criticize the performance of West, a tenured university professor who reports to him. Another Harvard professor (who remained anonymous) told the *Chronicle of Higher Education*, "Once someone's a tenured professor, if he wants to write articles for the *Wall Street Journal* and the *New York Times* instead of doing his scholarship, he has every right to do so. . . . Once someone is a tenured professor they answer only to God. Its as simple as that."[22] I do not know who this Harvard professor might be, but would love to sit down with him(?) and discuss issues of tenure. It's no wonder the general public, reading similar cynical statements, judges professorial tenure negatively. Does a university president not have the right to sit down with a colleague, even one who possesses an exalted title, and express opinions about that professor's performance? As president of Cleveland State (a university whose reputation is not comparable to the eminence of Harvard), I was pilloried for being critical of a black colleague who was neither a faculty member nor tenured.

The Cornel West episode took place on the campus of one of the strongest and greatest universities in the world— at the top of the stairs. It came twelve years after the Winbush affair at Cleveland State, further down the stairs—a lower tier mass-market campus with high energy, high hopes, and ambitions to be realized. But the racial dynamics are the same. The Al Sharptons and Jesse Jacksons are not about to go away. It will be years, perhaps generations, before these racially based academic misadventures no longer occur. They have no relevance to the real problems of minorities in inner cities—crime, drugs, poverty, and disenfranchisement.

Closure and New Beginnings

I was in my seventy-first year in 1991 when, counting student days, my active time on university campuses passed the half-century mark. Some leftover choler from the Winbush controversy remained in corners of the CSU campus, but circumstances were returning to normal. I was able to preside over the appointment of Winbush's successor, an accomplished woman of color who is successful in her role at Cleveland State and is doing creative work. (Quite incidentally she married a white professor who used to be a firebrand and was addicted to awful clothes. She has calmed him down and, of all things, he now wears suits.)

Clearly the time for retirement was at hand. Lanette had passed away in September of 1991, her bout with breast cancer ending our forty-one years of marriage. Her presence in my life strengthened my being.

I retired from the CSU presidency on July 1, 1992, but stepped into the CSU Foundation presidency to serve for two years as a bridge until a new administration was in place. Concurrent with these changes I was offered, and accepted on a part-time basis, the executive directorship of the Northeast Ohio Council on Higher Education (at that time the Cleveland Commission on Higher Education). This is a consortium of twenty-two northeast Ohio colleges and universities which fosters cooperation between campuses and interacts with the business community to connect campus academic programs with the needs of businesses. I worked with the presidents and operational officers of these colleges and universities for eight years. It was a felicitous experience. My life was reinvigorated during this time: Maxeen Joy Stone (to whom this book is dedicated) and I were married. That we found one another was one of those events that could not have been blue-printed. Maxeen accepts none—absolutely none—of the conventional wisdom and mythology about the impacts of chronological age on an individual. To her, a person is endlessly fresh, an attitude she requires of me, leaving little chance of compromise on my part.

THE SELECTION OF MY SUCCESSOR

In almost exponential ways the presidential search process for my successor exemplified problems that can emerge— and employing Murphy's Law will emerge—when special interest group politics intervenes in university affairs. (Something a retiring academic officer does not do is involve himself or herself in the appointment process of a successor. Nor did I. My recounting of the following episode is therefore anecdotal. I cannot produce particular citations substantiating it. But anyone who would want to verify it, even ten years after the fact, will have no problem doing so.)

The CSU Trustees conducted the presidential search and after doing all the right things came up with a final slate of three: a white woman, a black male, and a white male. Understandably, the intense racial issues surrounding Cleveland State during the preceding five years produced pressure for the appointment of a black president. Thus the trustee intent to appoint the black candidate on the final slate to succeed me was not unexpected. A board meeting was scheduled in accordance with state statute and the "sunshine law" to confirm the presidential appointment and announce it publicly.

Then, only hours before the board meeting was to begin, the black candidate withdrew. The attendant consternation and dismay of trustees, particularly the black membership, can only be imagined.

One cannot enter into the mind of the candidate, but it might appear that after he considered the pressures that would be exerted upon him by the more assertive members of Cleveland's black community, along with their possible expectation that he serve as "their representative" at CSU, he decided he wanted no more to do with it. Even though it was the eleventh hour he got out while the getting was good.

The black activists had overplayed their hand. They badly wanted and could have had a black CSU president (someday, obviously and appropriately, there will be a black president) but in this instance they blew it. Following a decorous period, the white woman was appointed. After eight years she is no longer in office. Her successor, the highly respected and accomplished former president of Kent State University, Michael Schwartz, was chosen from a slate of three white males.

CHAPTER 13

Problems in Shared Governance: How They Relate to Detached Professors and Their Disconnects in Teaching Students

It has been said that democracy is the worst form of government except all those other forms that have been tried from time to time.

Winston Churchill

A NOBLE PROCESS MISUSED

If Winston Churchill's famous aphorism was applied to university governance most faculty members, administrators, and staffers would agree with what he said. But that does not mean campus shared governance succeeds. State college and university presidents, along with trustees, confront demands for greater accountability. At the same time, faced with tightened tuition and tax-dollar support, they need to make adjustments within their organizations and management structures in order to cope with emerging forces. In the world of universities a major problem exists. The authority of presidents to accomplish necessary and difficult internal change is limited. Their decision-making and follow-up actions are compromised to an extent much greater than corporate CEOs. Chief among the reasons is faculty shared governance, a brooding omnipresence of proliferated management. The needs of today's complex and at the same time fast-moving world of university administration have outpaced the capacities of shared governance. As reported in the *Chronicle of Higher Education*, this thorny issue is addressed not only privately by campus presidents, but now the forebodings of the twenty members of the Commission on the Academic Presidency (sponsored by the Association of Governing Boards of Universities and Colleges) are being expressed publicly.[1]

A high-minded purpose motivated the American Association of University Professors when it crafted shared governance in the early decades of the twentieth century. It created mechanisms so that faculty members became involved in the management of campus affairs. In so doing, they could protect their rights, which heretofore had been subject to infringement by dictatorial presidents. Faculty unionism would have been as alien in those days as creatures from outer space, not only because the union movement as we know it today was still coalescing, but because faculty members then could not have fathomed transferring individual initiative to a collective union entity. Compared to what existed in the early days of the AAUP, this protection against arbitrary treatment by deans and presidents is no longer needed. Individual faculty rights are now protected by layer upon layer of state and federal statutes. Officials who abrogate these statutes or make procedural errors find themselves tied up in knots of litigation. But, spawned from out-of-date shared governance procedures, faculty committees with octopus-like tentacles continue. Of course the shoe can sometimes be on the other foot. Examples occur from time to time where a blockheaded president or university officer makes a decision, in the face of contrary advice by faculty members, which turns out to be absolutely wrong. The faculty was right, the administration wrong. In such situations the officer or officers should be held accountable, and to use another of Churchill's pithy phrases, the culprits "should be pole-axed" by the board of trustees. But too often the board itself is complicit.

CAMPUSES AND THE MARKETPLACE

In those less bureaucratic days a century ago most colleges and universities were private and had little dependence upon their surrounding communities. They catered to privileged Americans who provided support. Today, by contrast, the vast majority of public campuses cannot be separated from the marketplaces and special interest groups in their surrounding populations. Academic traditionalists decry this as being detrimental to campus integrity. They cite pressures from those who make up these diverse constituencies. For example, in matters of curriculum they point to a proliferation of so-called "culture studies" such as Hispanic studies, Afro-American studies, gay and lesbian studies, women's studies, all of which respond to pressure groups. This, they say, has caused a weakening of Western civilization courses as the backbone of undergraduate degree programs. They believe that in place of disciplined humanities, math and science regimens, a smorgasbord of courses has been cobbled together to make programs that cater to different cultures and vocations. The constituent groups will respond to this by saying, "That's right! The college has to listen to those who support it and act accordingly." These forces will not abate. The fact is irrefutable; accountability to the surrounding publics continues to grow. All of these arguments illustrate a small part of what the late Bill Readings of the Université de Montreal had in mind when he said that "It is no longer clear what the place of the university is within society nor what the nature of that society is."[2]

TIMELINESS OF RESPONDING

Because of increasing changes in the activities of our communities and an expansion of campus community relationships, campuses are sometimes forced into situations that require rapid responses, not so much involving curriculum or research work, but in management or planning issues such as, for example, property acquisition. The out-of-date forms of shared governance which function through committees, especially those dealing in budget issues, make timely responses difficult to impossible. Presidents find themselves in untenable situations, caught by faculties demanding their procedural share of governance, which as an abstract principle is understandable. The trouble is it flows like molasses that sometimes congeals.

In my more than fifty years as a faculty member and administrator, I spent what seemed like eons of gainless time in committee meetings. Not only does this sometimes endemic committee silliness gum up orderly processes but, due to bureaucracy and inefficiency, bureaucrats of all types (faculty, staff, and administrators) create paperwork that would fill up the Grand Canyon. The faculty members involved are forced to divert themselves from teaching and research. Equally destructive to reasonable management is the massive amount of money consumed (directly and indirectly) through committee bureaucracy, perhaps as much as 5 percent of a university's operational budget. For example, in medium-sized state universities of 15,000 to 20,000 students, with operational budgets of somewhere between $150 to $200 million, this could amount to more than $9 million, a good portion of which goes down the drain. Extrapolate that to hundreds of regional colleges and universities, varying in size from fewer than 5,000 up to 30,000 and more students (excluding the flagship group of state universities which present different management issues), the waste of student tuition and tax dollars adds up into the billions. This cannot be sustained when budgets are tightened.

DIFFERING VIEWS OF SHARED GOVERNANCE

Joan Wallach Scott, professor of social sciences at the Institute for Advanced Study in Princeton, took the opposite point of view in an opinion piece for the *Chronicle of Higher Education*.[3] The reasoning of defense is removed from public campus realities. This is not uncharacteristic of distinguished professors at the best campuses, who deliver homilies defending shared governance, and in so doing miss the mark by disregarding how shared governance is actually carried out on hundreds of regional state campuses by thousands of faculty members. They plead the praiseworthy concept of sharing governance between trustees, presidents, and faculty members, but ignore the distressing specifics of how this shambles of a system actually works. Her argument, which cites John Dewey, reflects the situation of a hundred years ago, when higher education was elite, mostly private, and, compared to current times represented a miniscule cut of the spectrum of U.S. citizenry. She suggests that John Dewey believed that, "without changes in knowledge, societies would not grow or move in new directions. Tenure and academic freedom exist to protect vulnerable faculty members from the 'intense emotional reactions' that Dewey thought characterized resistance to change."[4] Who can argue with that?

She is in the right church but the wrong pew. First, today's faculty members who are tenured are not vulnerable. They probably have more protections than any professional group. (Civil servants have ironclad job protection, but they do not have the freedom to establish their own work schedules and chart the direction of their personal careers to the extent professors do.) Second, changes that took place in curricula a hundred years ago were essentially in the realm of ideas, as for example in the classics and mathematics and the developing sciences. Today's pressures for programmatic changes in the hundreds of regional public universities are essentially practical and vocational. They bear a greater relationship to trade schools and vocational training, in other words the marketplace for jobs, than to the traditional university liberal arts curriculum. Governance processes that emerged from privileged ivory towers of a century ago cannot be translated verbatim into egalitarian, sometimes pungent and unsmooth public campuses.

Still another reason is that currently appointed faculty members are no longer culturally homogenous, but are diverse and even fractured, sometimes to the point of trauma. At Cleveland State, as provost and president, I regularly dealt with faculty members of broadly diverse ethnic backgrounds from within the United States and from Asia and the Middle East. Some had serious problems of personal adjustment, along with problems of verbal communication with their students. They do not and cannot be expected to behave like the Victorian holdover faculty members of a century ago. Neither do they as individuals have the heritage of the kind of collaborative behavior which is indispensable to shared governance. Not unusually a lack of the milk of human kindness is evident, replaced by a built-in adversariness. No wonder elements of disarray exist in regional public universities and community colleges.

Writers of articles about the cherished world of shared governance who hold appointments in medallion institutions (and there are lots of them, to say nothing of professors at mass-market institutions who yearn for posts at prestige campuses) do not understand the different realities of faculty participation in shared governance between the elite few and the democratic many. If Professor Joan Wallach Scott, a sociologist, were to address the nitty gritty of the reactions of diverse faculty types in the actual carrying out of shared governance, instead of concentrating upon the defense of its tradition in the abstract, her commentary would be more useful.

On the other hand, the lighthearted contribution made by Pennsylvania State English professor Michael Berube in a *Point of View* piece for the *Chronicle of Higher Education*, "Dither and Delay: Personalities of Faculty Committees," gets to the point with effectiveness.[5]

> I've begun to analyze the peculiar academic aversion to decision making and have come up with an interim list of four personality types who are sure to sandbag any decent committee. Only one of those is actually malevolent: the person who sits silently through a two-hour meeting, and then, as everyone is getting up to leave, delivers himself or herself of a single, orotund proclamation that effectively unravels whatever fragile consensus has hitherto been achieved. . . . The second type is the person who cannot recall from meeting to meeting, what has previously been agreed upon. That type is the natural prey of the first type. . . . The third faculty type is the advocate of multiplicity, who, after three months of deliberation, suggests it might be a good idea to submit to the provost *two* strategic plans, or maybe even three so as not to close down viable options (as if one plan weren't enough fodder for further administrative caviling down the line). . . . And the fourth type is the benign cousin of the first, who, just as the penultimate draft proposal has been circulated to all committee members (and maybe a friendly dean or two),

pipes up and says, 'You know, I've had very serious misgivings about this enterprise from the start . . . and frankly, I'm not even sure we should be drafting a proposal at all.'[6]

If only the legion of crabbed malcontents had the lightness of touch and deftness of characterization that Berube practices so expertly. His good-natured satire about shared governance as practiced by many faculty members produces an outline which those who know what goes on cannot gainsay. He disassembles the laments and the handwringing of the complainers. They refuse to recognize themselves in concert with the legions of egalitarian professors from mass-market campuses (but elsewhere too) in the practice of shared governance. In so doing they have tied it up in knots.

UNACKNOWLEDGED DIFFERENCES

There are vast differences in types between colleges and universities within both private and public sectors. These institutional differences derive from equally vast differences in the educational backgrounds and in the socializations of students and groups of faculty members. This follows inevitably from the widely varied experiences of students and faculties who come from different parts of the social, economic, and cultural worlds. These differences beget diverse institutional roles and missions which call for varied structures of governance. In the plethora of books and articles about the problems higher education faces, the nature of these many differences is insufficiently plumbed.

Historically the term "college education" had been reserved for the kind of study that educates students to think in the realm of abstract ideas and to understand, rationally and critically, universal human values. Throughout western history most individuals within the masses of humanity had little or no time and energy to reflect and conceptualize about universal values. This has not changed. If we accept it as valid that a university education should prepare students to think better, in addition to being trained in vocational skills, then a significant portion of today's curricula is not what universities have been dedicated to accomplishing since the Middle Ages. Much of American higher education suffers under the delusion that the vocational and training curricula now predominating over the humanities, sciences, and the arts represent authentic university-level work. This is a mistake which developed from our American "feel-good" syndrome. People don't want to call this a trade school function but want it referred to by the more exalted term university. But these campuses are not universities according to the historic meaning of the word. They are trade schools or at best polytechnics with smidgeons of the humanities. They are concerned more with *training* rather than with *educating*. This has been the emphasis since the end of World War II, the result of the practical needs of students enrolling in college under the G.I. Bill.

This in no way denigrates the human and economic value of training which is absolutely requisite in our information/knowledge society. But as American higher education evolved during the second half of the twentieth century, we mixed our categories. We like to subsume all training beyond high school under the umbrella of the university, including the nicely evocative title of McDonald's "Hamburger U." When compared to professors educating student minds in the verities of universal human values, faculty members who are dedicated to teaching students what to do to get better jobs work in a different world.

Cardinal Newman believed the function of the university curriculum was to teach students to be moral and better human beings. Elevating the mind through teaching the works of the best thinkers humankind has produced helps to achieve this. It requires time, reflection, and quietness on the part of students and faculty, which is why professors perceived themselves as removed from the marketplace and why campus governing authority sedulously avoided outside influences, often leading to town/gown problems. Clearly this kind of educational experience is not for all people. But our society somehow has promoted the notion that a traditional university experience should be for everybody. Many believe, however, that the nation would be better served if, instead of egalitarianizing that which has been traditionally elite, we should strive to inculcate humanistic values into the training that is necessary for students to get better jobs.

Despite the barrels of print media ink critical of higher education, embodying a significant change in national attitude toward higher education, there remains a mystique in the minds of the public that derives from the teens, twenties and thirties of the last century about what a college experience is. It comes from perceptions of so-called traditional students—attractive, ages eighteen to twenty-three, interacting with helpful faculty members and tutors, living on a nice campus in dormitories or fraternities and going to class, to parties and to football games on crisp, sunny days. It is definitely upperclass and upscale, which is what working classes and immigrants who had not gone to college wanted to provide their children—an upward thrust. The image came from well-off private campuses and what are now the flagship state universities. The limited world of state universities was expanded by the entry of normal schools, which were subsequently transformed into teachers' colleges, thence into state colleges, and finally into regional state universities. They were followed by trade/technical schools, whose courses of study influenced degree work at state colleges, further altering and leavening the state campus mix.

Student experiences today at these many hundreds of

institutions do not resemble the continuing and mistaken perception of upscale, upstairs identities. In place of homogenous groupings of white students and faculty members, newer campuses enroll students from every part of our society, as well as foreign students. "Nontraditional" students have become "traditional". They include women returning to school after rearing their children, divorcees seeking job skills, inadequately prepared high school graduates enrolled through open admissions, welfare mothers desperately trying to improve the lot of themselves and their families, tired and overworked fathers and mothers seeking job-skill improvement by enrolling at night and on weekends, trading off baby-sitting or rushing home after class to tend a sick child. Could one imagine the academic rigors and conceptual demands of, say, Columbia's famous undergraduate core course Literature-Humanities being visited upon this group of nontraditional students, many of whom have never mastered reading skills, to say nothing of writing? This explains the diverging roles and missions spread through contemporary campuses in all fifty states. Students by the millions are unprepared for the historic academic regimens. To cope with these masses of students in an academic setting requires skill and uncommon dedication on the part of individual faculty members.

TOP OF THE HEAP

On the other hand, at the upper tier of venerable and generously endowed private and hallmark state institutions, the agreeable environment described above still exists (transformed into a contemporary form), though diversity through affirmative action has somewhat changed its substance and complexion—not greatly, but somewhat. However, those upper-tier institutions enroll only a miniscule percentage of today's approximately 15 million college students. This small percentage of students is at the top of the heap. Their institutions on average spend many tens of thousands of dollars a year (in some examples beyond $100,000) on each individual student, compared to an average of about $12,000 at state schools. There is no such thing as open admissions in these elite and selective institutions. It would be inconceivable for students with only B or C high school grade point averages to enroll at Cal Tech, or that hordes of freshmen, through open admissions, could enroll at Williams College.

In like manner faculty members at upper-tier campuses are at the top of the heap. It is within these faculties, especially at professional and graduate schools, that the Nobel Laureates, the National Book Award and Pulitzer Prize winners hold appointments, and where advisors to presidents, cabinet members and other top publicly appointed figures are invited to teach. Here, faculty attitudes and postures about shared governance are considerably more casual. They don't always pay that much attention to it. There are obvious reasons for this.

A sizable proportion of these professors are supported by funds from endowments identified with chairs to which specific individuals have been appointed. These appointments are selective and meritocratic. The level of academic and professional accomplishment of upper-tier university endowed chairholders, who are an exalted class of professors, is the highest in the nation. The endowments provide the income to compensate the appointee, and by virtue of the dependability of the cash flow, furnish research and ancillary benefits to the chairholder. This guarantees freedom and independence from the central administration. Involvement in shared governance is casual (with inevitable exceptions here and there). It is nice but not a high priority. "My research comes first. That's why I'm here. Let the administration run the place." In addition, project and research-oriented faculty members, whose funds derive primarily from grant sources and not from university or college operating funds, function more on the order of individual entrepreneurs. They have worries other than shared governance. Also, the central administration usually feels somewhat beholden to them simply because of income from overhead and indirect recovery they generate for the university.

LOWER DOWN THE ACADEMIC TOTEM POLE

But at the hundreds upon hundreds of mass-market institutions, individual faculty members are much more dependent upon the central administration in matters relating to day-to-day campus affairs. Endowed chairs are few and far between. Further, they find themselves in an essentially homogenized, as opposed to a meritocratic, environment. They tend to see themselves as employees who deal with administration as management, where they are simply hired to teach X, Y, or Z courses as degree requirements or to fulfill credentials for students seeking jobs.

The noble idea of shared governance protecting the search for truth, as conceived by the AAUP in 1915, has degenerated. This shows up in public opinion of the professoriate. In November of 1999, the Gallup Poll surveyed 1,013 adults to determine their opinions about, "which professions best demonstrate high ethics and honesty?" (Thirty professional groups were identified.) College teachers came in tenth, with 52 percent of those surveyed believing college faculties demonstrate high ethics and honesty. Nurses, pharmacists, and veterinarians came in at the top, one, two, and three, at 73 percent, 69 percent, and 63 percent. Newspaper reporters, building contractors, and labor leaders sat on the bottom three rungs with a meager 19 percent, 18 percent, and 17 percent of those surveyed believing them to demonstrate ethics and honesty.[7] Developed earlier as a mechanism to achieve the ideals of shared governance, the faculty committee system has become an instrument of power, not to protect truth but to protect jobs. At many public universities, shared governance because of the misuse of its committee system is crushing needed campus change and adaptation.

As long as faculty members take the shortsighted view of themselves as employees rather than as academics for whom teaching is a high calling, shared governance will not improve. Faculties who see themselves as employees rather than as appointees would do better to emulate their counterparts in the industrial world and join quality circles, interacting with management to improve the accomplishments of employees and management. Quality circles in the corporate world have a better record than campus shared governance in achieving improvement.

There is logic in proceeding with a shared governance system conceived for faculty as appointees. As such they are legitimately a part of governance. But when faculty members behave not as accountable members of a shared higher education enterprise, but as hired employees merchandizing their skills, shared governance breaks down. Given today's forces this will continue to bring undesirable results.

PROFS AND THE STREET

Never in the more than three hundred fifty year history of American higher education has it been as important as it is today for professors who teach the liberal arts to understand the different forces which drive the nation. Because of the varied resources of our national communications systems, these forces—political, religious, business, social, educational, ethnic, racial among others—can generate a broader and potentially more effective base of human interactions than ever before. Misused, these communicative forces can also erode our ethical and moral base. Professors are positioned to demonstrate the relationships between these forces. To do this it is necessary to step aside from the lectern, the seminar room or academic computer terminal and interact with realities beyond the university, rather than just the ones inside. In a professional world as complex and varied as the one professors inhabit, this cannot be accomplished simply by generalizing. Specifics must be dealt with. Three issues are involved.

The first consists of those professors who are themselves trained (and frequently have "hands-on" experience) in fields where there is a professional and technical constituency beyond that of the college or university. Some examples of these fields are business administration, engineering, computer technology, and journalism, along with the myriad other business and technical fields making up today's professions. Usually academic programs in these fields are clustered on campuses within so-called professional departments and units. Some professors in these programs identify, through consulting work or other involvements, with their professions as practiced beyond the campus, usually to the benefit of both. Examples do exist where a professor's lucrative consulting contracts get in the way of teaching responsibilities. A fine line exists here between teaching responsibility and professional responsibility. It becomes counterproductive for the university when professors neglect responsibilities to students in order to pocket extra consulting fees. Faculties have not done a good job of monitoring and controlling excesses in outside consulting or outside business involvements by some of their members. But at the same time it is extremely important that professors interact with their colleagues who practice their disciplines in the marketplace beyond campus borders, simply so they know what is going on in their fields.

With the emergence of E-commerce and the internet bonanzas in the late nineties a cadre of professors have combined their computer science knowledge with surpassing entrepreneurial skill and created high-tech companies that have made them millionaires many times over. A significant number retain their professorships, dubbed their "day jobs." The March 3, 2000 issue of the *Chronicle of Higher Education* devotes a cover article to this spellbinding story.[8] Profiles of some of these individuals, most quite young, who have amassed great individual wealth, covered aspects of their dual lives between business and the university. All said they wanted to retain their academic involvements but admitted that their businesses encroach upon their professorships. These academics have created a new paradigm by virtue of the massive assets they have created and obviously are not beholden to the same rules that an $80,000 a year professor of management is held to when he consults with the local seed company. The debacles encountered by dot-com companies at the turn of millennium have reduced the entrepreneurial opportunities to make vast sums of money, but in our innovative, high-tech world there will always be some who succeed sensationally.

The second issue comes under the heading of human health and human help programs of which there are two broad types: the scores of "allied health" programs (so called to separate them from those preparing doctors of medicine, dentistry, and veterinary medicine), and the broad array of community interactive programs developed to help poor and disadvantaged people learn how to help themselves and adjust to our complex and demanding society. Those within the first type involve educating and training, for example, physical therapists, X-ray technicians, occupational therapists, various kinds of nursing specialists, along with those in many other fields related to medicine. The second grouping consists of social service fields, the substance of which cannot be separated from the human behaviors and pathologies that collectively add up to the ills of our society. Within this second category there are individual and community interactions through hands-on involvements by faculty and students.

These human health and help programs emerged as college-level degree and associate degree programs in the period after World War II. The extent of the efforts of faculties and students to help people in direct ways illuminates their dedication to service. They know they will never make much money, but they believe in what they are doing and hold constant.

K THROUGH 12

Through student teaching assignments, primary and secondary schools are part of undergraduate programming in colleges of education. This compares to the community involvement on the part of human health and human help programs alluded to above. Education faculties are generally conversant with the issues and problems of the schools. Today's monumental problems in the schools do not stem from lack of university faculty involvement in the public schools, or from the insensitivity of state bureaucratic curriculum code requirements, but from the depth and dimension of the human problems that disadvantaged children from inner cities bring to school with them. While school boards in most big cities have been notoriously lacking in civil discourse, and display incompetence and sometimes corruption, these shortcomings do not alone account for the terrible state of our urban and inner-city schools. The basic reason is the large component of disadvantaged students who are not actually part of the American system and its values. They are not related to our society in the same way that students were who grew up in neighborhoods during years gone by when drug dealers did not frequent street corners and when students were not in the habit of bringing guns and knives to school. Since our schools and their curricula come from the values that shaped America, the gulf between the disadvantaged and disconnected students thus far has been insurmountable. And yet our citizens expect these underclass problems to be solved by the schools and criticize them for not doing so. This is manifestly unfair. As a nation we have not faced up to the problems. We throw money and bureaucratic programs at them but we have not girded our loins, individually or collectively, to confront the human problems.

THE LIBERAL ARTS AND CONNECTIVITY TO THE CITIZENRY

Now we come to the third issue, that of university liberal arts teaching faculties being involved with citizens at large and thereby being connected to the forces that move our society. For the most part they are too much removed from what is going on in the world outside of academe. It can be forcefully argued that teaching the liberal arts and sciences is more important now than ever before. The meaning of the term liberal includes being liberated from our own prejudices. Our citizenry needs broadened perspectives in order to make reasoned judgments about the complex issues confronting the nation. Today, the reach of democracy into the populace is broader than yesterday. In the nation's earlier days, a type of representative government different from our present, popular form of democracy wove our national fabric. Senators were not popularly elected nor were women allowed to vote. "Negroes" were disenfranchised. The nation's leaders represented a much smaller cut of the national socioeconomic spectrum. Mostly, though certainly not always, they came from privileged eastern seaboard families. As the nation moved westward, the more rough and tumble aspects of democracy asserted themselves. Increasingly, citizens expressed dissatisfaction with twice or thrice removed representation, and pushed for more direct involvement in their government. Today an equivalent of this hands-on citizen involvement is the plebiscite, which various states are perfecting as one of the instruments of governance. As a nation we will never return to the kind of representative government where elected officials can statutorily be once or several times removed from citizens. A counterforce to the increasing democratization has been created in the growth of appointed officials in federal and state governments and in the bureaucracies surrounding them. The actions of this officialdom, such as that exercised by regulatory agencies, has in many ways exacerbated the sense of citizens being removed from the processes of government. This is one of the causes for the increasing use of plebiscites. It is against this backdrop of the expanding enfranchisement for all types of U.S. citizens that humanities and liberal arts faculties should do their teaching in mass-market campuses. It is axiomatic that as a nation, if we are to be governed by involved citizens, the more enlightened the citizenry, the greater the chances for effective governance.

How well are humanities faculties on these mass-market campuses doing to help students achieve this enlightenment? Poorly, very poorly.

Crosscurrents roil enlightened expression, from Asian Indian philosophy to that of Western civilization's "dead white males;" from Judeo-Christian thought to that of Zen Buddhism; from feminists to third world Nobel Laureates. Enlightened thinking is just that—enlightened thinking— regardless of its source. But too many humanities departments substitute political correctness in the presentation of literature through an emphasis on gender, or racial and ethnic issues regardless of whether or not the literature deserves to be included on its merit.

Academic concern for diversity explains this. Teachers of the liberal arts now must identify with all categories of citizens, not just those with an elite background. Privileged people are no longer the only ones going to college. Neither are they the only citizens who should be expected to be concerned about and understand universal human values. This is inherently true for everybody who has a functioning mind and conscience. Faculties have tended to segment the applicability of the liberal arts to the privileged components of society. This is not necessarily done consciously, but simply because it is so much easier to teach the liberal arts to students who come from privileged backgrounds. It is much more difficult to explain abstract concepts involving truth and beauty to a student from the inner city worried about getting shot at in the home neighborhood than to a student from a suburban community whose home has books in it. In like manner first generation college students whose parents are working class and whose desire is to rise on the socioeconomic ladder, want something practical that has value in the job market, not something abstract. Because the dizzying pace of technical change makes the job market changeable it is precisely more important than ever before to teach students how to think and adapt. Training in tangible skills for a specific purpose will not do this unrelated to larger issues.

MARKETABLE SKILLS VERSUS TIME-TESTED PRINCIPALS

This is our problem. We must train students in today's specific skills, but we must also educate them in time-tested basic human principles from western, eastern, and third world civilizations. It is extremely difficult to teach the values of critical and objective thinking to students who are conditioned by Damocles' sword of economic survival hanging over them. But we must learn how to do it. It is a safe hypothesis to say that college education will become even more democratized than it is now. We must, therefore—we absolutely must—see to it that the curricula in our increasingly democratized colleges, both two-year and four-year, are not relegated to technical education only, but to education that seeks the truth in value and idea. It can come from east, west, north, south. It must convey to all of our students basic concepts of humanity, and basic disciplines in thinking. Cultural relativists, and postmodernists who profess that the truth is not absolute but merely relative, will decry this as being hopelessly out of date because, as they say, values and even truth itself "is not absolute but relative." Let them. But, regardless of faddish rhetoric that plays around with the meanings of words, there are in fact matters of truth that for all practical purposes are absolute. People from different cultures and with different needs may put to different uses that which emerges from absolute truth, but from whatever human perspective you may view it, gravity is gravity whether you are a woman, a man, a Laplander, or a Tibetan monk. Truth in fact is truth regardless of what relativists or deconstructionists say about it.

WHAT HUMANITIES TEACHERS COULD DO TO HELP

I believe we must teach liberal arts to every one of the millions of current college students. For the most part, (excepting upper-tier private colleges and not always those), I believe faculties are not doing a very good job of this kind of teaching. What do I think would help? It would help if humanities professors understood the motivations and ways of thinking of their students from the mass market. The differences in thinking between these professors and their students inhibit the transfer of vitally important concepts and ideas. Thus, liberal arts and humanities professors periodically should get themselves out into the marketplace and onto the street in order to learn how to communicate better with their students. At regular intervals they should venture beyond their protected positions behind lecterns, in seminar rooms or library carrels, where too many of them churn out neverending streams of papers and reports which have little or no significance and for all practical purposes are read by no one.

How to do this? The academic year plus the summer, which together have many more periods of recess than businesses and public organizations, afford opportunities for professors of the liberal arts to do different things. Too many of them simply mow their lawns and paint their houses. A creative liaison between business and university departments (perhaps encouraged by some modest foundation funding) could provide opportunities for liberal arts professors to experience what is going on in the worlds outside their academic departments. How wonderful it would be for a philosophy professor to have an internship at the City Council. What a fine opportunity it would be for a language professor to have an internship at the welfare office. Think how a history professor could benefit from identifying with an emerging business, or with an office in venture capital. This is what is needed in many hundreds of liberal arts and humanities units serving the mass market of students. It has far more importance than sitting in shared governance committee meetings.

Do I think the troubles in mass-market higher education coming out of the issues discussed above will improve? In the near term I do not. Chief among the reasons is a deterioration of the public financing of these institutions, along with outdated management. Whenever this occurs an inward, centripetal force takes place trying to reinforce a status quo.

This is happening now.

CHAPTER 14

Rising College Costs, Less Support, Outdated Administrative Management, the Dilemma of Increased Part-time Faculty along with Graduate Student Unionizing

They hired the money, didn't they?

Calvin Coolidge

BLUE SKIES OF THE 1950s

During the 1950s universities were seen as providing answers to the nation's problems. The high esteem in which they were held was unprecedented. State university operating subsidies received generous yearly increases. Academic and administrative support programs proliferated and were added to what existed. They were not substituted for those that could or should have been phased out. Faculties and support staff multiplied. There seemed to be no limit. Little to no oversight of faculty members was exerted from any quarter and trustees exerted little to no supervision over presidents. Because of campus expansions faculty members were recruited with insufficient or no experience and after minimum probationary periods received tenure. They were drawn from parts of the spectrum of citizens that previously had never contributed to the ranks of the academy. This changed the sociology of faculties, especially at open-admission state universities that had to expand to accommodate the influx of new students which by statute they were required to admit.

Presidents were not called to fiscal account. Anecdotes were legion about presidents with regular budget deficits and who never had to balance those budgets, much less handle the anxieties of meeting a payroll. Why should they have worried? Each year their institutions received state tax dollar subsidies that increased by 5 to 10 percent. All they had to do was roll over the deficit into the next budget cycle, where it was covered by the increase. If necessary, toward the end of the fiscal year they waited a month or more and delayed paying bills, until the new money came in at the turn of the new fiscal year. And so on for each succeeding year until they moved on or retired. They never had to face up to hard fiscal reality. Operations were loose and relaxed. No one learned how to say "No."

FACULTY MEMBERS SETTING THEIR OWN WORK ASSIGNMENTS

Practically everybody outside of the academy who has an opinion about tenured faculty members thinks they do not spend enough time teaching students. For the most part I agree, obviously excepting faculty members who are authentic scholars and researchers and who are engaged in efforts that will potentially increase the worthwhile store of knowledge. However, faculty members whose research activity centers on bean counting are not included in this exception.

Principle among the causes for public negativity about the workloads of regular, fulltime faculty members is that oversight by deans, provosts, and presidents over what it is that faculty members actually do with their time is generally lax to non-existent. It isn't that faculty members are not busy. They are. I have read many workload reports from individual faculty members telling me that they work seventy, or eighty, even ninety hours a week. I believed them and still do. But the salient question remains; how do faculty members use the time they are so busy filling up? Teaching assignments are reported on the conventional campus forms documenting workloads, along with office hours. Also reported are community activities and university service such as committee work. In some examples the term "academic politicking" might be a better substitute for committee service. Various other campus involvements are listed, research work being the most important to many. All too often this research work possesses dubious value to society, but it is included in a resume to be used at promotion and raise time.

Taken together these activities add up to time and energy on behalf of the individual faculty member. The question of whether there is any guarantee of faculty members' adherence to the university mission in their work schedules, other than teaching, is not posed. If it were, the answer in far too many examples would simply be no. The individual's teaching schedule remains the only assigned part of her/his job responsibility. This is done by the department chair who is often junior to various departmental faculty members, so the assignment authority in many examples is *pro forma*. For the remainder, the faculty member's contracted time remains essentially unspecified. This inevitably results in disconnects between the professional desires of individual professors, and the needs and missions of the university in its service to the larger community.

CAMPUS MISSIONS RELATED TO REGIONAL
CONSTITUENT NEEDS

During the second half of the twentieth century professors
in mass-market institutions adopted for themselves the system of shared governance that had been developed earlier
for smaller institutions serving a smaller cross-section of the
citizenry. These newer public institutions (sometimes brand
new, sometimes built upon the foundation of preexisting private or municipal institutions) inevitably identified with the
needs of their communities. Community leaders had normally been involved in their founding. Often roles and missions were imparted to the colleges that did not quite fit the
education of faculties recruited to staff them. This was a
changed situation from earlier autonomous campuses which
were separated from the communities. Their campus missions, by contrast, did indeed emerge from the preparation
and needs of the faculty, not the needs of the community.
Also, to use a term adopted by many community-oriented
universities, the "engagement" of campus with community
necessitates the involvement of campus units other than the
faculty. While this in no way diminishes the faculty, it places
the faculty in a different perspective and to an extent makes
the shared governance system anachronistic.

Not uncommonly the mission of the university had not
been clearly delineated. It is at mass-market institutions represented by regional and inner-city, urban, public universities, where most of the problems lie that stem from lack of
mission clarity. From the standpoint of rational planning, the
gaps separating individual faculty members and university
missions are a paradox of organization. They illustrate the
inordinate complexity of state universities, which grew like
Topsy, demonstrating a lack of logic in management. The
proliferation of budget units along with separate hierarchies
of administration resulted in incoherence. The former chair-

man of the Massachusetts Board of Higher Education, James F. Carlin, in a *Point of View* piece for the *Chronicle of Higher Education* asserted that, "never have I observed anything as unfocused or mismanaged as higher education. . . . Clearly the reason that tuition is so high is that college costs are high. Why are college costs high? Nobody is in charge. . . . This year the University of Massachusetts, over my strong objections, put into place a post-tenure review program that specifically prohibits administrators from using the results of a review for disciplinary purposes. Sponsors of the program are calling it a national model. Please!"[1] Mountains of operating monies go to faculty members, to staff bureaucracies, and to programs that are not congruent with a university's mission.

Further confusion exists in the lack of connection between the university mission—to serve the needs of mass-market students—and the specialized academic-research and programmatic desires of faculties. Working-class, first-generation college students for the most part have not had adequate preparatory academic instruction in such subjects as English, mathematics, and basic sciences. It is not exalted academic work to remedy these deficiencies in students (not to mention public school teachers, who also need remediation in the same subjects), but it is a priority that grows in direct proportion to the growth of our our information/knowledge-based society. It stands out in relief as a dilemma in the structure of our higher educational systems. Doing remediation is not college-level work, but at the same time it is the most effective way faculties can serve students from the mass market who are unprepared.

How should this be done?

There is no clear cut, tidy answer. The City University of New York City has valiantly embarked upon an initiative to remand remedial work to the community colleges in the system and return to the faculties of four-year institutions their expected role of teaching at the actual college level. But to accomplish this in New York City alone will take years. Other initiatives just aborning in a number of states involve instituting higher standards in teacher-training programs in colleges of education so that future public school students will receive better instruction and thus be better prepared upon reaching college. But this will take even longer. In the meantime, given the predicted growth in numbers of college students in the near future, the problem increases. So for the better part of this first decade of the twenty-first century the issue remains, messy as it is, that the best way tax-assisted, public institutions and non-selective private colleges can serve the majority of their students, and thus serve the needs of their regions, is to fill in this gap of student learning by adjusting to the remedial needs of students.

The Teaching Desires of Faculty Members

This does not square with the desires of well-educated, specialized, faculty members. They want to offer courses and do research in their academic specialties. But at institutions serving the mass market this seldom provides help to working-class students who come to college to improve their job prospects. It is not to say that faculties with specialized backgrounds pursue worthless projects. Many have authentic value to the academic fields involved. The issue boils down to the ethics of campus priorities. Do you serve students or faculty? Do you use public tax dollars to subsidize instruction in the courses the great majority of students need, or do you allocate the funds to subsidize faculty members to teach and do research work in the specialties that captivate their interest?

Earlier, when campuses were elite, private, and independent of public tax support, the issue did not arise. Faculties (sometimes in the shadow of strong, dictatorial presidents or deans) comprised colleges and universities. Programming emanated from what they knew and stood for. Student needs, in a practical sense, were not part of the equation. Today it is totally different. Students enrolled in public universities serving the mass market have pressing educational and training needs, often different from what faculty members want to teach. Obviously this creates not only a contradiction in campus roles and mission, but adds up to a diversion of operating dollars meant to carry out that role. How can you be fair to both faculty and students in public institutions?

One of the ways for faculty and administration to bring about and operate special academic projects which may or may not coincide with student needs, is to fund them through outside fundraising. In so doing, tax and tuition support for campus operations and for the basic teaching mission is not diverted. (Private institutions have done this for generations.) But it is much more difficult for mass-market public institutions to do this kind of fundraising than it is for monied private campuses and flagship state universities, simply because wealthy alumni and affluent old-boy networks are not as available to them. Even so, for a creative, worthwhile academic research or teaching project, particularly if it has an outreach function into the community, special external funding can usually be found.

POTENTIAL OF GOVERNMENT OVERSIGHT

University management in general has not contained costs, which are curving upward faster than income to pay for the increasing costs. It is no wonder that elected federal officials express concern. Senator Christopher Dodd of Connecticut brandished the sword of possible legislation to take control of tuition increases away from the public institutions themselves. The National Commission on the Cost of Higher Education created by the Congress and reporting to it turned into a political hornet's nest. With a number of well-known representatives from campus constituencies on it, the commission's preliminary report offered rationales and excuses for the steep rate of tuition rises. Members of Congress reacted with unadorned antipathy, refusing to accept the findings and sending the commission back to the drawing board. Education committee member of the House suggested that a Commission on College Costs be formed. If it were to be established, and cost-control experts from the business world were to staff it, they would dig into issues of how faculty workloads are developed, along with identifying the costs of much faculty research work perceived as having little or no consequence. Wrenching upheavals would take place in academic hallways. If public resentments about campus costs continue, and the outside momentum for establishing controls grows, it is conceivable that wholesale campus management restructuring will be forced, along with staff cuts, not dissimilar to what many business experienced during the eighties.

CRISIS OF FINANCE AND ACCESS

A signifiant report of a two-year study by the Commission on National Investment in Higher Education was released under the auspices of the RAND Corporation in the academic year 1996/97. Entitled *Breaking the Social Contract: The Fiscal Crisis in Higher Education*,[2] the report presents a frightening array of facts and predictions coming from escalating campus operating costs outrunning predicted sources of college and university support. At its outset the report says, "at a time when the level of education needed for productive employment is increasing, the opportunity to go to college will be denied to millions of Americans unless sweeping changes are made to control costs, halt sharp increases in tuition, and increase other sources of revenue."[3] While the second half of the 1990s were stellar economic times which resulted in significantly better state tax-dollar support of higher education and which took some of the pressure off higher education, the ominous facts and predictions in the report *Breaking the Social Contract* are not vitiated. Even though state tax-dollar support increased during the late nineties, costs have escalated at a substantially higher rate, as has tuition. The longer term (projected to 2015) foreshadows grim conditions that call for drastic, corrective action. Here are some of the facts and projections in *Breaking the Social Contract*:

> The higher education sector . . . is facing a catastrophic shortfall in funding. Given current trends in both funding and costs of higher education, the deficit in operating expenses for the nation's colleges and universities will have quadrupled by 2015. Assuming tuition increases no faster than inflation, by that year U.S. colleges and universities will fall $38 billion short (in 1995 dollars) of the annual budget they need to educate the student population expected in 2015. If, however, tuition increases at current rates—basically doubling by 2015—the impact on access will be devastating: effectively half of those who want to pursue higher education will be shut out. . . .
>
> The population of the United States has doubled since 1930 but the enrollment in higher education has expanded tenfold. . . .
>
> Clearly, government support for higher educations has declined both economically and politically over a long period, and it will be difficult to bring it back to previous levels. . . . [T]he government is beginning to ask the same kinds of questions of colleges and universities that it has asked of the health care industry—questions about cost, productivity, efficiency, and effectiveness.

The main reason why institutions have not taken more effective action is their outmoded governance structure— i.e. the decision making units, policies and practices that control resource allocation have remained largely unchanged since the structure's establishment in the nineteenth century. Designed for an era of growth the current structure is cumbersome and even dysfunctional in an environment of scarce resources.[4]

The predictions of the above 1996–97 Rand-sponsored report were buttressed by statistics released in November, 2000 from a study done by the National Center for Public Policy and Higher Education in San Jose. States were graded on various categories of higher education opportunities provided in all states both from public and private institutions. Affordability was one of the categories. It received the lowest grade. In my own state of Ohio, for example, a typical family pays approximately 30 percent of its annual income for the cost of an education at a public institution, and 59 percent at a private school. This is pricing families out of the market.

OUTDATED STRUCTURE OF MANAGEMENT

Increasing complexity has become a thorn in the flesh of campus management. As universities have become more pluralistic, academic departments and other units that always enjoyed considerable autonomy have turned into Balkanized hierarchies. When crucial issues coming from today's fiscal, social, and political forces affect the university as a whole and require prompt action, the dispersed and fragmented stakeholders erect separate turf protections that not only delay but prevent institutionally coherent action. When this happens, dysfunction sets in. Increasingly, government steps into the vacuum left by this dysfunction, an example being the state of Virginia, where a 20 percent cut in tuition was mandated, with the presumption the state would make up the lost income to colleges and universities, a presumption perhaps better described as a hope. This shows the growing apprehension of the public officials about the cost of and access to higher education. Stories and editorial comment in the print media illustrate this growing concern. *Synfax Weekly Report* quotes figures from the Institute for Higher Education Policy that show that "from 1976 to 1996 . . . the costs of college rose 49 percent while family income rose 10 percent, and the average Pell Grant award dropped 23 percent."[5]

The roots of the governance and management problems I have just called attention to are usually laid at the feet of university faculties. The James F. Carlin piece cited earlier is a typical, if somewhat vehement example. There is no question that faculties find themselves set upon from all sides, so much so that champions from many different quarters inside and outside of academe spring to their defense. They make valid points that are applicable to many faculty members. Washington D.C. attorney Martin Michaelson, in *Trusteeship*, the journal of the Association of Governing Boards of Universities and Colleges, says that, "without doubt, the strength of American higher education and the reason for its world leadership is the faculty." He goes on to say that the tendency for increasing criticism of faculties, "[C]an be likened to biting the feeding hand."[6] What inspired Mr. Michaelson was the Fall 1997 issue of *Daedelus* entitled "The American Academic Profession."[7] This issue consists of a collection of essays preceded by a superb editorial preface. The authors are respected, contributing academics from well-established institutions. They deal with higher education concerns going far beyond the ill humor experienced by

discontented faculty members on the inside and their constituencies on the outside. The tone of the authors is positive, even idealistic.

But the realities of mass-market institutional staffing,
and how it affects the basic values of higher education, is not
discussed in this specific collection nor is it dealt with adequately in the general literature.

THE CADRE OF PART-TIME, ADJUNCT FACULTY

The need to deal with expanding knowledge and convey
greater amounts of information coincides with universities
having to confront escalating costs. This creates obvious
budget pressures. Among the consequences has been a
growth of part-time, less traditional faculty members, many
with specialized skills related to the marketplace and not
possessed by traditional faculties. From the perspective of
administering campus budgets, part-time faculty appointments relieve pressure. Part-timers, usually identified as adjuncts, are not ordinarily eligible for fringe benefits, and
proportionately teach heavier loads than regularly appointed
and full-time tenured faculty members. Depending on the
field, it is possible to replace one full-time tenured faculty
member with three adjuncts for the same cost and at the
same time realize twice the equivalent amount of teaching. (I
realize that my pointing this out causes regular faculty members to squirm and makes me vulnerable to being castigated
for appearing to substitute corporate management measures
for academic values. In terms of pure educational value this
logic cannot be faulted. But neither can the reality of fiscal
problems, which are getting worse, be denied. No matter
how firm the academic values of an institution might be, if it
goes bankrupt they go for nought.)

There has been growth in the administrative practice of
not replacing a retired or resigned full-time tenured profes-

sor, with another, comparable appointment but instead to reassign the money to the part-time budget and hire part-timers. This practice comes under fierce criticism from unions, and from the American Association of University Professors which has extended its function as a professional organization into academic unionism. The point being made is that part-timers cannot have the commitment to the institution that regular faculty members do, being as a group involved in shared governance of the institution, and who are also involved (or at least should be) in research and service work. The logic in these assertions is apparent, postulated on the assumption that regular faculty members, as contrasted to part-timers, do in fact do research and service work in the search for new knowledge or for new and improved ways of teaching.

This is the justification for lighter teaching loads. But unfortunately far too many faculty members in mass-market institutions do not do research, or aren't much good at it, nor do they put their shoulders to the wheel of community service, which is one of the ways of transferring to the surrounding regions the knowledge and skill that accrues at universities. Some get involved in faculty politicking and represent this as service work to the institution. Not a few deans, provosts, and presidents do not exactly view this as service but rather the opposite, namely making it more difficult to achieve what should be the orderly process of campus management. Other regular faculty members have simply lapsed into the comfort of tenured positions with the minimum possible teaching responsibility. As such, their roles are not much different from part-time teachers except they have offices, privileges and compensation far beyond the part-timers. It is a two-tier system with a vengeance.

There are strong countervailing forces at work against the two-tier system which now exists throughout higher education in America but causes embitterment most clearly in community colleges and mass-market four-year institutions. In the fall of 1997, a *Daedalus*-published report compiled by ten academic organizations made up of faculty groups and learned societies cited numerous statistics concerning the use of part-time faculty. The report said that "the proportion of adjuncts has doubled over the past twenty-five years, to more than 40 percent of all faculty members. . . . At community colleges, 64 percent of faculty members hold part-time posts, compared with 29 percent of the faculty members at four-year institutions. The latter often rely on graduate teaching assistants—nearly 200,000 of them in 1993." With the turn of the twentieth into the twenty-first century the use of adjuncts continues to grow as does the adversariness this issue has generated. In the state of Washington, part-timers from the state's community colleges have filed no less than three actions against the system. Two of them (joined in a class action) allege they have wrongfully been denied retirement and health care benefits. Another suit sought damages because the plaintiffs alleged that for years they were not paid overtime for work outside the classroom. "[T]he hours spent on class preparation, student counseling, test preparation, grading, and department meetings—the sort of work for which full time faculty members are compensated."[8] Since this action was filed, the state court where it was heard has ruled that time spent in student advising, class preparation, and grading papers must be counted, along with the time spent in class, when a part-time teacher is evaluated for retirement benefits.

This shows that there are other issues which go beyond budget implications. The hand-wringing by traditionally vested, full-time faculty members sends false signals. A significant component of the part-time teaching cadre relates to the vocational needs of students better than traditional faculty members do. Many, if not most, of these adjuncts continue to pursue careers in their chosen professions, and as such have more hands-on experience than full-time faculty members. Since their graduate school days, the full-time tenured group has been enveloped by academe. In my own profession of music performance, which I realized in an academic setting, it would be impossible to maintain viable music degree programs without the appointment of professional musicians as adjunct faculty members. Maintaining the wide variety of performance categories on today's campuses—instrumental, vocal, ensemble, theatrical, classical, commercial—can only be accomplished with the cooperative interaction of full- and part-time faculty. The same holds true in dozens of other professional pursuits now part of university programs. The crux of the issue is the goal of professionalism and the real world experience that adjuncts bring to the programs.

PART-TIME STUDENTS

Concurrent with the growth in part-time faculty has been a growth in nontraditional part-time students who are not concerned with earning a formal degree. They have jobs that do not permit them to attend college classes on schedules established for the convenience of comfortable, tenured faculties, weekdays from 10 A.M. to 2 P.M. Because faculties in many regional public universities have not sufficiently accommodated the nontraditional students, more and more of them are turning to other providers of training, including corporate training programs and instruction provided by proprietary for-profit institutions. Given the unyielding necessity of gaining knowledge in our information/knowledge economy, continuing education has become a lifelong requirement for career success. The so-called nontraditional group, which includes a significant percentage of part-time students, is becoming the norm. Many traditional faculty members have not yet come to realize that other providers of higher education and training have broken the generations-old monopoly of post-secondary instruction held by private and state universities. There is a perceptible shift in enrollments, especially in practical coursework, to these newer institutions who are user-friendly and who adapt the logistics of their offerings to the needs of students, a contrast to the rigidity and bureaucratic constraints of conventional public campuses.

This contributes to a growing separation between past and present. A university education had been tailored for the relatively few students, mostly upper crust, in contrast to today's avalanche of millions of students in higher education who cross the spectrum of all socioeconomic groups. When higher education was divorced from the marketplace and took place in the ivory tower, "gown" separate from "town," its curricular values tended to focus upon larger issues in the realm of concept and idea and were meant to last a lifetime. Today's college curricula increasingly cater to the immediate, practical needs and desires of students who have vocational goals related to the job market. There is no alternative, either for the students or for the mass-market institutions. Vast numbers of students have nowhere else to go. The president of the University of Phoenix, Jorge Klor de Alva, indicates the U.S. labor force has been turned upside down. He comments that, "in the forty years between 1950 and 1991, the percentage of skilled workers in the workforce increased by 25 percent. Yet this unprecedented feat in economic history has been nearly duplicated between 1991 and 2000 . . . with the same sector of skilled workers increasing by 20 percent."[9]

If you take the values inherent in the curriculum and residential living characteristics of private higher education

during generations gone by and compare them with the purposes of today's utilitarian curricula at mass-market institutions to which part-time students of all ages commute, you
are comparing examples of the unlike. They are simply not
the same. Mass-market institutions go by the title of "university," but large parts of most of them, were you to apply historic educational criteria, are not universities. To apply the
European designation "polytechnic" would be more accurate. But it won't happen in America because of damage to
faculty egos.

Plenty of criticism and carping exists on the part of professors on all academic fronts over this massive shift from the
historic meaning and intent of university learning into
polytechnic–trade-school curricula and methods. In a recent
book Professor Stanley Aronowitz from the Graduate Center of the City University of New York takes up the cudgel
against the de-emphasis of the "loftier goals of higher education," something he reiterated in an interview with Elizabeth
Greene of the *Chronicle of Higher Education*. He stated that,
"[U]niversities have become glorified employment agencies,
churning out people who can meet the immediate needs of
Corporate America but are poorly equipped to think for
themselves."[10] No one knowledgeable about American
higher education today will deny the element of truth in this
assertion. Taking into account the larger reality of university
learning, i.e., over 15 million students spread out over 3,887
U.S. institutions, pure intellectual value has deteriorated.
This view is buttressed by Stephen Balch, President of the
National Association of Scholars who, in the same article,
takes a swipe at administrators: "Now this calls for more administrators who are themselves serious scholars or who
have been recently serious scholars and who see the university in more than just vocational dollars and cents terms."[11]

But what is not set forth in these admonishments is

today's context of inclusiveness in mass-market public universities, non-selective liberal arts schools, and specialized institutions, a contrast to earlier times. Teaching the humanities to privileged students who have been reared in surroundings of well-bred moderation and culture, and whose parents have been educated, comes naturally. I taught music and its theory to this sort of student when I was head of the honors program in music at the University of Michigan School of Music in the late fifties. But things are different in the scrambled, rough and tumble of today's open admissions. Joe Sixpack (yes, he now enrolls in non-selective public universities) has no interest in literature or in philosophical subtleties. His serious side desires practical training so he can do better in the job market. Politicians in state legislatures who want his vote, to say nothing of local business associations, increase the pressure on campus administrators to accommodate his wishes. Professors Aronowitz and Balch admit that to put their noble aspirations in place would require smaller classes and a dramatic shift in the application of university fiscal resources. Given the tidal wave of vocationalism manifest in mass-market universities, Aronowitz and Balch have about as much political clout to achieve their objectives as do dogcatchers in Smalltown, USA. Indeed, their lofty purposes are realized in various selective liberal arts institutions still dedicated primarily to developing the minds of students. But that is upstairs. The downstairs is what is defining the realities of undergraduate higher education in America.

The Dilemma of Part-time Faculty Appointments

Statistics show a dramatic pattern of growth in part-time faculty appointments on campuses everywhere in the country during the eighties and nineties. Data is hard to come by, but the National Center for Educational Statistics (NCES) produced the two most comprehensive studies to date (released in 1994 and 1997) documenting the swelling ranks of part-timers.12 These studies together document full-time and part-time staffing patterns for the fall of 1987 and the fall of 1992. A continuing survey of postsecondary faculty staffing patterns for subsequent years is being conducted by the NCES but is not available yet. The data released by NCES in 1994 and 1997 reveal major shifts in percentages of part-time faculty compared to those with full time appointments at the different types of universities by 1987 Carnegie classifications.

Higher Education Instructional Faculty and Staff, 1987 and 1992

Fall 1987	Fall 1992	Percent Increase from 1987–92
Full-time, 67%	Full-time, 58%	Full-time, 3%
Part-time, 33%	Part-time, 42%	Part-time, 48%

Source: Data from NCES, published by Council of Graduate Schools, *Communicator*, January 1998. Prepared by Peter D. Syverson and Stephen R. Welch.

The tabulation shows data snapshots of 1987 and 1992, the most comprehensive available. They were old by the time the twentieth turned into the twenty-first century. Use of part-timers has continued to increase during the intervening years.

A concerted effort by a number of higher education organizations to get a handle on the facts continues. The most recent information (November 2000) was compiled through survey work by a consortium of no less than twenty-five disciplinary associations called the Coalition on the Academic Workforce. The data concerns what and how much adjuncts teach and how they fare in salaries and benefits, along with what other support they are provided, such as office space and a telephone. Ten social science and humanities fields were covered. While the information is not comprehensive, it reveals the continuing growth in the use of adjuncts and illustrates their second-class status. This growth of part-time personnel has escalated into a major faculty/administrative issue across the country. Richard Moser had this to say about the latest data in an interview with the *Chronicle of Higher Education*: "This report is going to reveal a shameful truth. Administrations have abandoned the notion that the university should set an example of good citizenship, that they have turned away from the pursuit of justice and instead set up the sweatshops of the future for the greedy to imitate."[13] Could one imagine Professor Lovejoy, who helped found the AAUP, talking like that?

Part-time teachers, it is implied, do not bring to the campus the commitment to learning that regular, full-time faculty members do and because of this, the larger learning environment is diminished. In residential campuses this cannot be denied. But neither can it be contradicted that, at public flagship and research-oriented campuses, because the research interests of full-time faculty result in less teaching, large numbers of adjuncts and doctoral students are needed to fulfill the needs of undergraduate students. They have assumed major undergraduate teaching responsibilities, too often with little or no supervision. These responsibilities are assigned largely in the humanities and sciences in the basic curriculum, which is precisely where the experience of mature teachers and thinkers is needed. There is nothing new in this practice. Herein lies the dilemma.

GRADUATE STUDENT UNIONIZATION

The use of graduate students as part-time teachers (usually called teaching fellows or teaching assistants) cannot be separated from that of the non tenure-track adjunct faculty. Both graduate students working as part-time teachers with unfinished doctorates, and adjuncts who are simply hired to teach are mobilizing on their campuses to improve their circumstances. This movement has been gaining momentum. At some public universities graduate students teaching part time have already unionized, but private universities had been exempt from a requirement to bargain collectively. This was changed in October of 2000 when the National Labor Relations Board declared that at New York University (a private institution) graduate student teachers had the right to organize and bargain over their working conditions. They had earlier formed a union. What the NLRB decided was that the issue of being employees trumped the issue of being students. University administrations pointed out that the teaching done by graduate students could not be separated from their larger learning situation as students, which was the reason they came to the university in the first place. Therefore it would not be logical for graduate students to bargain over their responsibilities with a university's faculty. But the NLRB reasoned that teaching was not a universal requirement for graduate students, nor did it afford academic credit. It could therefore be separated from student status compared to employee status and could be subject to bargaining.

The union movement among teaching fellows and adjuncts will continue to grow. "At Temple and Michigan State University, T.A. unions won elections. At the University of Washington, teaching assistants went on strike. At Columbia University and Brown University, T.A.s filed petitions seeking recognition. And campaigns proceeded at Pennsylvania State University, the University of Pennsylvania, and the University of Maryland at College Park."[14] Cornell is an exception, where T.A.s voted against becoming unionized.

The distinction between the roles of teaching assistants as employees as contrasted with students is now crucial. This is the crux of the issue. The dean of Yale's law school said: "I believe passionately that unionization of graduate students is not the best solution to the problems. . . . If anything it solidifies the sense that they are primarily employees and only secondarily students, which completely reverses the order of things."[15] In response, Jon Curtiss, a union organizer for the American Federation of Teachers in Michigan responded somewhat more colorfully: "Give me a break. All sorts of professionals are unionized—airline pilots, nurses, teachers. Just because philosophy Ph.D.s aren't carting lunchboxes to the factory floor doesn't mean they can't bargain collectively."[16]

During my own graduate-student years I was a part-time instructor and had a *de facto* teaching independence supposedly accorded only to regular faculty. The difference between then and now is that I had the good fortune of being in that position during a period of expansion and budget affluence, and had the opportunity, upon completing the Ph.D., of moving over onto the regular, tenure-track faculty at Michigan, which I did, and remained to be tenured and promoted up through the ranks.

Such opportunity for doctoral students today is almost nonexistent. The exceptions are the rare but recognized near-geniuses in fields such as mathematics or physics in departments of one of the top research universities. These prodigies can proceed to a full professorship in another research university at age twenty-six. But this can scarcely represent a benchmark in the normal course of academic events, anymore than Mozart could be considered routine in music, or Bertrand Russell in mathematics and philosophy. What normally happens to doctoral-level, part timers is that when the Ph.D. is finished the person is cut loose to enter the job market, and then another part-timer is appointed, and so on. The part-timers who are finished with their degrees, but who have taken part-time, non tenure-track positions because they could not find a regular teaching job, have become a "shadow" academic constituency. In order to patch together enough paychecks to live, they teach courses at more than one campus, sometimes flitting between two and three campuses. They are called "gypsy faculty," and they save U.S. universities hundreds of millions of dollars. In urban universities it has been estimated that 60 percent of faculty members are adjuncts, i.e., not permanently appointed, but that they account for only 15 percent of the payroll. Human interest stories about the problems encountered by these itinerant faculty appear regularly. This cadre has grown substantially, and is now the subject of serious union organizing and discussion in state legislatures, due to the discrimination they suffer.

But neither is the use of part-timers all that bad. There can be no question that in the mass-market institutions with substantial vocationally oriented technical programs, part-time faculty are basic to academic programs. Many of these faculty members have full-time careers in their own fields of expertise, are not dependent upon the stipends they receive from their campuses, and teach part-time at night and on weekends because they like doing it. They are not discriminated against by university administrations.

The Council of Graduate Schools says: "Obviously there are both positive and negative aspects to the increased reliance on part-time faculty. As discussed at 1997 CGS Annual Meeting, part-time faculty are a proven way for universities to bring in expertise from business and arts communities to supplement the full-time faculty and to help institutions meet teaching needs in a period of heightened financial constraints. However, the practice of using part-time faculty to replace full-time positions increases responsibilities of per-manent faculty for departmental and institutional gover-nance, maintaining the research and service programs of the institution, and advising and mentoring undergraduate and graduate students."[17]

It is a group of patchworks. The issue has not been sorted out. But the trend is clear. Not only are graduate stu-dents and part-timers being heard and listened to more and more as they utter concerns and complaints, but the answers are increasingly in their favor. They see it as a larger moral issue against which they contend.

CHAPTER 15

Morality and Ethics on Campus: The Replacement of Accepted Verities by Relative Values

> *Lay then the axe to the root, and teach governments humanity.*
>
> *It is their sanguinary punishments that corrupt mankind.*
>
> Tom Paine

BLURRED MORAL BOUNDARIES

On most campuses the lack of emphasis on moral education and student ethical development parallels a lack of emphasis on ethics and morals in our communities. Exceptions are found on campuses controlled by religious denominations and to an extent those where strict honor codes prevail. Also, since 9/11 a resurgence of patriotism has taken place, similar to what always happens in wartime—although it is not quite a resurgence of morality.

Throughout the generations since the colonization of

America the general acceptance of moral principles concerning right versus wrong served as a foundation for the citizenry. They were breached in countless human ways in the everyday personal lives of citizens (scoundrels cheerfully did their thing), but these moral and ethical boundaries and norms were recognized and accepted as part of life on farms and in communities. The structure of society was such that a man's word was supposed to mean something. If he did not abide by his word, life was made difficult for him. The vast continent of America, with its beauty, differentiated landscapes, and natural resources presented opportunity and freedom of action never before experienced by the waves of immigrants. However, adherence to what were accepted as verities in matters of right and wrong served as community moral boundaries. Even though they were sometimes expressed in doctrinaire ways by preachers in Sunday sermons, they established norms for behavior that were approved by common consent.

By contrast on today's campuses, cheating, for example, tends to be treated by faculty and administration not so much as a moral misstep but simply as a fact of life. Two emeritus professors from Teachers College, Columbia, and Queens College, CUNY, Harold J. Noah and Max A. Eckstein, are continuing their long-standing research work on cheating within higher education. "Perhaps more disturbing than the prevalence of cheating," according to Eckstein, is that "it is now widely tolerated."[1]

The fear of civil lawsuits for violation of individual rights of accused students inhibits university officials in dealing with the situation. Glenn C. Altschuler from Cornell provides further information:

> Measured by recent surveys, cheating has reached epidemic proportions in high schools and colleges. In a survey of 21,000 students by the Josephson Institute of

Ethics, 70 percent of high school students and 54 percent of middle schoolers admitted they had cheated on an exam. That is up sharply from a study cited in 'The State of Americans: This Generation and the Next,' edited by Urie Bronfenbrenner and others. That study found that 33.8 percent of high school students used a "cheat sheet" on a test in 1969. By 1989 the percentage had risen to 67.8 percent . . . A recent study by the Center for Academic Integrity at Duke University yielded results similar to the Josephson study, with almost 75 percent of college students acknowledging some academic dishonesty.[2]

THE POSITION OF COLLEGES AND UNIVERSITIES

Where do colleges and universities stand on the issue of cheating and morality? They have been ambivalent.

In statements of purpose and in covenants, the panoply of U.S. colleges and universities usually express allegiance to morality, often by implication rather than explicitly. They fear being perceived as doctrinaire if they use simple language to identify moral principle. (Have you ever sat with a committee of faculty members and administrators drafting a mission statement and marveled at how skillfully executed is the dance around straightforward words?) Campus communities inevitably salute free speech, but sometimes the salute misrepresents what it is that is being saluted. (How much freedom of speech might an assistant professor up for tenure have if that assistant professor's words, no matter how well reasoned, do not conform to conventional departmental norms or to what the chairwoman's research work espouses?) In my administrative career as a provost and president, whenever I referred to moral values, cynics and skeptics from the faculty usually made light of the reference as "rhetoric."

Rarely are ethics and moral values taught or promulgated in any regularized way; not even in the ubiquitous orientation sessions imposed upon incoming students. Colleges of business usually have a course or two on ethical business practices; the content of these courses tends to be tailored to the specific discipline, not to individuals behaving in ethical ways. Philosophy departments teach ethics, usually from the standpoint of epistemology, the theory and basis of knowledge, but the field is so vast that students, to say nothing of faculty members, easily get lost as they wend their way from Aristotle through Marx to Derrida. Other professional disciplines may include specialized instruction such as the ethics of dealing with human subjects or animals in research work. But basic, straightforward ethical instruction for students related to moral human conduct in everyday living is lacking. There is, however, a heartening concern surfacing in some quarters of higher education about the importance of student ethical development. Two issues of *SYNTHESIS: Law and Policy in Higher Education*, (Winter 1999 and Spring 1999) are devoted to the topic of the ethical development of students. In the Spring issue Patricia King of Bowling Green State University responds in an article to an entreaty by the Association of State Universities and Land Grant Colleges to "Attend more conscientiously to issues of character development."[3] In the same issue Gary Pavela, editor of *Synfax*, authored an article with the purpose, "To lay a framework for implementing an ethical development program."[4]

LACK OF ETHICS IN STUDENT DEGREE PROGRAMS

The general lack of ethics as part of student degree programs shows vividly in the reaction of CEOs and human relations staff to on-the-job behavior of employees recently hired from colleges. A survey of over 300 business and professional organizations in Ohio conducted by a consortium of northeast Ohio colleges and universities (on which I served) showed disturbing results.[5] A sizable majority of the hiring officers of companies generally indicated dissatisfaction with attitudes toward ethics and morals that new employees brought with them. Obviously employers need acceptable levels of competence in skills as basic as arithmetic, English communication, and computer manipulation. (Over 60 percent of supervisors were unhappy with the level of quality in these skills of new employees.) But employers are as much or more concerned about employee ethics and integrity, ability to work with other people, and the willingness to adjust to the inevitability of change in the ecologies and needs of the workplace. The glaring deficiencies in these traits on the part of new employes hired from work-related programs on college campuses have reached alarming proportions. Faculties have done a poor job of teaching ethical values to students and by example demonstrating that these values are important to individuals and society. For the most part faculties have rejected the responsibility. This contrasts to days gone by when, even at state colleges and universities, faculty members frequently lectured or "preached" at Sunday night services in campus chapels.

It is true that in those days the services were anything but "multicultural," at least in the sense we understand the term multicultural today. They were essentially Protestant and usually presided over by white, male chaplains. Except on Catholic campuses, it was not the order of the day for a Catholic priest to celebrate mass, nor for a rabbi to instruct Jewish students in lessons from the Torah. A Muslim call to worship facing Mecca, a Buddhist service involving meditation, or even an African-American service (with the exception of a handful of black campuses), with its vibrant singing and preacher-congregation interaction, would have been inconceivable. And certainly gays, lesbians and radical feminists did not openly participate in services. But despite the lack of inclusiveness, at least there was the acknowledgment of moral principle with concomitant accountability and responsibility applied directly to the individual.

Imbued in college faculties were the historic principles that had coalesced from the religious doctrines of post-Reformation Europe and from ideas that stemmed from classical Greek and Roman authors. They were buttressed by the concepts of Saint Augustine, Thomas Aquinas, Immanuel Kant, John Locke and subsequent Enlightenment thinkers. The nation's founders (some not being Christians, but Deists) were profoundly influenced in their ethics by the ideas of these thinkers. That they were almost all white, mostly Anglos and male, and that this background might taint them would have been incomprehensible. The concept of race and ethnic diversity in the authorship of ideas taking precedence over the evaluated substance of the ideas, or that diversity of authorship, of and for itself, should be a requirement for inclusion in a curriculum had not occurred to anyone. The founders had a base in principle. Relativism, where values could change depending upon how they are perceived, played no part. (Could one imagine the Declaration of Independence being cast in the subjunctive?)[6]

Catholic, denominational Christian, Orthodox Jewish, and Islamic institutions abroad, in contrast to what has been a broadening stream of relativism, remain supported and controlled by the tenets of their faiths. They still frame morality in statements emerging from firm principles of religious faith and philosophy. Responsibility for moral behavior is placed on *individual students* who are sometimes even monitored regarding their adherence to moral strictures both on and off campus.

In parts of the U.S. population there also exists a current resurgence in the acceptance of Christian practices (I use the term "practices" instead of "faith" since this well publicized resurgence is selective). Some practices are adhered to and others not. The use of birth control devices by many Catholic couples, in contradiction to the teaching of the Church, is an example. But testimony to Christian resurgence along with Islam and Buddhism in sectors of the population shows up. The Council for Christian Colleges and Universities, for example, with a membership of about 120 liberal arts institutions and Bible colleges, reports that from 1990 to 1996, ninety of their evangelical institutions showed enrollment gains of 24 percent compared to 5 percent at private campuses and 4 percent at public campuses.[7] However, this gain represents only about 129,000 students, a small fraction of the more than 15,000,000 student enrollment of American higher education.

PROLIFERATION OF RESPONSIBILITY

For most of the millions of students at the majority of colleges and universities, morality as an institutional responsibility takes many forms within multicultural relativism. Responsibility is proliferated through *groups* which embody the human diversities of cultural backgrounds, race, color, gender, sexual orientation, age, physical disability, economic status, and other differences. What comes to the fore are not clear statements of moral principle, but campus dicta, most often crafted by administrators in offices of student services—deans, assistant deans, assistants to deans for cultural diversity, and others with even more gobbledygook titles. These rules have set forth patterns of acceptable behavior and patterns of prohibited behavior in a welter of diversity. The concern is not transcendent moral principle, but rather how to speak (or not speak) and behave (or not behave) so as to avoid offending groups often identified as having been historically oppressed.

These patterns of acceptable or prohibited speech and behavior are usually expressed as speech codes, and have as their genesis the monumentally significant Civil Rights Act of 1964, specifically Title VII, along with Title IX of the Education Amendments passed in 1972. This Congressional action, and in subsequent years, the countless examples of statute and regulations at federal, state, and local levels, have now replaced the religious and philosophic principles that heretofore established the moral base of higher education. The purpose of the codes is to "level playing fields for historically disenfranchised groups" by pointing out their "vulnerability and oppression by the white majority" and, by prohibiting actions or words by university students and staff, whether intended or not, that would create "hostile environments" for them.[8]

VIOLATIONS OF FREE SPEECH

A mega-issue continues to exist in that examples of these prohibitions of expression have violated First Amendment principles. Examples of codes struck down by federal courts have been those at Stanford, the University of Wisconsin, and the University of Michigan. District court decisions determined that speech codes on these campuses infringed constitutionally protected free speech. It looms as a large negative that such infringement has occurred on U.S. campuses, the historic citadels of freedom in the realm of speech and ideas. That the courts had to be petitioned to step in and halt the actions of campus administrative personnel responsible for the infringement is a gloomy commentary on the altered values of the university officials involved.

To invoke this judicial protection of free speech requires time, energy, and resources on the part of courageous individuals—often students. It is no small undertaking to pursue the necessary litigation in court. Individuals have to go counter to the current tide of institutional, bureaucratic officialdom and be willing to submit to publicity where their own motives can and probably will be misunderstood. In so doing they could place their own positions and careers as students or staff in jeopardy. Thus for individuals to take these risks remains comparatively rare, and codes continue in effect at hundreds of campuses.

The Wisconsin speech code, judicially barred in 1991, referred to students. The faculty speech code (never alluding to academic freedom) remained in place. Subsequently, faculty, students, and staff argued over what to do about it, and in a surprise move in March, 1999 the Faculty Senate (perhaps with an idea that another federal suit might negate it) passed a set of alterations to the code that essentially eliminated its force. The older code had contained wording exemplified by the following:

> A faculty or academic staff member's expressive behavior in an instructional setting may be the basis for discipline [if]—the behavior is *commonly considered* [italics mine] by persons of a particular gender, race, cultural background, ethnicity, sexual orientation, or handicap to be demeaning to members of that group.

The new code by contrast includes considerably modified wording:

> Adherence to the right of freedom of speech and to the principles of academic freedom requires that all thoughts presented as ideas or the advocacy of ideas in instructional settings, if they are germane to the subject matter of the course being taught, must be protected.[9]

It took eight years, after a federal court spoke bluntly, simply to reassert a principle of free speech at one of America's premier flagship state universities. That the faculty vote for revision was narrow and the debate acrimonious speaks volumes about continuing faculty attitudes at Wisconsin. One associate professor in Afro-American and Women's studies spoke against amending the faculty speech code to include the phrase "right of freedom of speech" reacted by saying, "There is no recognition that there is a cost *to this business of free speech.*" [Italics mine].[10] But she did not prevail, with the result being that the Wisconsin Faculty Senate by the less than resounding majority of seventy-one to sixty-two became the first Big Ten campus to assert that free speech takes precedence over proscriptive faculty speech codes. Even so, this scarcely presages a stampede on campuses elsewhere to do away with them.

SHIFTS IN ACCOUNTABILITY FOR USE OF WORDS

The language of codes usually indicates that the person hearing another's words on campus has the prerogative of determining whether or not discrimination, racism or a hostile environment is engendered, and then of filing a complaint, which must be investigated and heard. The intended meaning of the words of the person against whom the complaint is filed (regardless of how innocent) becomes secondary to the interpretation (regardless of how subjective) of the hearer. The wording quoted above, *commonly considered by persons of a particular gender* (read female), *race* (read essentially black—certainly not Chinese), *cultural background, ethnicity* (read other than mainstream American), *sexual orientation* (read gay-lesbian), *or handicap* (the only word without a coded meaning), places the term *commonly considered* in a special advocacy context. It is anything but a common consideration. This is a 180-degree shift in the way American citizens have always used words. The common meanings of words, absolutely requisite to civilized and comprehending human discourse, gives way to the Babel of tongues.

Even though, case by case, these perceived individual

"violations" of campus-imposed speech codes are often pal-
try, taken altogether they have had prodigious implications
for campus free speech. This is a rasping contradiction to the
centuries-old tradition of free and open discourse on campuses. During the last decade college and university presidents, who are not usually involved in constructing the
codes, have for the most part supported them, not wanting
to deal with the roil that would come from special-interest
groups among faculty, staff and students if they had been
resisted.

ALICE IN WONDERLAND TWISTS

Alice in Wonderland twists in the interpretations of words
can result in freakish controversies. One took place in
Philadelphia at the University of Pennsylvania. Dubbed the
"Water Buffalo Affair" it resulted in a misbegotten and
freakish controversy over a racist interpretation of what the
term water buffalo implied. The episode involved an Orthodox Jewish student, Eden Jacobowitz, who was a freshman at
the University of Pennsylvania. He was disturbed late at
night while working on a paper for an English class by a
group of partying African-American sorority students outside his university residence hall window. First he asked
them to please be quiet, but ultimately shouted "Shut up you
water buffalo," which was taken as a racial slur. Other students in the dormitory, who were also annoyed and had
shouted objections to being disturbed called out worse
things to the sorority sisters, but none came forward to
admit having said anything. In contrast, Eden Jacobowitz
freely identified himself as having used the term "water buffalo." Five of the sorority sisters alleged water buffalo to be a
racial term of abuse; staff in the office responsible for student
life agreed and charged Jacobowitz with having violated
Penn's speech code. He responded that his religious up-

bringing forbade him to engage in any behavior even remotely related to racism and that the word water buffalo
bore no racial connotation whatsoever. Subsequently this
was corroborated by linguists, who indicated the term was
and never had been a racial epithet or a derogatory stereo-
type of blacks. Even so the official charge against Jacobowitz
was continued, and consistent with practice on most campuses he was offered a settlement involving, among other
things, residential probation. On the basis of his own principles he refused to settle and at this point the well-known
Penn historian Alan Charles Kors became his advisor. Given
the heaviness of the university bureaucratic apparatus coming down on Jacobowitz, it would seem doubtful that without the help of Kors he could have continued his effort to
achieve what he believed was fair.

Almost always at this juncture in speech code violation
cases, students yield and accept settlements, even though they
believe themselves treated unfairly. The students charged are
usually white and like most white Americans are afraid of
being cast in the lurid light of being called racist. It is this
psychology that gives the tactical advantage to those who pre-
fer the charges.

As facts in the case became known beyond the Penn campus reporters concentrated on it and media coverage spread.
The general tenor of stories and articles was incredulity. But
despite this, staff wheelhorses in the administration continued the case. It went on from January to May of 1993, with
bizarre twists and turns, themselves a sad commentary upon
governance as it is practiced on university campuses. The
stuff and nonsense in this episode of alleging "water buffalo"
to be a racial insult made Penn the butt of media jokes nationwide. Finally, in May, university personnel threw in the
towel and dropped the charges.[11]

It could be understood that, if an African-American

woman, perhaps of substantial physical proportions, were to hear herself called "water buffalo" she could construct it as a racial slur. But in this situation had both sides been reminded of the meaning of civil behavior, and reasoned with in calmer circumstances, the ensuing foolishness might have been avoided. Because of the apparatus in the enforcement of speech codes, this affair got out of hand.

As president of Cleveland State I experienced how a phrase can be twisted by experts in word spin. In March of 1991 I gave a speech in which I set forth my beliefs about what it takes for a student to acquire knowledge. The speech was covered by the press. I said that the process of learning comes from a mutual commitment between student and teacher and that the discipline of this human commitment is moral in its nature. Learning is not the same thing as product development, making cars or aspirin. "Learning cannot be manufactured," I said and discussed the contrast between learning itself and the opportunity to acquire it. In this nation the opportunity to learn is a citizen's right and entitlement, but learning itself, by its very nature, cannot be an entitlement "as, for example, food stamps." The reporter covering the event recognized a good thing when he saw it. The reference to food stamps provided an opportunity for a controversial story, which he wrote in such a way that my example of food stamps could be construed as derogatory to blacks. The story aided and abetted the inevitable outcry of racism that followed, which included words from the black mayor of Cleveland.

HORNS OF THE POLITICAL CORRECTNESS DILEMMA

Political correctness transfers the function of understanding words away from the person saying them to those hearing them, even if that hearing is subjective. This can then impart meanings to the words not intended by the speaker, which in turn makes the speaker potentially culpable. Also, placing spin on speech and gauging its political correctness is an uneven process. For example, political correctness is essentially a non-issue between whites and Chinese, or between white males and other white males. It is almost always enforced in the context of women against men, lesbians and gays against straight white men, blacks against whites, and, especially in California and Florida, Hispanics against mainstream whites. It has not developed as a two-way street. Blacks can and do use the word "nigger" in the context of other blacks.[12] But if a white employs the "N word" regardless of context, he or she might run into an untoward situation.

We as citizens need to reflect upon how we reached the point where we are so suspicious of perceived bias in expression that, in the hope of eliminating it, we rebuff the First Amendment. Historic bastions, such as university campuses, that should be the protectors of openness in discussions of gender, race, and preferences have become its enemies.[13]

I think campus speech codes should be scrubbed and the campus hacks and lightweights responsible for them be put on bread and water for a year. The residue of white guilt deriving from black slavery has encompassed other groups and continues to be a potent force which unfortunately has been used negatively.

FIVE POWERFUL MOVEMENTS

The moral issues we now encounter on campuses have roots in five philosophic, social and political movements that took over a century and a half to develop and consolidate. They are:

1.) The evolution of the concepts of Karl Marx and Friederich Engels, starting in the 1840s.

2.) The struggles of women to achieve their just human rights and legal parity with men, exemplified by Elizabeth Cady Stanton and the first women's rights convention in Seneca Falls, New York, in 1848.

3.)   The ideological struggle for the proper way to conduct the civil rights movement of black people, exemplified at the beginning of the twentieth century by the controversy between W. E. B. DuBois and Booker T. Washington. It was ultimately determined by the acceptance of DuBois' ideas within the developing black civil rights leadership.

4.)   The influence of the philosopher Herbert Marcuse, in the 1960s, drawing students into the New Left. His thinking highlighted the polarities between groups possessing power, who were strongly perceived as oppressors of groups who had no power.

5.)   The spread of moral and ethical relativism during the last twenty-five years of the twentieth century.

MARXISM

Over one hundred fifty years ago the principles that came to be known as Marxism were first enunciated by Marx and Engels. Their work was added to and developed by a myriad of nineteenth- and twentieth-century thinkers.[14] The late philosopher Sidney Hook wrote about how Marxism provided a [rationale] "to overcome human alienation, to emancipate man from repressive social institutions, especially economic institutions that frustrate his true nature, and to bring him into harmony with himself and his fellow men, and the world around him so that he can both overcome his estrangements and express his true essence through creative freedom."[15] Marxism had no particular racial emphasis, but identified and synthesized forces and methods that would lead to the emancipation of oppressed masses who were victims of dominant groups wielding power. Excepting the Sermon on the Mount, never before in western history had such powerful philosophic expression been given voice in the cause of oppressed people.

WOMEN'S RIGHTS

The seeds of Feminism actually sprouted during the French Revolution, when an Englishwoman living in Paris, Mary Wollstonecraft, composed the tract *Vindication of the Rights of Women* in 1792, although several years earlier no less formidable a personality than Abigail Adams had unsuccessfully twisted George Washington's arm to include the emancipation of women in the U.S. Constitution. But for all practical purposes, the women's movement in the United States began in 1848 at a convention in Seneca, New York. Primarily organized by Elizabeth Cady Stanton and Lucretia Mott, the convention produced a declaration of independence for women, demanding equality of treatment and the right to vote, as well as giving voice to other women's emancipation issues. These early initiatives were led by some of the most remarkable women America has produced, perhaps the best known being Susan B. Anthony, famed for her militant leadership of the Daughters of Temperance, the first women's temperance association. She and Stanton became close friends, colleagues and continuing collaborators, organizing the National Women's Suffrage Association in 1869. Both lived long lives into their eighties. The fact that women did not get the right to vote until the Nineteenth Amendment was ratified by the states in 1920 (only one year before I was born) shows the difficulties and resistance encountered by these pioneers of women's rights. Had it not been for their brilliant, unselfish, single-minded, and total dedication to women's emancipation, the Civil Rights movement of the 1960s could not have coalesced as it did.

THE RIGHTS OF BLACKS

As the nineteenth gave way to the twentieth century, issues of oppression by whites as the reason for lack of progress by blacks and how the "negro problem" should be dealt with were spelled out in quite different ways by two men, W. E. B. DuBois, author of the classic, *The Souls of Black Folk* and co-founder, in 1905, of the Niagara Movement (which in 1909 became the NAACP), and Booker T. Washington, one of the most accomplished speakers of his day and the founder of the Tuskegee Institute in 1881. The dichotomy between these two men of towering character and intellect, and how subsequent civil rights initiatives were influenced by the arguments of DuBois, speaks volumes about the dynamics of civil rights leadership later in the century. These dynamics were shaped by the oppression of working-class people in the early decades of the twentieth century, whether imposed by business practices inherited from nineteenth-century steel and railroad robber barons, or in sweat shops, or in the lowest level jobs, often degrading, as the only employment available to blacks. DuBois believed fervently that blacks, regardless of their skills and training, should be given economic and political equality, to say nothing of full civil rights. Booker T. Washington, on the other hand, argued that it made no sense for blacks to agitate for social equality until they had gained the practical and professional skills to achieve economic equality. To say the least, this was an unpopular view among blacks, and was attacked by most black leaders, including DuBois, whose concepts prevailed as guiding principles in the struggle for civil rights. Today, Shelby Steele[16] is perhaps the best-known exponent of black self-help and reaps the same invective as did Booker T. Washington, who died as a disillusioned man in his fifty-ninth year in 1915. DuBois continued his writing and involvements into his nineties, but equally disillusioned, moved to Ghana for the last two years of his life. He died there in 1963 at age ninety-five.

HERBERT MARCUSE AND THE RIGHTS OF OPPRESSED PEOPLE

The cause of civil rights emerged slowly during the first half of the twentieth century, exploded with a rush in the late fifties, culminating in the civil rights legislation of the sixties. During this decade the brilliant Marxist philosopher Herbert Marcuse and his idea that liberty in a pluralistic society is a "zero-sum game" exerted an influence still felt. He said the prerogatives of action and expression that should justly be enjoyed by oppressed groups, as contrasted to groups possessing power in society, were in fact finite. He believed that in order for civil rights to be obtained by those without power, these rights would have to be taken away from those in power. His 1964 book, *One Dimensional Man*, motivated radical students of the New Left, many of whom, after their graduate student days in the sixties, moved into campus academic positions during the seventies, became tenured, and in so doing infused their doctrinaire politics into student life on campus. (Interestingly it is this left-oriented contingent of our academic citizenry, historically the staunchest defenders of free speech, even if selectively, that metamorphosed into the enemy of free speech in the eighties and nineties through the mechanisms of speech codes.) Adherents of Marcuse elaborated upon his ideas relating to the different allocation of prerogatives of freedom of speech. His adherents say that restricting the free speech of those possessing power (thereby infringing the First Amendment) does less harm than permitting its untrammeled use whereby those without power are harmed.

RELATIVISM

Finally, the academic spread of relativism from the 1960s on and its impact on the nation's historic values has turned the moral climate on campus upside down. Relativism is a suitcase word that carries many connotations and implications. Basically it means that there aren't any universal truths. This is not a new idea. The fifth-century Greek sophist Protagoras, who knew Socrates, talked about it and coined the expression "Man is the measure of all things,"[17] by which he meant that truth is relative to the individual who perceives it and that it has no meaning beyond the perceiver. Because of his agnosticism, he had to run away to escape retribution from his fellow Greeks. This was in contrast to Socrates who, being unreasonably accused of corrupting the youth by citizens of Athens who were afraid of his probing questions, stayed where he was, refused to plea-bargain and went to his death by drinking hemlock.

AN ACADEMIC FLAP

In 1996 a much-publicized academic flap took place between those who on the one hand profess that truth exists in the world outside an individual's perception of it, thus it is natural and to that extent absolute, and on the other those who say truth resides in how one constructs the words to define it: since individuals differ, it is thus relative. The commotion was started by New York University physicist Alan Sokal, who, as a parody wrote an ostensibly serious article entitled, "Toward a Transformative Hermeneutics of Quantum Gravity" and sent it to the journal *Social Text*.[18] This journal, concentrating on cultural studies, was not juried, i.e. articles submitted for publication were not reviewed by external scholars, but only by the journal's editors. Cultural studies encompass many disciplines, which are then viewed in light of the dynamics within the societies in which they exist. Women's Studies, Ethnic Studies, Science Studies, Afro-American or Gay and Lesbian studies are examples. The late Alan Bloom, who wrote *The Closing of the American Mind*, wryly observed that "There is this big rock of *transcultural knowledge*, [italics mine] natural science, standing in our midst while we chatter on about the cultural basis of all knowledge. A serious non-Western *putsch* would require that students learn 50 percent non-Western math, 50 percent non-Western physics, 50 percent non-Western biology and so forth."[19] (As if 2 plus 2 equals 4 is different in its substance if calculated by non-Westerners.)

The pursuit of cultural studies, often broadly subjective, can be a touchy issue to scientists, who depend upon objective, verifiable proofs to prove or disprove their hypotheses. I relate to this quite personally since I've spent a good part of my life as a performing pianist. As a performer you "do" music, just as a gymnast you "do" acrobatics. You don't talk about it. In a keyboard performance, if you blunder over the notes no amount of talk will restore them. The same is true of science. You do it, rather than talking about it, which is why many scientists are skeptical of professors of "science studies" who can talk and write but, in the opinion of the scientists, do not have the knowledge and skills to *do* science.

Sokal's piece was full of big words with which he related quantum theory to radical politics and indicated "that physical 'reality' is at bottom a social and linguistic construct."[20] Sokal himself of course did not believe any of it and wrote it as a parody. He sent the piece to *Social Text* where the editors took the bait and printed it as a serious contribution. Sokal then published an article in the May-June 1996 issue of *Lingua Franca* where he revealed the trick he had pulled on *Social Text*. A lively hubbub followed in which the editors defended themselves with seriousness and *gravitas*, while a good part of academe, along with the media, had a belly laugh at the expense of the "culturists."

Accomplished scholars in cultural studies regretted the episode which cast a shadow on legitimate scholarship in their fields, saying, "scientific knowledge comes not only from nature, but also from social forces," and that "our *knowledge* of natural phenomena such as gravity—not the phenomena themselves—are shaped by social forces."[21]

DIFFERENT ASPECTS OF RELATIVISM

Thus within the social and moral context in which the term "relativism" is used, it simply means that people look at, interpret, and thereby act and react upon similar circumstances differently. Different individuals and groups with varying acculturations therefore impart different meanings to the same words and events. Moral and esthetic values come from the subjective feelings and reactions of individuals and have no status independent of their perceptions. In the realm of morality this variety of interpretation and action by people in a diverse, multicultural group takes the place of consistent responses and actions based on accepted principles of right or wrong. No constant moral base exists, whether it be a neighborhood, a town, a campus, or a nation.

Related aspects of relativism are called "poststructuralism" and "deconstructionism." These high-protein terms represent ideas developed by post-World War II thinkers of the French Left who believed, as Protagoras did, that truth is totally a creation of the human mind. "This is a view developed by French thinkers on the left in the 1960s that sees 'truth' entirely as a creation of the human mind—an illusion frequently propagated by those in power to exploit those who are weak and gullible."[22] The term "deconstruction" was coined by the French philosopher Jacques Derrida in the 1960s and it challenged any certainty in determining the meaning of texts. ("Do unto other as you would have them do unto you" deconstructed has no certainty of meaning.) It rejects the analysis of texts where the analysis had the purpose of determining the meaning and knowledge conveyed by the words. That which is not said can have as much importance as that which is said. Like that of Marcuse, Derrida's thought has had immense influence.

For many faculty members and campus student support personnel, basic principles are a painful rub. For them, since moral practices will vary from culture to culture, a transcultural set of moral principles cannot exist. This compilation is replicated on campuses through multiculturalism and diversity, where speech codes, *de facto*, replaced officially expressed moral precepts that heretofore had transcended cultural bias. These codes, descended from relativistic thought, identify with the "diversity thesis" which holds to the idea that morals are relative. The elimination of hostile environments by limiting the freedom of speech of oppressor groups is determined to be necessary to remedy the wrongs visited upon historically oppressed groups.

I have attended a number of workshops and sensitivity sessions presided over by handsomely reimbursed consultants. They were well-dressed, smooth facilitators brought in from comfortable academic positions at well-known campuses, most often African-American, almost never Hispanic, and in my experience never Asian. Characteristically they begin with the assumption that majority whites represent an oppressor group and must be made aware of their culpable behavior and sensitized to their unconscious but obvious biases toward minorities. (It never seemed to occur to people in attendance that the paid consultants who did the facilitating were themselves about as far from being oppressed as cosseted individuals in a romantic nineteenth-century novel.) If an individual in the audience presumed to question just what specifically was meant by "oppression" in the context of the present group, the individual automatically became a pariah with racist inclinations. This brand of groupthink minimizes the responsibility of the individual, and maximizes the importance and significance of the group.

THE MORAL BOTTOM LINE ON CAMPUS

The problem of the moral climate on campuses boils down to two parts. The first is a de-emphasis of the responsibility of the individual to herself or himself. It is coupled with added emphasis upon the role of the group as contrasted to the individual. The second is a denial that moral principles in fact transcend cultural boundaries. In the first instance there is an unwillingness to acknowledge that the character of individual persons transcends group identity. In the second, hierarchies of cultural value are represented as existing only within separate cultural groups—not also between groups themselves.

I believe both of these hypotheses are inadequate. The individual in fact can and does transcend the group. There can be, and are, qualitative differences between cultures. Until we recognize the validity of these two basic principles we will encounter continuing problems with the moral climate on campuses.

The Impact of Today's Forces for Change: What Will Happen?

Things do not change; we change.

Henry David Thoreau

THOUGHTS OF THE FUTURE

Today's forces thrust against the historic foundations of higher education with increasing impact. For colleges and universities that accommodate and serve masses of citizens, time-honored ways of doing things on campus no longer suffice. Necessary changes extend beyond only the managerial or ministerial. They are basic. The essence of higher education is undergoing a transformation.

A mass citizenry goes to college; information and new knowledge increase exponentially; vocationalism dominates degree programs; communications technology revolutionizes teaching and learning; a consumer attitude pervades student bodies; faculties often merchandize their expertise rather than profess it; politics, bureaucracy and pressures from special interest groups buffet campuses; fiscal pressures pound against all but the richest campuses; statutes mandate, through open admissions, that academically un-prepared students be admitted to state universities if they have graduated from high school. These forces emerged with a rush during the last third of the twentieth century and the changes coming from them have had more impact on higher education in America than everything that oc-curred during its evolution since the founding of Harvard more than three and a half centuries ago. College for the masses, with all of its vocationalism, i.e., training essentially as a substitute for education, can be traced to the G.I. Bill of 1944 and the Morrill Act of 1862 which created land grant colleges and universities. While land grant campuses devel-oped practical job-oriented programs essentially related to agriculture, and the GI Bill accomplished a breathtaking in-crease in access to a college education, neither of these leg-islative initiatives changed the basic nature and process of higher education. It used to be cohesive and consolidated. No longer is this true.

The world of U.S. higher education today consists of an accumulation of varying types of institutions which serve dif-ferent purposes and possess divergent curricular and opera-tional structures. Most of this proliferation of types emerged after World War II. The extent of their variations and intrin-sic dissimilarities impose a sense of wonder. The physical appearances of campuses vary, from elegant, period edifices surrounded by nature's beauty to brutal, concrete fortresses next to downtown commercial establishments; from disci-plined and reassuring New England architecture to store fronts. For virtual learning environments there is no physical appearance at all. Even so, these physical disparities fade into insignificance by comparison to the differences in what is taught, how, and to whom. Whereas pre-World War II higher education cut a relatively narrow swath across the U.S. pop-ulation, twenty-first century students come from every walk of life and all classes of society. During the seventeenth, eighteenth, and nineteenth centuries it was possible to construct a unified view of higher education. Such a picture is impossible to construct today. If Cardinal John Henry Newman were to set himself to the task of writing *The Idea of a University* encompassing today's mind-boggling universe of higher education, his task would be impossible.

The changed function of higher education through its non-selective accessibility to the mass market of students, as contrasted to its historically selective function, provides the reason. The social purpose of this is high-minded and good. Obviously its purpose is to teach and train individual citizens, thereby providing them opportunities for a better life, while at the same time improving the citizen base of the nation. Utopias to achieve this have been hypothesized since Plato wrote the *Republic*. But for us, as this relates to universities in the twenty-first century, the question has not been adequately presented: *Can the essence of a college education, which has always been to educate, not just train or remediate, be retained if through open, non-selective admissions anyone who happens to have a high school diploma can enroll?*

The answer is, of course not. The trade school, polytech function will continue and grow. The needs of the nation require it. Because of this need, mass-market universities have had to step into the role of training and remediating, which has been added to the traditional role of educating. Merging these disparate curricular elements has, thus far, been inadequate.

Courses That, By Tradition, Are Not Bona Fide College Work

Staggering numbers of courses and programs are being offered at colleges and universities in every state of the nation that, by historical standards, are not bona fide college work. Scores of institutions with the exalted title of university are not universities at all, but various types of training organizations. They have a difficult row to hoe. They try to make up for what students did not learn in the public schools and they also train students in specific vocational skills, which, earlier in the nation's history, was not done at universities. Much of what takes place in this campus teaching environment is not university teaching. It ended up in higher education partially by default and partially because students from the mass market demand it. This has drastically altered the role and function of hundreds of mass-market, regional, public, universities and non-selective liberal arts colleges. In a sense this has resulted in a bipolar curriculum—education on the one hand and training on the other.

The demand for technical training was so great that businesses organized training programs to provide instruction in the skills needed by their employees to do their jobs. The companies would have preferred that university faculties provide this instruction through contract relationships with campus continuing education units. Significant numbers of faculty members resisted, because they did not want to adjust their teaching habits by conducting classes at night and on weekends to fit the needs of students who were themselves employed. The corporations, in their own self interest, had to get into the business of teaching. They organized units to provide instruction, mostly for their own employees in practical subjects appropriate to their needs in manufacturing and commerce. These corporate universities have now grown, numbering in the hundreds, and collectively add up to a multibillion dollar enterprise. Many of them take students beyond the cadres of their own employees. On traditional public and private campuses, many faculty members resisted the addition of vocationalism to their curricula. They

were out of sync with the national need for training programs. This speeded the formation of corporate universities,
which for the nation, is a good thing. They are now siphon-
ing off students from regional universities because, earlier,
faculties refused to be cooperative. Corporate, for-profit universities are now forcing mass-market, tradition-oriented
universities and non-selective liberal arts colleges to re-think
what it is that their responsibilities should be.

These forces highlight the stark contrast to what the universities had always been—selective in enrollment processes—
either institutionally selective or self-selective on the part of
students. Unprepared persons were not even considered as
candidates for admission at elite upstairs campuses, unless of
course they were the sons of major benefactors. But these
were the rule-proving exceptions and were sufficiently small
in number that they could be handled. Today in the public,
open admission universities, what had been a small number
of academically unprepared admittees into academic hallways has now grown into a tidal wave.

Open admissions has pushed the function of colleges
outside of the historic, academic envelope, into the needs of
the mass market. It can never, like toothpaste out of a tube,
be pushed back in.

NEW KNOWLEDGE AND TECHNOLOGY

Knowledge has been the primary concern of higher education since before the University of Bologna was founded in
1088. The issues our age brings are not only those of coping
with the nature of knowledge, but with the logistics of its
preservation, acquisition and dissemination. These logistics
involve teams, powerful computers, and elaborate equipment. To verify that teams are indispensable to the pursuit of
knowledge, particularly in the sciences beginning in the sixties and seventies, one need only scan the lists of Nobel lau-

reates to see that what earlier were usually separate awards to individuals are now, more and more often, divided and awarded to more than one individual. (Literature remains the exception.) It isn't that individuals of uncommon talent and genius no longer ponder and seek inspiration alone in the middle of the night, but that the nature of projects of discovery now are sufficiently complex that it takes the efforts of many to carry them out. The expense of the projects, personnel, and equipment means that consortiums of universities, along with business and governments, are involved. The Human Genome Project is an example. Project interaction in the realm of research and discovery will continue.

In the instructional realm, faculties on conventional, regional campuses have not been adept at mastering new teaching technologies in user-friendly ways. By contrast, the newer institutions, many in the for-profit sector, have embraced newer techniques. They now enroll students who previously had no choice other than conventional institutions. Obviously this is shifting patterns of enrollment, which will have profound implications for regional state universities and non-selective liberal arts colleges.

Every year for the last decade (and before) there have been small colleges that close their doors because of an inability to adapt to a changing world.

HUMAN DIVERSITY

Human diversity at universities should relate to diversity of intellectual achievement by individuals as they pursue learning. When, in the name of diversity on campus, the pursuit of group rights is leveraged so that it takes precedence over individual rights in ways that supersede intellectual diversity, then true diversity is tarnished. This has happened on campuses. Chapter twelve of this book is a chronicle of the threat to campus integrity that could happen when group rights are seen as taking precedence over individual rights.

The U.S. Supreme Court decision in the Michigan case (*Grutter v. Bollinger*) now guarantees that race can continue to be used as a factor in individual student admissions decisions. The Court declared that "student body diversity is a compelling state interest." This justifies the use of closely watched, "narrowly tailored" racial classifications in university admissions in order to achieve a "critical mass" of minority students. Those who watch the Court closely indicate that the majority of five justices who rendered the decision sought "nuance and context" in carving out the opinion. As this applies to admitting processes, it will mandate much more care on the part of admissions officers. They will have to take into account and make judgements about the totality of experiences and accomplishments of individual student applicants, each being evaluated within the context of her or his previous education and background. Mechanical application of test scores and grades will not suffice. For the large, highly selective admissions campuses that consider tens of thousands of applications (Michigan being but one example) it will require large numbers of added admissions officers be hired and trained. Also, the terms nuance, context, and critical mass lend themselves to a wide variety of interpretations that will inevitably generate lawsuits and controversies. For example, how do you define and determine what constitutes a critical mass in order to achieve diversity?

The top-tier schools with large treasuries will continue to attract those minority applicants who can meet the competition with offers of scholarships and other subsidies. The non-selective, mass-market institutions and those still partially selective institutions will easily absorb the disadvantaged applicants who cannot make it onto elite campuses. This cascading means that some black and Hispanic applicants who, because of earlier and looser applications of racial preferences, would have made it into medallion schools, will have to settle for lower-tier institutions. But does that mean they are being denied higher education? Of course not. Abigail Thernstrom, mentioned earlier, who has done extensive research work on black admission patterns in selective schools says unequivocally that progress made by blacks since the 1950s cannot, to any significant extent, be attributed to race-based affirmative action at elite schools. The belief in many quarters holds that color-blind admissions practices would not inhibit the progress of blacks and other minorities toward better lives. A contrasting view, held by most selective university presidents and by a significant number of business and military leaders, is that race-related preferences are necessary for social progress. But the opposite view has also been expressed by equally accomplished federal judges and members of the American Association of Scholars. Thus, there will continue to be argument and controversy. Further, it must be kept in mind that affirmative action as an ingredient in college admissions affects a relatively small number of students headed for college in the United States. It amounts to somewhat less than 10 percent. The other 90 percent enroll in mass-market institutions where preferences essentially do not exist.

"CUSTOMER SERVICE" FOR STUDENTS

Staff and teachers in corporate and for-profit universities are running circles around traditional, regional state universities in establishing user-friendly relationships with students. Among the reasons for this marked contrast is the encrustation on regional, state university campuses of faculty types that still look back to the way campuses were operated sixty and more years ago. Then it was a teacher-based academic environment, essentially residential, with students beholden to faculty members in ways that could be perceived as almost farcical in today's world. (Take another look at the movie *Paper Chase*.) Higher education in America in essence is now a student-based learning environment, with an extensive array of student types and student needs. Faculty members need to adapt to students, no less than students adapting to faculty. The for-profit higher education sector, along with special-purpose, niche institutions have recognized this need and behave and configure programs accordingly. As a result they are growing in enrollments. Three other reasons exist for the success currently enjoyed by the corporate and for-profit group.

The first is that they target particular student constituencies with specifically configured programs that fill readily identifiable needs. They set forth delineated missions for the programs they configure.

The second relates to the fact that they are concerned primarily with teaching; not with research work or service. They focus their work and provide clear programmatic rationales for what they do. This reason alone gives them an advantage as they carve out program logistics. Traditional faculty members at mass-market institutions complain that without research carried out by the faculty the substance of academic programs will wither, and the corporate and for-profit sector shortchanges higher education. There is logic and common sense to this contention by traditional faculty members, but it requires that they actually do research that has value. The undeniable fact is that on mass-market campuses across the nation where much of the criticism comes from, faculty research performance is spotty—sometimes almost non-existent. The argument holds no water. Also, a counter argument exists that teachers in the for-profit sector are almost all part-time in higher education. They have jobs beyond academe involving the subjects they teach and they make a living doing it. In many examples they are closer to the cutting edge of the fields in their vocations than traditional faculty, who do not usually practice their professions off campuses. They might consult, but consulting is not the same as practicing a profession.

The third reason is that teachers in for-profit institutions, being overwhelmingly part-time and possessed of career jobs in their own fields, have not shown interest in academic politics and in unionizing. Thus their attention and efforts are not proliferated.

The difference between many of the part-time teachers (adjuncts) on regular campuses and the part-timers appointed in corporate institutions is that adjuncts in traditional institutions do not usually have career positions beyond the campus. They have to function in what has become an inherently unfair but fiscally inevitable two-tier system—fiscally inevitable at least as long as regular faculty members, in terms of the percentage of teaching they do, siphon off a disproportionate share of salary dollars. By contrast, part-time professionals in the new battery of for-profit institutions teach because they like to and enjoy interacting with students. They usually do not have to depend on the money they are paid from part-time teaching to make their mortgage payments. Also, they are willing to teach at night and on weekends. By contrast, regular faculty members on traditional campuses have, in too many examples, been unwilling to make these schedule adjustments. These faculty members resist adjusting their own schedules from Monday-Wednesday-Friday sequences, which sometimes change to only Tuesday-Thursday. They tend to be in the senior ranks and control, for their own ends, the campus politics of academic program development.

The newer and younger group, both tenure and non-tenure track, are less conditioned in their thinking and have far fewer problems in making the adjustments to the new age of higher education. The obvious reaction of an outside observer to this dichotomy between the intransigence of the old and the flexibility of the young would be simply, "Just wait. The older group will fade away. Then things will change." Unfortunately, federal legislation outlawing mandatory retirement in public institutions slows things. Not as many old, tenured fogeys of the academy are retiring as was anticipated; thus the adjustment to the new age moves slowly. Younger faculty members are not able to replace older ones at the rate at which they should for the greater good of higher education. Of course, the realities of infirmity and the finiteness of life will ultimately take hold. But the question is: will this occur in time for regional state institutions to avoid serious and long-term incursions by the for-profit group?

I do not think it will but at this point the answer is not yet definite.

INDIVIDUAL AND GROUP INCIVILITY AND INCONSIDERATENESS ON CAMPUS

That the incidence of incivility on campuses is high cannot be denied. The question to be asked is, what does this portend for the future? If we tear our hair and predict further declines in civility we are simply predicting the future in linear fashion according to what we have observed in the recent past. Human behavior does not always work that way. It is not always extrapolated from the past. My own observation of what seems to be happening in today's millennial generation and older nontraditional students as they enter college is that these students seem to be showing a greater sensibility and awareness of the needs of society. It is a reasonable prediction that this will be be conducive to an improvement in civil behavior on campus.

Despite hand-wringing by the older mossbacks I think this is beginning to happen.

STANDARDS

Academic standards are something else. This issue reaches beyond the campus from kindergarten through high school. It is apparent that education officials in most states are trying to improve standards. One of the mechanisms includes proficiency tests at various levels throughout the public school system, the testing often tied to a student advancing from one grade to the next. But an outcry from parents has slowed the effort. The contention against tests is buttressed by a bevy of rationales, such as that testing of this sort is unfair to minorities, or that the tests create a situation where public school teachers inevitably "teach to the tests" rather than teaching so students will learn. This has not played itself out yet across the nation. In the meantime there seems to be no appreciable improvement in standards nationwide and American public school students continue to fare poorly in comparison to many other nations, even though we spend more than they do on education.

The problem of lowered levels of academic standards for the most part carries over into mass-market, public universities and non-selective liberal arts colleges, especially in undergraduate programs, but to an extent also in graduate and professional schools. Ask law school professors about the problems they encounter with students who cannot write coherently. Most law schools have had to appoint teachers to provide instruction in writing, which should have occurred in high school. In the meantime higher education has no alternative but to provide remedial instruction, essentially through the community colleges. Any significant improvement of academic standards in the near future is quite unlikely. However, I applaud the movement to place more emphasis on statewide, standardized testing in the public schools. The initiative is now buttressed by federal legislation, specifically the "No Child Left Behind" act signed by

President Bush in January of 2001. The resistance from academic malcontents saying this will jeopardize learning because teachers will teach to the tests rather than for students to learn is a thin argument.

Regardless of hindrances by mushy-minded parents afraid of any pressure being applied to their kids, as in Wisconsin, testing will provide both motivation and increasing discipline. This will be an effective start in the effort to improve public school education.

INTERCOLLEGIATE ATHLETICS

A positive appraisal of the value of big time intercollegiate basketball was made by the former and the current presidents of the University of Connecticut, Harry J. Hartley and Phillip E. Austin, in a March 1999, interview in the *New York Times*. They did not wax eloquent about class and race equalization or bonding coming out of their university's teams. They were realistic and practical as they pointed to the benefits of having winners. They said in plain English that the University of Connecticut's fundraising, legislative support, and student applications for admission increased very significantly as a result of the 1995 women's national basketball and the 1999 men's basketball championships. They indicated that the first magnitude national visibility these teams brought the campus was responsible. When they are winners, other powerhouse universities in competitive sports will echo these sentiments. The reality of this cannot to be denied. It is a commentary upon what generates support for higher education from the American public.

There is a an insatiable desire of citizens (whether in stadium seats or as TV couch potatoes) to be entertained by the physical mayhem on the football field. This is not unrelated to Roman crowds watching gladiators kill off one another, or crowds in seventeenth-century England being entertained by watching public hangings. I still remember being turned off by the physical violence on the field the first time I saw Michigan play football in the monstrous stadium. This is not to gainsay the remarkable skill displayed on the field. The complexity of a well-executed play can be a marvel to behold. But gladiators had skill too. Big-time universities provide this kind of entertainment. When this dynamic is tapped into through incandescent media visibility, fundraising benefits accrue, sometimes dramatically.

In an earlier days of the twentieth century sportsmanship still prevailed. But in today's world the context is different. When the University of Chicago football team played Michigan and Louis Elbel could write the Michigan fight song "Hail to the Victors," or some years later Notre Dame's immortal Knute Rockne, Red Grange of Illinois, and the University of Southern California's charismatic and diminutive Cotton Warburton held forth, they did not compete for multimillion-dollar television contracts. Professionalism in terms of dollar bills and recruitment of athletic talent, unrelated to academic talent, was not the order of the day, at least not to the extent that it is now.

In the second half of the century things changed. As a result, the question looms: what do many universities and colleges have to do to themselves in order to field winning football and basketball teams? The number of universities and colleges that are members of the NCAA Division I add up to 312; not an insignificant number. Within this group there occurs a corrupting compromise of campus integrity in the quest for winning teams, particularly in the totally unethical treatment of the throwaway minority, black athletes. Somehow they have been led to believe that athletics is the best, if not the only, route for them to break the barrier of discrimination. (Why couldn't this have been the academic route?) The first prominent minority college football star, Paul Robeson, at Rutgers, was not recruited to play football.

In the pursuit of winning teams by means that go far beyond the individual human value of sports participation, universities have created a crisis for themselves. Integrity and credibility are at stake. For example, the University of Minnesota-Twin Cities dealt with an infestation of athletic scandal for several years and the NCAA had no choice but to come down hard on them. In October of 2000, the university was cited for no less than twenty-five violations of NCAA rules, including what has been identified as academic fraud and unethical conduct. The NCAA Committee on Infractions determined that the head coach had given members of the basketball team money and that, of all things, a departmental secretary had completed more than 400 tests and papers for members of the basketball team, all *with* the knowledge of the coach and the academic advisor.

What are the remedies? Presidents simply must exert a stronger hand in the administration of intercollegiate competition. This is tough—extremely so—in the face of influential persons who are sometimes trustees, pressuring for winners. But rehabilitation will not happen otherwise. Better academic counseling and personal guidance must be provided for individual student athletes. Most athletic programs do have such counseling but it is insufficient. Declining graduation rates attest to this. In some cases, responsibility for this counseling should be taken away from the athletic department and placed in faculty hands, with the faculty empowered to declare athletes ineligible to participate if their academic performance falls below established levels. It must be made clear that athletic participation on campus is contingent upon academic success.

The remedies suggested above, along with others, have not solved the problem, in part because the power of the constituencies clamoring for winners is too strong. In many examples their power over big-time sports exceeds that of the president. Now comes the Emeritus President of the American Council on Education, Robert Atwell, who says, in effect, call big-time sports, mostly football and basketball, what they are: entertainment. Cut through the hypocrisy. Separate them from the educational mission of the university and identify them with the entertainment wing of the campus. Do not require athletes to be students (unless they want to be), pay them, and call them professionals, fulfilling the function of entertainment provided by the university—not education.

Will this happen in the near future? No; given the power of the NCAA and that of athletic boosters in alumni echelons. But calling big-time sports what it is, entertainment, and separating it from the educational mission of the university, is the only non-hypocritical way to go.

TENURE

In all industrialized nations in the world, worker job security has increased. (At the beginning of the twenty-first century, Japan is an exception, but does not alter the trend across the globe.) It is ironic that in the United States, where university faculty tenure arose and was codified, the resistance to it in sectors beyond campuses continues to grow. Reasons for this resistance can be found in public views of its abuse and misuse, which include perceptions of tenure protecting laziness (two-day workweeks) and pure and simple incompetence. The extent of the abuses clearly are not legion but they are visible enough to provide a rationale for the attacks upon tenure. Nor has the professoriate as a professional group seriously set to work remedying aberrations within its own ranks through the establishment of professional self-corrective mechanisms that have enforcement teeth. (It is said with wry snickering in campus hallways that getting rid of an incompetent, tenured professor is a career in itself.) If the procedural aberrations were corrected, attacks upon tenure could be countered with logic and effectiveness. Designs of post-tenure review programs crop up on various campuses but for the most part they do not come to grips with the issue of the misuse of tenure. Rather than getting at the heart of the problem, those speaking for the professoriate, predominantly representatives of the AAUP, counterattack the attackers. This gets the profession nowhere.

The increased tendency of academic budget officers to rely upon part-time, adjunct teachers and limited-term, contract teaching appointments to replace tenure-track appointments is in part a reaction to the low academic productivity of a component of tenured faculty members. If officers of universities move to terminate a nonproducing, tenured faculty member, the procedural and technical hurdles are so high that they are essentially insurmountable. Therefore they have taken the easy way out and when the opportunity comes, they bring in part-timers not eligible for tenure. The abuse of this practice has generated intense reaction in faculty unions, and in the state of Washington, legislative action. The smoke and fumes erase the lofty purposes of tenure and academic freedom. What does the future hold?

Contract appointments, as contrasted to tenure-track appointments, will grow, even though some unionized faculty contracts have put a brake on the practice, and in the mass-market public and non-selective private campuses the percentage of tenured faculty members will diminish.

PROFESSIONAL POLITICS AND BUREAUCRACY

These obliquities are on campuses to stay, and will continue to become more prevalent in state university organizations. However, politics derived from local wards and precincts is now reaching into previously immunized private campuses, as, for instance, Yale will no doubt ruefully testify.

SHARED GOVERNANCE

The locus of shared governance problems with its attendant tensions exists primarily in the mass-market, regional state universities and to an extent at community colleges. Among the reasons is the divergence and a general lack of fellowship between faculties and administrations. The "we-they" attitude is prevalent. Faculties on other types of campuses, especially those at selective admissions schools within higher education, also experience adversarial relationships between faculties and administrations, but their nature is somewhat more abstract. When there are smaller pies to divide among competing campus constituencies on the mass-market front (to verify this simply compare levels of faculty salaries between regional and upper-tier campuses) the antipathies rise to the visceral level. Quite naturally, in our era of collective bargaining, these antipathies have brought about the higher rate of faculty unionism on mass-market campuses. It is no wonder that faculty shared governance today extends beyond its historic intent of managing the institution for the good of students and all concerned, but instead is bent into a weapon to use in ways that are meant to benefit faculty and staff.

Professors at mass-market institutions don't have as much individual leverage as professors on medallion campuses. Because of their influence, status and support—for example endowed chairs and external grants—these professors from upstairs can essentially go their own way and are less dependent upon the central administration. The downstairs professors at regional state university campuses and community colleges, by contrast, are highly dependent for fiscal support upon administrators. Because of this dependency a "worker-boss indisposition" has become prevalent, more so on community college campuses than state four-year institutions, and it continues to grow.

In 1996 the Association of Governing Boards of Univer-

sities and Colleges, which comprises 1,100 boards that gov-
ern 1,700 campuses in the U.S., Canada, and abroad, released a carefully crafted document entitled "Renewing the
Academic Presidency." The study dealt with many governance issues as they related to presidents, boards and faculties. It has had wide circulation and generated much
discussion, not all positive, particularly in the wake of the
AGB President's comment that faculty senates are dysfunctional. Nonetheless the study has had significant impact. In
November, 1998 the AGB published a sequel, the "AGB
Statement on Institutional Governance." These two documents are windows through which the issues of governance
can be seen. The language and rhetoric are not transcendent
and soaring when compared to the 1915 statements by
AAUP founders, but though couched in committee prose,
the AGB statements represent the best work that has been
done on the intractable problem of governance in the last
quarter of the twentieth century. Obtaining clarity of the institution's role along with board responsibility; review and
accountability of presidents; responsibility and accountability of the faculty in the context of today where faculties remain central but are by no means the university's only major
on-campus constituency: these are issues permeating the report. The AGB cautions that the governance document is
not a prescription but a "template of good practices and policy guidelines."

Do I think faculties within the mass market are paying
much attention or are even that much aware of it? No. This
means that in the lower-tier, downstairs institutions, governance of the campuses will shift from faculty to administration and shared governance on the faculties' part will
become more and more advocacy for their special interests.

TEACHING THE LIBERAL ARTS AND HUMANITIES

On the mass-market campuses of today's multicultural world with all of its group partisanships, to profess the values of the liberal arts as they have come down to us from both western and eastern civilizations presents a grueling intellectual and teaching challenge. Teaching the disciplines of the many vocations and professions, while never easy, is direct by comparison to teaching in fields of the humanities. Craft, technique, and skills lend themselves to straightforward presentation. There is not a lot of interpretation in a medical student learning how to suture and tie a knot (or, nowadays, using adhesive material instead of thread to reconnect skin and tissue). For a budding composer it is an intellectually simple process to learn how to read a musical score, regardless of the difficulty of what is on it. Learning the basic principles of grammar is really not all that hard, although teaching students what to do with it is.

But in the their essence, the humanities and liberal arts, as they deal in realms of idea, interpretation, and expression, challenge the human mind in its struggle to find meaning in the realities of the world. The finest minds of all epochs have unceasingly struggled with this. So how do faculty members in mass-market institutions deal with the intractable problems of communicating the values of the liberal arts to students who have never before had exposure? Not very well.

Perhaps one or two teachers in a hundred, if that many, have any significant skill teaching the liberal arts in the context of the higher education mass market. The reasons for this failure are not hard to grasp. Multitudes of students have little interest, or none at all, in the subjects involved. The liberal arts have no immediate practical application. In order to come to terms with them intellectually it is necessary to read and read and read. Many in this vast assemblage of students come from homes with few, if any, books. Many cannot even read that well. Nor are they habituated to think in the realm of abstract ideas, especially, competing ideas that compel analysis. Some possess sincere religious faith which they accept unquestioningly. But this is not the same as trying to understand what Saint Thomas Aquinas, the Book of Job, or the Buddha propounded. Further, many are part-time students with full-time jobs. They have spouses, children, and family responsibilities. They are physically tired. Often they have trouble staying awake in class. It is a daunting task to awaken these students even to an awareness of the awesome intellectual achievements that great thinkers throughout the ages have effected.

Teaching the liberal arts on mass-market campuses cannot be approached in the same ways that are effective in elite schools with selected students from privileged homes providing well-prepared backgrounds. Their conditioning makes an approach to humanities subjects much easier for the teacher. But in the mass market of students on regional state university campuses and community colleges, where students' aims are, first, to train for jobs, and only second to become educated, teachers must first create an intellectual environment where humanities subjects can be credibly approached. This is an inordinately difficult assignment. Given the obstacles inherent in the lives these students have lived, sometimes it can be a well nigh impossible task. Most teachers of the humanities do not know how to create this environment, particularly in unreceptive circumstances. There are some teachers who cannot bring themselves to make the attempt.

The liberal arts in the mass market loom as one of the discouraging contrasts in the upstairs-downstairs of college life. We have not begun to build bridges between these contrasting groups. But we have no alternative but to continue to try.

Rising College Costs, the Dilemma of Part-time Instruction, and Outdated Management

Rising costs that outpace both increases in the consumer price index and family income presage problems that menace student access and budgets in higher education. Professional experts in management reiterate that one of the major causes is outdated management practices on campuses. These exist on practically every pluralistic university in the nation. Can universities contain costs? Not if they continue to operate as they have in the past. On most campuses funds to run the university on a day-to-day basis come from so-called operational budgets. They are separate from capital budgets, which pay for construction, major renovations, land acquisition, and permanent equipment. In public universities, usually by state regulation or direct statute, these two budget categories cannot be commingled. In the operational budgets of universities, the allocation of funds for salaries and benefits to pay faculty and staff, in other words, the human element, account for by far the largest percentage of budgeted dollars. They require on average somewhere between 75 and 80 percent of the amount budgeted to cover operations for the fiscal year. It is within this 75 to 80 percent that most budget problems exist. If there is a decline in faculty and staff productivity (faculties despise the word) and the personnel budget rises, troubles emerge. Of course, the administration can sometimes be at fault here by requiring so much paperwork from the faculty that it eats into the faculty's teaching and research time, which is what the faculty is supposed to be doing.

What is the initial objective of academic productivity? Obviously the teaching of students. If faculty members individually or collectively through unions or faculty senates bargain for reduced teaching loads they lower their productivity with respect to students. If they do research work not paid for by external grants instead of teaching, the imbalance is widened even more. Universities with generations of research heritage have mountains of external grant money to pay for it. This is not true of mass-market institutions. Such research that the faculties do through release from teaching puts a higher percentage of strain on the campus operational budget. Part-timers, both adjuncts and graduate students, are characteristically hired to fill in the teaching gap left by regular faculty who teach less. This has been happening for years and is what created the problematic two-tier system of appointments between regular faculty and others.

Raising student tuition and fees has been the easy way to alleviate some of the imbalance between rising university personnel costs and productivity. The increases are now coming to the point of diminishing returns. In February of 2003 the National Center for Public Policy and Higher Education released a report which said that current rises in tuition are "the worst fiscal news for higher-education and their students in at least a decade." Studies also point to outdated management as a principal deterrent to corrective actions. Getting personnel costs more in line with the inherent capacity of campus operational budgets means that individuals are going to have to be dealt with in ways they will not like. Shared governance has not been able to do this. Faculty members in shared governance seats of influence are not likely to endorse cutting back, firing, or reassigning faculty members to help balance budgets, especially when the same faculty members might occupy offices next door or live down the street. Administrators themselves, all too often being turf-oriented, resist combining or merging units in order to conserve operational money. More often than not the alternatives settled upon are across-the-board cuts with the principle expressed that everyone has to share in the solution to the budget problem. The trouble with this is that everyone does not give equal professional contribution to the institution; thus across-the-board solutions impose a lowered common denominator.

What do I think ultimately will happen? Two things. First, boards, presidents, and legislative committees will exert more direct authority in overseeing detail of fiscal management, particularly as it relates to the supervision and control of what faculty members do. This means that shared governance as it has been practiced, and perhaps even tenure, will be altered, and that there will be a rise in the level of adversariness between administrations and faculties. Second, as incumbent, tenured faculty members retire and submit to the finiteness of human life the new generation will take over. Members of this group have different attitudes. They have not had the academic privileges and freedoms that the fading generation has taken for granted and will more compatibly adapt to the administrative and management controls the new age will engender. This does not mean that they will be pushovers, but their approach will be different from that of their predecessors.

How long will it take for this metamorphosis to occur? Ten to fifteen years. In the meantime faculties and administrations at the elite, medallion and fiscally well-off institutions will continue to live upstairs and proceed according to their own plans.

MORAL ISSUES ON CAMPUS

It is reasonable to say that some moral impoverishment exists on campuses, as we understand morality in its historic context within the United States. A principle reason for the impoverishment is the rise of relativistic thinking within universities. Obviously the issue extends beyond campuses. An objective assessment produces the conclusion that at this

stage in the nation's history, the conditions leading to our
moral dilemma are inevitable. Why? Because we are so diverse. Why should that make a difference? For the obvious
reason that diverse racial, ethnic, and cultural groupings not
only see things differently, but believe in different values and
essentially behave differently. Further, we venerate the altar
of diversity, almost to the point of prostrating ourselves before it. The dynamic of our society tends to proliferate values rather than cohere them. When the nation was colonized
there was some diversity of immigrants, but that diversity
existed essentially within the unity of Protestant Caucasians
from Europe. Agreeing upon a common set of moral values
did not present a problem. This was clearly exemplified by
the ratification of the U.S. Constitution in 1788. If the Constitution were offered for ratification today, as a fresh document, the prediction could well be made that it would not be
ratified, given the ideological differences between the differing groups now making up the nation. At the time of the ratification debates in 1787 and 1788 the partisan problems
were essentially political and by comparison to today existed
in a reasonably homogeneous populace. Political issues are
always subject to compromise, which did occur then. Ideological issues present much more difficult hurdles for compromise. Today the issues are more ideological than political,
thus less subject to compromise. Of course we have political
problems, but the ideological differences loom ever larger.

The waves of immigrants during the latter half of the
nineteenth century did not change the immigrant infusions
of these Protestant Europeans, with the exception of German and Russian Jews and the Irish Catholics after the
Potato Famine of the 1840s. (No less than 1,600,000 Irish
emigrated to the U.S. between 1847 and 1854.) Others followed, not the least being the Chinese, who immigrated as
workers building railroads. The immigrants throughout the

nineteenth century and the first half of the twentieth, saw themselves as becoming Americans, meaning that becoming U.S. citizens took precedence over the ethnic and cultural loyalties of their prior lives. They suppressed their previous cultures, even to the overreaction of not permitting children to speak the languages of their heritage. To achieve agreement and consensus on values and morality was no problem. Morality for them, as understood in the U.S., was simply built into the woodwork to an extent greater than now. Today we deal with different forces. Racial and cultural diversity scatter the unifying elements that previously bonded the citizenry. Instead of celebrating unity ahead of difference, diversity is lauded. The melting pot is long since out of date, superseded by the stir fry.

Among the reasons for this dramatic shift in attitude can be traced to the huge problems of the millions of blacks involuntarily brought to the United States through the slave trade. They were not given the rights of citizens and did not have the same opportunity to become Americans that voluntary immigrants did. Emancipation for black slaves came after generations of legal black subjugation, during which time racism toward blacks and discriminatory attitudes solidified. The Emancipation Proclamation could scarcely be even a start in solving the class, economic and human problems of blacks. Overt white discrimination against blacks, in part with awful physical violence, and much of it with a legal basis, continued for another one hundred years after Lincoln's proclamation. It was not until the civil rights initiatives of the fifties, sixties, and seventies that made overt discrimination in most aspects of American life illegal, that blacks even had the opportunity to enter the mainstream. But the damage inflicted over a previous 300-year period did not vanish with the Emancipation Proclamation of January 1, 1863, or with civil rights victories a century later. Blacks did not necessarily buy into the values of the white man's world. The thinking was different. That remains true to this day. Even though overt discrimination is illegal and special benefits for blacks have been put in place, millions of blacks do not want to be integrated into white society. And millions of whites do not really want to live next door to blacks, although they don't talk very loudly about it. Integration cannot be legislated, which is why bussing did not work. Beyond the black communities this energy of blackness—black is beautiful—and the values of celebrating it separately as opposed to integrating it into the mainstream has resonated in other ethnic and cultural communities. It has given impetus to reducing the importance of the melting pot.

On campuses this has resulted in separateness, not only in personal behaviors, but in the various mechanisms of campus life. I could see this emerging over the decades as minority students grew in numbers on university campuses.

These issues are perhaps the most intractable moral issues of our day, at home and throughout the nation. Fault exists on both sides of the black-white ledger. In white communities, while overt discrimination simply cannot be practiced today, covert discriminatory attitudes continue in many corners. These attitudes deeply affect blacks on the receiving end, and tarnish the realities of the significant progress that has been effected by programs for blacks, both collectively and on a person by person basis. In black communities too many leaders, both national and local, continue to fight the old racism battles, and use demagogic language, as if lynching and separate water fountains still existed. In today's knowledge- and information-based economy no responsible labor leader uses the 1930s battle cries of John L. Lewis. The issues, while real, are different now. Similarly, it is an anachronism for black civil rights leaders to revert to or continue the use of inflammatory rhetoric used before the civil rights revolution of the fifties and sixties.

In today's United States no one has a ready-made answer. Nor is there one. As genetic research continues to gain momentum, it will ultimately become a transparent reality that the intrinsic differences between all human races are miniscule when compared to the similarities. Further, in the United States at least, given the increasing number of intermarriages of all racial categories, so-called pure racial categories diminish with each passing year. No one has illustrated this with more drama (and discipline) than Tiger Woods.

The only answer, both in the near and longer terms, lies in the integrity and moral fiber and its application to other human beings, on the part of individuals from all colors of the rainbow.

Campuses No Longer Separate Enclaves

Today's campuses can never return to ivory towers surrounded by ivy-covered walls. They will continue to interact with off-campus community leadership and with interested and active citizens. There is no way this can, or should, be avoided. It is reasonable for citizens in a community to express themselves—even pressure—campus leadership in order that faculty and staff provide programs appropriate to the higher education needs of the community. This is an expectation that developed in the sixties and has grown during the seventies, eighties, and nineties. It is here to stay. Town-gown separation is out of date. The issue is not whether, but how, the interactions should occur.

In order for faculties and administrations to interact rationally, not only with citizens from the external community but amongst themselves, the purposes of higher education as a crucially important part of America generally and the specific goals and missions of the particular university itself must be clear and up front. State universities have not been good at expressing these values in straightforward, understandable words. This leaves a vacuum which makes it much easier for individuals or groups with partisan agendas to step in and gain leverage.

For the condition of higher education, particularly in the public sector, to be maintained and improved, faculties, staff, presidents, boards of trustees, and government officials must learn to work together better than they have during the past twenty-five years. This means that greater clarity must be introduced as the purposes and values of higher education are set forth and described. The educational effort must be directed not only to students but to citizens in general. It goes beyond conventional instruction and degree programs. Educating the larger community about the values of higher education, as they relate to citizens individually and the nation at large, is an indispensable part of higher education's mission. Integrity on the part of those individuals comprising the university is an absolute requisite to achieve this. We have concentrated too heavily on group behavior and on packaged solutions. What has been lacking and needs emphasis is the crucial role that individual integrity plays within the faculty, administration, board, and students. This is the only base on which to build lasting solutions for American colleges and universities.

Herein lies the wake-up call. Not only downstairs, but upstairs.

Notes

Introduction

1. The lack of willingness to discuss class as an issue, in contrast to the never-ending studies of race and gender, is beginning to change. Studies of class now are emerging as a corollary to or included in cultural studies. Noteworthy is the Center for Working Class Studies at Youngstown State University in Ohio, certainly given Youngstown's history an appropriate location. For a description of the Center see, Jeff Sharlet, "Seeking Solidarity in the Culture of the Working Class," *Chronicle of Higher Education* (July 23,1999): A19.

2. The approximated total endowment amounts for American colleges and universities and the percentages identified are my calculations. They are thus my responsibility. They came from statistics compiled by the National Association of College and University Business Officers, published in the *Chronicle of Higher Education* (January 24, 2003): A24. The ranking of 654 institutions are included. Below, I have listed the top twenty-five institutions by endowment size (in billions) for the fiscal year 2002.

Institution	Endowment in billions
Harvard U	17,169,757
Yale U	10,523,600
U of Texas System	8,630,679
Princeton U	8,319,600
Stanford U	7,613,000
Massachusetts Institute of Technology	5,359,423
Emory University	4,551,873
Columbia U	4,208,373
U of California System	4,199,067

Texas A&M System and Foundations	3,743,442
Washington U in St. Louis	3,517,104
U of Pennsylvania	3,393,297
U of Michigan	3,375,689
U of Chicago	3,255,368
Northwestern U	3,022,733
Rice U	2,939,804
Duke U	2,927,478
Cornell U	2,853,742
U of Notre Dame	2,554,004
Dartmouth College	2,186,610
U of Southern California	2,130,977
Vanderbilt U	2,019,612
Johns Hopkins U	1,695,150
U of Virginia	1,686,625
Brown U	1,414,285

3. The Oxford Movement begun in the eighteen-thirties by a group of Anglican clergymen (located at Oxford University, with Newman being a prominent member), sought to reinvigorate the Anglican Church by reintroducing some Roman Catholic doctrines and rituals. Obviously this encountered vigorous criticism from the leadership of the Anglican Church.

4. John Henry Newman, *The Idea of a University*, edited by Frank M. Turner, (New Haven: Yale University Press, 1996.) Cardinal Newman believed that morality was the basic purpose of education. Of particular interest with respect to training is Discourse VII, "Knowledge Viewed in Relation to Professional Skill," 108.

5. The characteristic use of digital technique by performing pianists all over the world (as contrasted to knowledge about the technique) doesn't have to be replaced in regular cycles of advancing knowledge as do the techniques and the accruing of knowledge in physics or mathematics. It couldn't. Evolution is not going to change the configuration of the hand into a fin or flipper. As long as the keyboards of pianos, organs and harpsi-

chords remain in their present form, and there is no purposeful effort that I know about to realign these keyboards, basic techniques required for keyboard virtuosity will remain as they have for 250 years. (I leave out of this discussion those performers who have a taste for "preparing" the instrument, for instance putting thumbtacks in the hammers or spreading newspapers over the strings simply to obtain other than conventional sounds), but that is scarcely disciplined technical practice. This is not to say that knowledge *about* serious music and concepts *about* its interpretation, or that musical language itself does not evolve, particularly as we learn about the social context in which music existed. But the methods of performing it do not begin to change at the rate that science does. Stradivarius violins to this day are still better than contemporary ones.

6. Peter Drucker, "The Age of Social Transformation," *The Atlantic Monthly* (November, 1994).

7. The chapters in *Reinventing the University—Managing and Financing Institutions of Higher Education*, written by an array of notable men and women from both campus and the business world, compiled under the auspices of Coopers and Lybrand L.L.P. and published by John Wiley and Sons, 1998, provide insightful views on these issues of change.

8. For the perspective of a professor involved in committees of shared governance see Michael Berube, "Dither and Delay, Personalities of Faculty Committees," *The Chronicle of Higher Education* (January 22, 1999): A48.

9. Bill Readings, *The University in Ruins* (Cambridge: Harvard University Press, 1996), 2.

10. Comments in the following articles provide insight into the problem: Jeff Stratton, ed., "Limit the Damage a Single-Issue Board Member Can Do," "Key to Working Effectively on a Split Board," *Board and Administrator*, 15, no. 6 (February 1999) and, John Dibaggio, Steven B. Sample, and Gordon A. Haaland, "Confessions of a Public University Refugee," *Trusteeship, Association of Governing Boards of Universities and Colleges* (May-June 1996): 6.

11. See "The Future of Universities—Turning Students into Customers," *The Economist Review*, October 19, 1996, and three publications concerned with broad issues of change on campus, Christopher Lucas, *Crisis in the Academy* (New York: Saint Martin's Press, 1996), Bill Readings, *The University in Ruins*, and Louis Menand (ed.), *The Future of Academic Freedom* (Chicago: University of Chicago Press, 1996).

Chapter 4

1. My comments were given at a faculty meeting of the College of Fine and Professional Arts on May 12, 1970, a week and a day after the shootings. The meeting did not take place on campus because of the injunction which prohibited it, but took place in the United Church of Christ. Even though I quote myself at some length, I include it because it illustrates the depth of the emotions in the aftermath of the events.
2. John Flower, "Youth Rebellion is Wider than Campus," *Akron Beacon Journal* (October 18, 1970), op. ed.
3. Anonymous letter to "Mr. John Flowers, [*sic*] Dean of the Communist Party." This letter in pencil (in possession of the author) contains such choice tidbits as, "Either straighten up and help prevent this country from going communist, or go to Russia, Red China, or Cuba where you belong . . . You are a big suck ass [*sic*] for the spoiled students who in turn are guided by the communist agitators."
4. David Hess, "A Profound Clash of Values," the *Akron Beacon Journal* (October 18, 1970).
5. Excerpted from The State of Ohio Grand Jury Report on Kent State University, October 16, 1970. Available at http://dept.kent.edu/may4/report_special_grand_jury.htm

Chapter 5

1. Following is an example: "If I see one more goddamned bureaucrat, with a s—eating grin on their face telling us how

everything is under control I'm going to f——stab somebody."
This was accompanied by a picture of the president with a line
pointing to her parted lips and the caption "The s—eating
grin in question." *The Vindicator* (August 16 to September 12,
1999), 16.

2. Alison Schneider, "Insubordination and Intimidation Signal
the End of Decorum in Many Classrooms," *Chronicle of Higher
Education*, March 27, 1998, 12–14. Also see, Peter Sacks, *Generation X goes to College* (Open Court, 1996), and, Stephen L.
Carter, *Civility: Manners, Morals, and the Etiquette of Democracy*
(New York: Basic Books, 1999), both cited in the article.

3. "Defamation and Civility," *Synfax Weekly Report* (March
11,1996), 457–458.

4. Ibid.

5. Ibid.

6. It would be impossible today, given current pathological bureaucracies in the administration of federal programs ensuring
hassles and frustrating delays, that a monumental entitlement
program could be administered as smoothly as the GI Bill was
in the forties and fifties.

7. Evelyn Tan Powers, "Average U.S. students trail those in Europe, study says," *International U.S.A. Today* (July 6, 1995).

8. Statistics in the survey came from "Education at a Glance:
OECD (Organization For Economic Cooperation) Indicators," 1998.

9. Chester E. Finn Jr. and Herbert J. Walberg, "The World's
Least Efficient Schools," *The Wall Street Journal* (June 22,
1998).

10. William H. Honan, "S.A.T. Scores Decline Even as Grades
Rise," *New York Times* (September 2, 1998).

11. John Leo, "A University's Sad Decline," *U.S. News and World
Report* (August 15, 1994), 20.

12. "Ways and Means," *Chronicle of Higher Education* (October
15,1999): A31.

13. Dick Feagler, "Striving is fine but Correct Answers are Better," the *Cleveland Plain Dealer* (September 19, 1999). In this
piece, Mr. Feagler inveighed against a research project in

progress at the Educational Testing Service (which administers the SAT) that would adjust SAT score upward for disadvantaged students called "strivers" who score more than 200 points above the average scores of students with a similar backgrounds. This has been compared to a tournament golf handicap. In effect it would ratchet them into a competitive position in the college admissions process with students who are not disadvantaged and whose average SAT scores are higher. The *Wall Street Journal* and the *Chronicle of Higher Education*, along with many other publications, ran stories about the project, although ETS officials declined comment. Feagler, who describes himself as coming from a background "marginally away from the right side of the tracks," called the idea preposterous and compared the thinking behind it to that which gave us the concept of "social promotion."

14. John Silber, "Teacher Colleges must Shape Up or Shut Down," the *Cleveland Plain Dealer* (July 7, 1998, op. ed. Reprinted from the *New York Times*).

15. Anemona Hartocollis, "Albany Toughens Standards for Teachers and Training," *New York Times* (September 20, 1999).

16. Kate Zernike, "Union is Urging a National Test for New Teachers," *New York Times* (April 15, 2000), 1.

17. Jacques Steinberg, "Academic Standards Eased as Fear of Failure Spreads," *New York Times* (December 4, 1999), 1.

Chapter 6

1. When my wife Maxeen and I were in Myanmar (Burma), which is controlled by a military dictatorship, the government had arbitrarily closed all universities because of student demonstrations—although professors were required to report to work anyway.

2. David Fellman, "Academic Freedom," *Dictionary of the History of Ideas* (New York: Charles Scribner's Sons, Philip P. Wiener, Editor in Chief, 1973), 11.

3. I recall one episode during my days as provost at Cleveland State University when a professor from the Law School was

involved in labor issues in the steel industry that were inimical to the management of a major company headquartered in Cleveland. The management put pressure on me to call the professor off, which I did not do. Had I, it would have been justifiably interpreted as an egregious intrusion into the professor's academic freedom.

4. "The American Council on Education," *American Colleges and Universities*, 15th Edition, (New York: de Gruyter, 1997), 5.

5. I well remember in the sixties when Michigan State College of Agriculture and Mechanical Science was finally renamed Michigan State University—to the accompaniment of derisive refrains from University of Michigan faculty and alumni referring to the "udder" college in East Lansing.

6. *The American Council on Education, American Colleges and Universities*, op. cit., 5.

7. Ibid.

8. Welch Suggs, "Graduation Rates Hit Lowest Level in 7 Years For Athletes in Football and Basketball. Percentage of black teams earning degrees is lower than at any time in the decade," *Chronicle of Higher Education* (September 10, 1999): A58. The detailed statistics in this article were supplied by the NCAA.

9. Steven Fatsis, "Another March, the Usual Madness," *The Wall Street Journal* (March 22, 2002), W6.

10. "Throw-away students: Court's decision against academic standards invites colleges to exploit their athletes," Lead editorial, the *Cleveland Plain Dealer* (March 18, 1999), 10B.

11. Douglas Lederman, "Misconduct Off the Field, Colleges struggle with athletes who break the law, agents who bend the rules." *Chronicle of Higher Education* (November 10, 1995): A35.

12. Welch Suggs, "College Presidents Urged to Take Control of College Sports," the *Chronicle of Higher Education* (July 6, 2001): A35.

13. Ibid.

14. Robert Atwell, "The Only Way to Reform College Sports is to Embrace Commercialization," *The Chronicle of Higher Education* (July 13, 2001): B20.

15. Ibid.

Chapter 7

1. Albert Einstein, *Ideas and Opinions* (New York: Crown Publishers, 1954), 36–52.
2. Stephen Hawking, *A Brief History of Time* (New York: Bantam Books, 1988), 175.
3. Paul Davies, *God and the New Physics* (New York: Simon and Schuster, 1983); also Paul Davies, *The Mind of God* (New York: Simon and Schuster, 1992), and Gerald Schroeder, *The Science of God* (New York: *The Free Press*, 1997), illustrate this unifying attitude attempt.
4. William B. Rees, "Life in the Lap of Luxury as Ecosystems Collapse," *Chronicle of Higher Education* (July 30, 1999): B4–B5. The data and commentary in this article by Rees (who is Director of the School of Community and Regional Planning at the University of British Columbia, and President of the Canadian Society for Ecological Economics) were essential to the author in writing this section. Also, William B. Rees and Mathis Wackernagel, *Our Ecological Footprint* (New Society: 1995).
5. Rees, "Life in the Lap of Luxury," B4.
6. Ibid.
7. Dan Carnevale, "Survey Finds 72% Rise in Number of Distance-Education Programs," *Chronicle of Higher Education* (January 7, 2000): A57. The figures were taken from "Distance Education at Postsecondary Education Institutions: 1997–98," released by the National Center for Education Statistics.
8. Frank H. T. Rhodes, "A Battle Plan for Professors to Recapture the Curriculum," *Chronicle of Higher Education* (September 14, 2001): B7. This article is adapted from his book, *The Creation of the Future: The Role of the American University* (Ithaca: Cornell University Press, 2001).

Chapter 8

1. Sometimes the period in which we live is referred to as the "Knowledge Age," but that is premature. Information and

knowledge are not one and the same. We confront a wash of information on all sides most of which never coalesces into knowledge.

2. In some programs the teaching of practical skills is no different in universities than in trade schools.

3. Obviously slavery was a glaring exception to this principle.

4. William J. Bowen, Derek Bok in collaboration with James A. Shulman, Thomas I. Nygren, Stacy Berg Dale, and Lawrence A. Meserve, *The Shape of the River: Long-Term Consequences of Considering Race in College and University Admissions* (Princeton: Princeton University Press, 1998).

5. In the early days of affirmative action, when schools were scrambling to assemble black persons into student bodies, authentic academic qualifications were downplayed. Egregious examples of preferential admissions, which spawned the criticism, occurred.

6. Bowen and Bok, "Merit and the Relevance of Race in College Admissions," *Los Angeles Times* (September 23, 1998), op. ed. article, portions reprinted in *Synfax, Weekly Report* (December 7, 1998) from which the quotation is taken.

7. Ibid.

8. Abigail Thernstrom, "A Flawed Defense of Preferences," *Wall Street Journal*, (October 2, 1998), A14.

9. Quoted in *Synfax Weekly Report* (December 7, 1998), 799

10. Nicholas Lehmann, "Taking Affirmative Action Apart," *New York Times Sunday Magazine*, June 11, 1995, 36.

11. The knotty problem of the performance of blacks on tests reaches into all corners of public and private education. A *Washington Post* staff writer, Michael A. Fletcher, came to Shaker Heights, Ohio, the community where I live, and produced a front page story, "A Good-School, Bad-Grade Mystery," *Washington Post*, October 23, 1998, A1. In journalistic fashion Fletcher looked into the dilemma of poor performance by black students. He wrote, "the 5,600-student Shaker Heights school system [of which African Americans make up just over half] might seem a strange place to find such racial disparities in student achievement. Far from the urban blight

commonly associated with underachieving black students, this suburban school system has a reputation for being one of the best in America. The vast majority of students, black and white, are at least from middle-class families. The schools spend $10,000 a year to educate each child, a level of funding nearly 50 percent above the national average. Advanced courses are open to any student who chooses to enroll. And after-school, weekend, and summer academies are available to bolster student achievement. Still, Shaker Heights officials acknowledge that they are as baffled as their colleagues elsewhere by the persistent achievement gap between black and white students. It is a problem that cuts across American education, from impoverished school districts to the most wealthy, and it is evident in a range of educational measures." Lehmann reported that, "[E]ducators are placing more emphasis on intangible factors that may hold the key to closing the gap: teachers, even black ones, who have higher expectations for white students and push them harder; parents who don't regularly cajole their children to work hard and take the most challenging classes; and black students who are sometimes ridiculed by their classmates for 'acting white' in the struggle to do well at school."

12. Lehmann, "Taking Affirmative Action Apart," 4.
13. I could write chapters about the twists and turns of dealing with the regulations coming out of the Office of Federal Contract Compliance.
14. *Regents of the University of California v. Bakke.* The decision in this case was rendered by the U.S. Supreme Court in 1978. The Medical School on the Davis Campus of the University of California had a 16 percent minority quota for enrollment. In fulfilling this quota, Allan Bakke was denied admission, even though a number of minority candidates for admission had lower scores than he did. Bakke sued on the grounds that he was discriminated against and the case worked its way up to the Supreme Court. Its decision struck down quotas as a device of affirmative action, thus clearing the way for his admission (he graduated from medical school in 1992) but the Court

also decided that race could be one of the "factors" in the determination of a student's admission.

15. *U.S. Constitution, Amendment XIV, Section I*, adopted in 1868: "All persons born or naturalized in the United States, and subject to the jurisdiction thereof, are citizens of the United States and the state wherein they reside. No state shall make or enforce any law which shall abridge the privileges or immunities of citizens of the United States; nor shall any state deprive any person of life, liberty, or property without due process of law; nor deny to any person within its jurisdiction the equal protection of the law."

16. *Synfax Weekly Report*, Gary Pavela, Editor, (May 17, 1999), 854.

17. Quoted from Scott Jaschitk and Douglas Lederman, "Appeals Court Bars Racial Preferences in College Admissions," *Chronicle of Higher Education* (March 29, 1996): A 26.

18. Ibid.

19. Timur Kuran, *Private Truths, Public Lies: The Social Consequences of Preference Falsification* (Cambridge: Harvard University Press, 1995).

20. Neil L. Rudenstine, "The Uses of Diversity," *Harvard Magazine* (March-April, 1988), 48.

21. Ibid.

22. An example of the criticism is in an op. ed. piece by Frank T. Rhodes (President Emeritus of Cornell University), "College by the Numbers," *New York Times* (December 24, 1999). After quoting Cardinal Newman, Dr. Rhodes says, "One by one, person by person: that is the basis for education success. It is also the basis for a free society; we should not abandon it for a system which, however swift, however simple, not only judges individuals by numbers, but uses numbers as ambiguous as those of class standings. Even in an age bedazzled by rankings, surely we can do better than that."

Chapter 9

1. Daniel J. Boorstin, *The Seekers* (New York: Random House, 1998), 82.

2. During the Middle ages and Renaissance, instruction in my
own academic field, music, was for the most part separated
into two parts, *musica theorica*—the theory of music—which
was part of the *quadrivium*, and *music practica*—practical
music—which taught you how to "do" music—not simply how
to think about it. There is a considerable difference between
these two categories. Practical skill in making music took place
informally, often with apprenticeship training. It occurred in
the countryside, in town squares (to say nothing of taverns)
and was an active and participative group endeavor involving
dancing, singing and performing on drums and other instruments of the day. This contrasts with our present era where
most of the group experience of music is passive, i.e. no participation of the group in actual music making takes place—for
instance listening to CDs, which is a wonderful armchair experience but not active, psychomotor musical realization.
Today's aging audiences at symphony orchestra concerts spend
as much time reading the program notes as they do actually
listening. (Group singing occurs today in houses of worship,
but except for the vibrancy characteristic of African-American
congregations it is usually so anemic as to be worse than no
singing at all.) At rock concerts plenty of audience activity exists, but it is not musical activity. It is, rather, a sociological experience—frequently a happening—mostly of the young adult,
teenage variety. The theory of music on the other hand, similar to the other disciplines in the seven liberal arts, holds a formal, intellectual history of over two and a half millennia. For
example, the Greek mathematician Pythagoras discovered that
musical notes could be expressed in numerical ratios, and from
the sixth century B.C.E., he and successive mathematicians and
philosophers did not separate music from mathematics. This
process of unifying the two disciplines continued for two millennia into the Renaissance. The two were not thought of separately. In the fifth century C.E. the Roman man of wisdom
Boethius possessed the monumental intellect of his day. He
served as a minister to the conqueror of Italy, Theodoric, King
of the Ostrogoths, but he made the fatal error of lining up on

the wrong side of the king's politics, was imprisoned and ultimately executed without trial. While in prison before his execution he wrote his transcendent *Consolation of Philosophy*. Through his writings and translations Boethius transmitted Greek philosophy, mathematics, and music to the early Middle Ages. He used the term *Quadrivium*, (arithmetic, geometry, astronomy, and music) as the fourfold path to the knowledge of "essences." Music, because of its structure and essence, was used by Boethius and subsequent thinkers over the centuries as a model to explain and describe the nature of the universe. His treatise *De institutione musica* made him the authority on music for over a thousand years. He believed that music was an uncommon component of the *Quadrivium* because not only was it related to pure knowledge, but it could not be separated from morality.

3. The year 2000 "Carnegie Classification of Higher Education" was developed by the Carnegie Foundation for the Advancement of Teaching, located in Menlo Park, California.

4. Julianne Basinger, "A New Way of Classifying Colleges," the *Chronicle of Higher Education* (August 11, 2000): A35. The following tabulation is derived from that article.

Doctorate-Granting Institutions
Doctoral/Research Universities—Extensive
Offer a wide range of baccalaureate programs; committed to graduate education through the doctorate; award fifty or more doctorates per year across at least fifty disciplines.
Doctoral/Research Universities—Intensive
Offer a wide range of baccalaureate programs; committed to graduate education through the doctorate; award at least ten doctorates per year across three disciplines or at least twenty doctorates per year over all.

Master's (Comprehensive) Colleges and Universities
Master's (Comprehensive) Colleges and Universities I
Offer a wide range of baccalaureate programs; committed to graduate education through the master's degree; awar

forty or more master's degrees per year across three or more disciplines.

Master's (Comprehensive) Colleges and Universities II
Offer a wide range of baccalaureate programs; committed to graduate education through the master's degree; award twenty or master's degrees per year in one or more disciplines.

Baccalaureate Colleges

Baccalaureate Colleges—Liberal Arts
Primarily undergraduate colleges; major emphasis on baccalaureate degree programs; at least half of the baccalaureate degrees awarded in the liberal arts.

Baccalaureate Colleges—General
Primarily undergraduate colleges; major emphasis on baccalaureate programs; less than half of the baccalaureate degrees in liberal arts.

Baccalaureate/Associate's Colleges
Undergraduate colleges with significant baccalaureate programs, but majority of conferrals at sub baccalaureate level (associate degrees, certificates).

Associate's Colleges

Offer associate degree and certificate programs, but, with few exceptions, award no baccalaureate degrees.

Specialized Institutions

Offer degrees from bachelor's to doctorate; at least half of the degrees in a single field; specialized institutions include only those listed in the Higher Education Directory as having separate campuses.

Theological Seminaries and Other Faith-Related Institutions
Offer religious instruction or train member of the clergy.

Medical Schools and Medical Centers
Can include dentistry, pharmacy, or nursing.

Other Separate Health-Profession Schools
These schools award most of their degrees in fields such as chiropractic, nursing, pharmacy.

Schools of Engineering and Technology
Schools of Business and Management
Schools of Art, Music, and Design
  Bachelor's or graduate degrees in art, music, design, architecture or a combination of such fields.
Schools of Law
Teachers Colleges
Other Specialized Institutions
  Graduate centers, maritime academies, military academies, and institutions that do not fit any other category.

Tribal Colleges and Universities
  With few exceptions they are located on reservations. All are members of the American Indian Higher Education Consortium.

5. Ibid. Alexander McCormick is quoted in the article, A 31.
6. George McKenna, "The Students City College Doesn't Need," *New York Times* (July 17, 1999), op. ed.
7. From an editorial by Ted Marchese, *Change* (March-April, 1998), 4.
8. Arthur Levine & Jeanette S. Cureton, "Collegiate Life: An Obituary," *Change* (May/June, 1998), 14. Over a period of years Levine and Cureton have done extensive studies on student attitudes and student life, supported in part by the Carnegie Council on Policy Studies in Higher Education. Extensive information on this subject can be found in their book, *When Hope and Fear Collide: A Portrait of Today's College Student* (San Francisco: Jossey Bass, 1998).

Chapter 11

1. Jon Debaggio, Steven B. Sample, Gordon A. Haaland, "Confessions of a Public University Refugee," *Trusteeship, Association of Governing Boards of Colleges and Universities* (May-June 1996), 6.
2. Arthur Levine, "Make Giuliani the Education Mayor," *New York Times* (January 8, 2000), op. ed.

3. Richard T. Ingram, "Sweeping reform of Public Trusteeship? YES. It's Time for a Change!" *Trusteeship*, *AGB*. (May-June, 1998), 11.
4. Ibid., 12.
5. Karen W. Arenson, "Union-Backed Pastor Runs for Seat on Yale's Board, and Yale is Upset," *New York Times* (April 11, 2002), A27.
6. Ibid.

Chapter 12

1. Carmen M. Whaley "CSU's Winbush addresses Black Minister's Conference," *Call and Post* (July 28, 1989).
2. Ray Winbush's attorney demanded that CSU release memos and internal information relating to the Winbush matter. This was prepared by my office and the university attorney. It was covered by a memo from me and included relevant documents. It was distributed on June 9, 1990. The material in the release was organized under nine "tabs" which included documents relating to a number of events. I possess copies of these documents. The four issues set forth earlier under "Problematic Involvements" are treated under tab E and tab F. Tab E contains two letters to Winbush by August E. Napoli, (associate vice president for university relations and development) dated May 14, 1990 and May 24, 1990. In these letters Napoli objected to Winbush's hiring persons to do work for his office, counter to university policy, instead of using staff members in university relations and development who are assigned to perform the service. Tab F contains my March 27, 1990 letter to Winbush in which I set forth problems he created, including his involvement outside of university policy in the allegations of the three doctoral students concerning discrimination in grading; his intrusion in the union grievance matter; and his intrusion in the law school assistant dean search.
3. From minutes the CSU Trustee Committee on Minority Affairs and Human Relations, (September 7, 1989), 2.
4. Raymond Winbush and Donna M. Whyte, "Some Goals of

the Office of Minority Affairs and Human Relations," 9, copy in possession of the author.

5. Ibid., 14.
6. Ibid., 12.
7. Marvin McMickle, "What did CSU Expect Winbush to do?" the *Cleveland Plain Dealer* (July 28, 1990), op. ed.
8. John Long, "White lambastes CSU," the *Cleveland Plain Dealer* (July 14, 1990).
9. Alan Achkar, "Sen. Johnson raises threat to CSU funding," the *Cleveland Plain Dealer* (July 5, 1990).
10. Ibid.
11. Alan Achkar, "Racism real at CSU, says Celeste after student talks," the *Cleveland Plain Dealer* (August 23, 1990).
12. Alan Achkar, "Celeste's help not needed, CSU says," the *Cleveland Plain Dealer* (August 24, 1990).
13 Editorial, the *Cleveland Plain Dealer* "Thank you Gov. Kneecapper," (August 26, 1990).
14. Quoted in *Synthesis: Law and Policy in Higher Education*, week of (July 30, 2001), 2033.
15. Shelby Steele, "White Guilt = Black Power," *Wall Street Journal* (January 8, 2002), op. ed.
16. Albert R. Hunt, "The Phony Protest . . . and Leaders," *Wall Street Journal* (January 10, 2002), op. ed.
17. Ibid.
18. Pam Belluck, "Black Scholar Looks Beyond Mended Fence and Harvard," *New York Times* (January 10, 2002).
19. Kate Zernike, "Can Crying Race be Crying Wolf?" *New York Times* (January 13, 2002).
20. Fareed Zakaria, "The Education of a President," *Newsweek* (January 14, 2001).
21. Shelby Steele, op. cit.
22. Robin Wilson and Scott Smallwood, "Battle of Wills at Harvard," *Chronicle of Higher Education* (January 18, 2002): A8.

Chapter 13

1. Commission on the Academic Presidency, "Renewing the Academic Presidency," (Washington D.C.: American Association of Governing Boards of Colleges and Universities), 1996.
2. Bill Readings, *The University in Ruins*, 2.
3. Joan Wallach Scott, "Defending the Tradition of Shared Governance," *Chronicle of Higher Education* (August 9, 1996): B1.
4. Ibid.
5. Michael Berube, "Dither and Delay: Personalities of Faculty Committees," *Chronicle of Higher Education* (January 22, 1999): A48.
6. Ibid.
7. Gallup Poll conducted November 4–7, 1999 (a margin of error plus or minus 3 points) reported in the *Cleveland Plain Dealer* (November 20, 1999), 9B.
8. Robin Wilson, "They May Not Wear Armani to Class, but Some Professors Are Filthy Rich," *Chronicle of Higher Education* (March 3, 2000).

Chapter 14

1. James F. Carlin, "Restoring Sanity to an Academic World Gone Mad," *Chronicle of Higher Education* (November 5, 1999): A76.
2. Commission on National Investment in Higher Education (established by the Council for Aid to Education), *Breaking the Social Contract: The Fiscal Crisis in Higher Education*, released under the auspices of the RAND Corporation, (1997).
3. Ibid., 4.
4. Ibid., 4, 14, 18, 21.
5. *Synfax Weekly Report* (August 2, 1999), 856.
6. Martin Michaelson, "Rising to the Defense of Faculty," *Trusteeship, Association of Governing Boards of Universities and Colleges* (January-February, 1998), 35.
7. "The American Academic Profession," *Daedalus, Journal of the American Academy of Arts and Sciences*, 126, No. 4 (fall 1997).

This issue consists of fifteen essays contributed by scholars and administrators from well-known and respected colleges and universities. They deal with a wide variety of issues confronting higher education.

8. Erik Lords, "Part-Time Faculty Members Sue for Better Pay and Benefits, A legal battle in Washington State reflects tensions evident throughout academe," *The Chronicle of Higher Education* (October 15, 1999).

9. Jorge Klor de Alva, "Remaking the Academy," *Educause Review* (March-April, 2000).

10. Stanley Aronowitz, *The Knowledge Factory: Dismantling the Corporate University and Creating True Higher Learning* (Boston: Beacon Press, 2001), and Elizabeth Greene, "A Sociologist Urges Colleges to Forget Careers and Foster Intellectual Growth," *The Chronicle of Higher Education* (March 17, 2000).

11. Ibid.

12. National Center for Educational Statistics, "National Survey of Postsecondary Faculty," released in 1994, and "Instructional Faculty and Staff in Higher Education Institutions, Fall 1987 and Fall 1992," released in 1997 by the NCES.

13. Ana Marie Cox, "Study Shows Colleges' Dependence on Their Part-Time Instructors," *Chronicle of Higher Education* (December 1, 2000): A1.

14. Scott Smallwood, "Success and New Hurdles for T.A. Unions," *Chronicle of Higher Education* (July 6, 2001): A10.

15. Ibid.

16. Ibid.

17. Peter D. Syverson, Stephen R. Welch, "New Report from NCES tracks changes in Teaching Faculty from 1987 to 1992, confirms rapid increase in part-time Faculty," *Council of Graduate Schools, Communicator* (January 1998).

Chapter 15

1. Alison Schneider, "Why Professors Don't Do More To Stop Students Who Cheat," *Chronicle of Higher Education* (January 22, 1999): A8.

2. Glenn C. Altschuler, "Battling the Cheats," *New York Times*, Education Supplement, (January 7, 2001), 15.

3. Patricia M. King, "Why Are College Administrators Reluctant to Teach Ethics?" *Synthesis; Law and Policy in Higher Education* (Spring 1999), 756.

4. Gary Pavela, "Designing A Citizenship/Ethical Development Program At The University Of Maryland," *Synthesis* (Spring 1999), 763.

5. Northeast Ohio Council on Higher Education, "Inventory & Assessment of Workforce Development Programs and Services," released Sept. 25, 1996. In the area of behavior skills of new employees, almost three times as much concern was reported by the businesses responding to the survey over the lack of "work ethic, interpersonal, customer service, team work, dependable, reliable, self directed, adaptable, flexible, willingness to learn," as was expressed about "basic academic skills, technical skills, computer literacy and thinking skills."

6. For a discussion of this issue see Derek Bok, "Ethics, The University, and Society," *Harvard Magazine* (May-June 1988).

7. Leo Resberg, "Enrollments Surge at Christian Colleges," *Chronicle of Higher Education* (March 5, 1999): A42.

8. A lead editorial, "Abolish the Speech Codes," *Wall Street Journal* (Friday June 11, 1993), quotes then-President Benno Schmidt of Yale; "Offensive speech cannot be suppressed under open-ended standards without letting loose an engine of censorship that cannot be controlled. Vague and unpredictable possibilities of punishment for expression on campus . . . are antithetical to the idea of the university." This was in 1993. The political correctness engine has not yet run out of gas.

9. Robin Wilson, "Wisconsin Scales Back Its Faculty Speech Code," *The Chronicle of Higher Education* (March 12, 1999): A10. Text material from the University of Wisconsin Faculty Speech code and reactive comments about it are printed in this article.

10. Ibid.

11. Following these events Penn State Professor Alan Charles Kors and Harvey A. Silvergate, a criminal defense attorney

and civil litigator produced a book with copious citations, *The Shadow University: The Betrayal of Liberty on America's Campuses* (New York: The Free Press, 1998), in which the facts of the "Water Buffalo Affair" are presented in excruciating detail.

12. For grotesque and ludicrous examples of this listen to a smattering of Gangsta Rap.

13. Kors and Silvergate in *The Shadow University*, op. cit., have gathered information from hundreds of campuses and identified comprehensive examples where due process in dealing with students dealing with speech code violations have been systematically trashed by campus student affairs functionaries. They show time and again where the doctrinarism of P.C. has taken over.

14. The collected works of Engels and Marx require forty volumes while the writings of others on the subjects fill libraries.

15. Sidney Hook, "Marxism," *Dictionary of the History of Ideas, Volume III*, (New York: Charles Scribner and Sons, 1973), 157.

16. Shelby Steele, *The Content of Our Character* (New York: St. Martin's Press, 1990), and, *A Dream Deferred: The Second Betrayal of Black Freedom in America* (New York: Harper Collins, 1998.)

17. Quoted in *The Cambridge Dictionary of Philosophy*, Robert Audi, General Editor, (Cambridge: Cambridge University Press, 1995), 690.

18. Alan Sokal, "Toward a Transformative Hermeneutics of Quantum Gravity," *Social Text* (Spring-Summer 1996).

19. Quoted in, *Synfax Weekly Report*, Gary Pavela, Editor, (May 27, 1996), P. 489.

20. From Sokal's article, Ibid.

21. Bruce Lewenstein, "Science and Society: The Continuing Value of Reasoned Debate," *Chronicle of Higher Education* (June 21, 1996): B2.

22. Quoted in *Synfax Weekly Report*, "Truth or Consequences," (November 27, 1995), 425.

Index

Aberdeen, Washington, 24, 28, 32
academic freedom and tenure
  1915 *Declaration of Principles,* AAUP, 106–7
  1940 *Statement of Principles,* AAUP, 108
  1966 *Statement on Government of Colleges and Universities,* AAUP, 109
  1967 *Joint Statement on Rights and Freedoms of Students,* 109
academic freedom, 104
  tenure, 105–6, 331–32
accountability in use of words, 302
Adams, Abigail, 308
affirmative action
Adarand case, 151
alternatives to, 157–58
  Bakke decision, 150
  beginnings of, as a substitute for "racial preferences", 146

"compelling governmental interest" and "narrowly tailored," 152
Hopwood case, 153–54
lawsuits against the University of Michigan. *See* colleges and universities
Altshuler, Glenn, 294
Ambrose, Stephen, 87
American Association of Higher Education, 173
American Association of University Professors, 10, 105–7, 281
American Civil Liberties Union, 110
American Council on Education, 117
American Federation of Teachers, 92, 101, 290
Apari to Okinawa, 39–40
Appiah, K. Anthony, 240
Aquinas, Thomas, 298
Arensson, Karen W., 208

Aristotle, 175, 201, 296
Armstrong, Louis, 54
Aronowitz, Stanley, 285
Association of American
    Universities, 144
Association of Governing Boards
    of Universities and
    Colleges, 203, 334
Atwell, Robert, 118, 331
Augustine, Saint, 298
Austin, Phillip E., 328

B-25, 34
Bach, J. S., 28, 54
Bacon, Sir Francis, 105
Baguio, Philippines, 35
bailing out, 38
Balch, Stephen, 285
Baptist Minister's Conference,
    213
Beethoven, Ludwig, 15
Berdahl, Robert M., 154
Bernstein, Leonard, 48
Berube, Michael, 252
Blackburn, John A., 154
Bloom, Alan, 312
Blossom Festival School, 62–63
blurred moral boundaries, 293
boards of trustees, 17–18
    trouble spots, 203
Boorstin, Daniel, *The Seekers*,
    164
Boston Latin School, 155
Boulanger, Nadia, 46, 51
Bowen and Bok, *Shape of the
    River*, 142–44, 157

Brand, Miles, 104
Breaking the Social Contract,
    277–78
Britton, Al, 56
Bronfenbrenner, Urie, 295
Buddha, 336
bureaucracy, 204–207
Burks, Walter, 221
Burns, Robert, 178
Busoni, Feruccio, 31
buttoned-up community, 50

Call and Post, 213
Campbell, Mayor Jane, 227
Campbell, Tom, 183
Carlin, James F., 273, 279
Carnegie Classifications, 167–68
Carnegie Foundation for the
    Advancement of Teaching,
    169
cascading, 144
caste system, 2–3
Caviness, Theophilus, 213
celebrity vs. deserved fame,
    87
Celeste, Governor Richard,
    228–29
Center for Academic Integrity,
    295
CETA, 189–90
changes
    differing rates and spread of,
        15
    forces for, 11–12
    specifics of, 13–15
    student expectations, 20

Charlotte, North Carolina, 34, 136
Chicago Academy of Sciences, 93
Chopin, Frederic, 53
Churchill, Winston, 17, 33, 246
Civil Rights Act of 1964, 147, 300
civility and decorum
    decline in civility, 82
    lack of decorum, 85
Clark Field, Philippines, 38
clash of cultures, 237–38
Cleveland Area Arts Council, 189–90
Cleveland Baptist Minister's Conference, 213
Cleveland City Club Forum, 235
Cleveland Press, 190
Cleveland Roundtable, 195, 211
Coalition on the Academic Workforce, 287
College Board, 93
Commission on the Academic Presidency, 247
Communications Workers of America, 215
colleges and universities
    American Express Quality University, 131
    Brown University, 232
    Cambridge University, 127
    California Institute of Technology, 257
    Chicago State University, xiv
    City College of New York, 64–65, 94–95

City University of New York, 65, 94–96, 273–74
Cleveland State University, 4, 18, 84, 149, 178–85, 210–15, 243–45, 251, 305
Columbia University, 73, 256, 289
Cornell University, 52, 132, 289, 294
Curtis Institute of Music, 30, 32
Duke University, 295
Eastman School of Music, 30, 32
Eton College, 127
Fenn College, 178
Grays Harbor College, 33
Harvard University, 5, 156–57, 179
Indiana University, 115
Jagiellonian University, 53
Juilliard School of Music, 30, 32
Kent State University, 5, 60–68, 72–74, 77–78, 156, 180–81
Mary Washington College, 46
Michigan State University, 289
Motorola University, 131
New York University, 289
Notre Dame University, 118
Oberlin College, 112–13
Oxford University, 127
Pennsylvania State University, 289
Princeton University, 5, 168

colleges and universities (*cont.*)
Queens College, 294
Rutgers University, 329
Swarthmore College, xiv
Temple University, 289
Teacher's College, Columbia University, 173, 293
Tuskegee Institute, 198, 309
University of Bologna, 165, 320
University of California, Berkeley, 73, 144
University of California, Davis, 150
University of Connecticut, 328
University of the District of Columbia, xiv
University of Maryland, College Park, 289
University of Massachusetts, 273
University of Michigan, 5, 4, 47, 65, 181
lawsuits against the College of Literature, Science and the Arts and the Law School, and appeals, 158
U.S. Supreme Court hearing on Michigan cases, 160
U.S. Supreme Court decisions on the Michigan cases rendered June 23, 2003, 160
University of Minnesota, 33
University of Minnesota, Twin Cities, 330

University of Oklahoma, 115
University of Pennsylvania, 289, 303
University of Phoenix, 169, 176, 284
University of Texas, Austin, 154
University of Virginia, 154
University of Washington, 33, 42, 289
Vassar College, xiv
Virginia Institute of Technology, 86
Western Governor's University, 177
Western Michigan University, 168
Williams College, 257
Yale University, 5, 45, 207–8
Connerly, Ward, 155
Coolidge, Calvin, 269
Copernicus, 122
Council for Christian Colleges and Universities, 299
Council of Graduate Schools, 287, 291
CSU Civic Committee on Race Relations, 195, 199, 211–12, 217, 238
Cureton, Jeanette, S., 164, 173
Curtis, Jan, 290
Czerny, Carl, 31

Daedalus, The American Academic Profession, 279
David, Hans, 52

Debussy, Claude, 28
December 7, 1941, 33
declining academic standards,
    92–96, 327–28
deconstruction, 313
Derrida, Jacques, 296, 313–14
Dewey, John, 44, 250
different sides of the tracks, 111
diversity
    group rights vs. individual
        rights, 138
    three reasons to merit
        diversity, 138
    the bottom line, 160, 322
distance learning, 131–32
Dodd, Senator Christopher, 275
Douglas A-20, 34–36, 38
Douglas C-47, 41, 43
Downstairs, Upstairs, xiii
Drucker, Peter, 127
Dubois, W. E. B., 198–99, 209,
    212

Early, Gerald. L., 240
Eastman Kodak Company,
    32–33
Eckstein, Max A., 294
ecological footprint, 128
education and training, xiii, 1,
    126, 127
Einstein, Albert, 35, 50, 121
Elbel, Louis, 329
Eliot, Charles, 156
Emancipation Proclamation, 341
endowments, college-university,
    7–8

Ervin, Senator Sam, 147
ethics in degree programs, 296

Farber, Donald A., 104
Farrakhan, Louis, 225
Feagler, Dick, 97
Finn, Chester, 92
Forbes, George, 193–94, 227,
    229
Fujiyama, 42
Fulbright, Senator William, 147
fundraising, 4

Gade, Marian, 203
Galileo, 122
Gallup Poll, 258
George, Henry, 59
getting shot at, 36
G.I. Bill, 7, 90, 317
Gilbert, W. S. 136
Goodman, Henry, 234
graduate student unionizing,
    289
Grange, "Red," 329
Greene, Elizabeth, 285
Green, Mareyjoyce, 223
Group of Sixteen, 185

Handel, George Friederich, 53
Hanson, Howard, 47
Harrow Public School, 127
Hartley, Harry J., 328
Hatcher, Harlan, 6
Hawking, Stephen, 121

Heraclites, 120
Hesburgh, Theordore M., 118
Hiroshima, 43
Holahan, David, 117
Hollandia, New Guinea, 35
Hook, Sydney, 307
Hubble Telescope, 124
Hudson, Ohio, 77
Hunt, Albert R., 240
Hunter Field, North Carolina, 136

increase of students at public
    campuses, 7
Ingram, Richard, 203–4
Initiative I-200 (Washington),
    155, 158
Institute for Higher Education
    Policy, 279
intercollegiate athletics
    desire of citizens for, 328
    Knight Foundation
        Commission on
        Intercollegiate Athletics
        June 2001 report, 117–18
    proposition 16, 115
    Robert Atwell
        recommendation, 118–19
    three major problems, 114–15
Itami, Japan, 41

Jackson, Jesse, 225, 240, 243
Jacobowitz, Eden, 303
Jefferson, Thomas, 24
Job, Book of, 336
Johnson, State Senator Jeffrey,
    228

Johnson, President Lyndon, 143
Johnson, Samuel, 153
Joseph, Frank E., 62
Josephson Institute of Ethics,
    294

Kant, Emmanuel, 298
Kennedy, Justice Antonin, 160
Kennedy, President John F., 147
Kerr, Clark, 203
keyboard performance in music,
    53–55
King, Reverend Martin Luther,
    147, 238
Klor de Alva, Jorge, 284
Kors, Charles Allen, 304
Kucinich, Mayor Dennis, 190
Kuran, Tim, *Private Truths,
    Public Lies,*156
Kyushu, Japan, 37

Lane, Louis, 63
Lehmann, Nicholas, 147
Leschetitzky, Theodor, 31
lessened academic quality, 6–7
Levin College of Urban Affairs,
    182–85
Levine, Arthur, 164, 173
Lewis, Councilwoman Fannie,
    229
Lewis, John L., 342
liberal arts, and humanities
    connected to the citizenry,
    263–65, 335–36
Lieberman, Senator Joseph, 208

Lingayen Gulf, 35
Liszt, Franz, 30–31
Locke, John, 298
Lovejoy, Arthur, 9–10, 106, 110, 114, 288
Ludwig, Friederich, 52
Luke Field, Arizona, 44
Luzon, Philippines, 35

Maius Museum in Cracow, 53
Mackey, Kevin, 231–32
Marchese, Ted, 173
Marcuse, Herbert, 310
marketing higher education, 170
Markham Valley, New Guinea, 35
Marxism, 307–8
  Karl Marx, 296, 307
  Friederich Engels, 307
mass market, 172
Massy, William, 167
McCormick, Alexander C., 169
McKenna, George, 171
McKeon, Congresswoman Nancy, 276
McMickle, Marvin, 229, 238
Merced, California, 34
Michaelson, Martin, 279
Millenial Generation, 88
Miller, Ruth, 220
Mindoro, Philippines, 35
Moore, Earl V., 47, 49, 55
Morrill Act, 317
Moser, Richard, 288
Mother Teresa, 88
Mozart, 55, 290
Muczyk, Jan, 186, 189

National Association for the Advancement of Colored People, (Niagara Movement), 309
National Association of Scholars, 285
National Center for Educational Statistics, 286–87
National Center for Public Policy and Higher Education, 278, 338
National Collegiate Athletic Association, 114–115, 329–31
National Commission on the Cost of Higher Education, 276
National Commission on Teaching and America's Future, 69
National Institutes of Health, 107
National Labor Relations Board, 289
Newman, Cardinal John Henry, 9, 86, 254, 318
Noah, Harold J., 294
North Central Association of Colleges and Schools, 176
Northeast Ohio Council on Higher Education, 243–44

Oakar, Congresswoman Mary Rose, 226
O'Connor, Justice Sandra Day, 161
Office of Federal Contract Compliance, 149

Ohio Grand Jury report, Oct. 16, 1970, 78
Okinawa, 37, 39–41, 44
Organization for Economic Cooperation and Development, 92
Osaka, Japan, 41

Paderewski, Ignace Jan, 31
Paine, Tom, 293
part-time faculty members
  budget issues, 280
  dilemma of, 281–82
  proportion of adjuncts to full-time faculty, 282
  two-tier system, 281
part-time students, 283
Pearl Harbor, 33
Perk, Mayor Ralph, 180
Plato, 48, 318
Powell, Justice Lewis F., 150–51
profs and the street, 259–60
Proposition 209 (California), 155, 159
Protagoras, 311
protest forces prior to May 4, 1970, 73–74
provost, 188
Ptolemy, 122

Rabaul, 35
Ravinia, 62
Readings, Bill, 1, 9
Rees, William E., 128
relativism, 311, 313

Riemenschneider Library, 52
Risegari, Silvio, 31, 32, 44
Rhodes, Frank H. T., 132–33
Rhodes, Governor James, 74, 178
Robeson, Paul, 329
Rockne, Knute, 329
Roosevelt, President Franklin D., 37, 90
Rudenstine, Neil, 156–57
Russell, Bertrand, 290
Ruthven, Alexander Grant and Mrs., 50

Scalia, Justice Antonin, 160
Schnabel, Artur, 31
School of Music, (University of Michigan) 286
Schwartz, Michael, 245
Scott, Joan Wallach, 250–52
seven liberal arts, 166
Shanker, Albert, 82
shared campus governance, 16–17, 246–51, 259
Sharpton, Al, 240, 243
Shepherd Field, Texas, 33
Silber, John, 99
Singer, Isaac Bashevis, xv
skirmish over academic turf at Kent State, 66–67
Sky Lancers, 35
Smith, Jerry E., 154
Smith, Joseph, 79–80
Socrates, 105, 120–21, 311
Sokal, Alan, 311
Some Goals of the Office of

Minority Affairs and Human Relations, 218–20
Southern Christian Leadership Conference, 225
speech codes, 300, 302, 314
stacked deck, 3
Steele, Shelby, 241–42
Steinbacher, Roberta, 184
Stinson L-5, 41
Stokes, Congressman Louis, 226
Stokes, Mayor Carl, 232–33
Strassmeyer, Mary, 229
Students for a Democratic Society, 84
Summers, Larry, 239, 240, 242
Swift, Jonathan, 86
Syverson, Peter D., 287
Szell, George, 64

Tanglewood, 62
teacher-training
    problems of, 68–69
    reaction against, 98–102
teamwork in science, 123–24
Thernstrom, Abigail and Stephan, 144, 323
Thompson, Randall, 48
Thompson, Virgil, 51
Thoreau, Henry David, 316
Tower, Senator John, 147
Trow, Martin, 144
trusteeship problems, 204
Truman, President Harry, 37
U.S. Army Air Corps, 33
United States Constitution, 340

U.S. National Student Association, 109

vast differences in college and university types, 253
Victoria, Queen, 83

Wackernagel, Mathis, 128
Waetjen, Walter, 193–94, 232
Walberg, Herbert, 92
Wallace, Jim, 57–58, 60
Washington, Booker T., 198–99, 209
Washington, George, 308
Waterbuffalo Affair, 303–5
Weatherwax High School, 32
Welch, Stephen R., 287
West, Cornel, 239–41
White, Mayor Michael, 226–27
White, Robert, 60–61, 63, 67
Whyte, Donna, 218
Will, George, 29, 151, 161
Winbush, Raymond, 209–43
Wolf, Johannes, 52
women's rights, 308
    Adams, Abigail, 308
    Anthony, Susan B., 308
    Mott, Lucretia, 308
    Nineteenth Amendment, 308
    Stanton, Elizabeth Cady, 308
    Wollstonecraft, Mary, 308
Zakaria, Fareed (quoting Leon Wieseltier), 241
Zemsky, Robert, 167